Transforming the Practice of Law: Reclaiming the Soul of the Legal Profession

Transforming the Practice of Law: Reclaiming the Soul of the Legal Profession

JOHN ALLISON

Books by John Allison

Choosing Your Lawyer: An Insider's Practical Guide to Making a Really Good Choice

Transforming the Practice of Law: Reclaiming the Soul of the Legal Profession

For all the lawyers who chose the profession in order to help clients and make a positive difference in the world.

Acknowledgments

My experiences as a practicing lawyer provide the foundation for this book. I am indebted to many people for those experiences, including colleagues, other lawyers, clients, judges and law professors. They are too numerous to acknowledge by name, and I do not want to mention some to the exclusion of others. Most of them taught me that lawyers can be instruments for the pursuit of justice as well as wise counselors serving the best interests of their clients. From others I learned valuable lessons about what not to do and how the power and privilege of the profession may be misused.

As a junior in high school planning the agenda for a summertime visit to our nation's Capitol, I wrote a letter to Justice Felix Frankfurter requesting a short meeting with him to talk about my dream of becoming a lawyer. Even though we had never met, Justice Frankfurter took the time to write a personal reply that was far longer than the letter I had sent to him. While his schedule did not permit a meeting during the time of my visit, he sent me a pass to attend a session of the Supreme Court and offered some guidance and practical advice to help me prepare to become a lawyer. I am very grateful to him for encouraging me to pursue my dream.

I want to acknowledge two other people by name. My friend Michael Grady, a scientist, read the entire manuscript and offered valuable feedback and editorial suggestions from the perspective of someone outside the legal profession. My wife Rebecca, a mediator and counselor with a background as a practicing lawyer, inspired the title. As my closest companion for the past twenty-two years she has influenced the development of the ideas that found fruition in this book. I, of course, take full responsibility for its contents.

Contents

Preface

I enjoyed practicing law for forty-three years. Most of my work as a lawyer was interesting, challenging and personally fulfilling. I learned a great deal about human nature and about how people relate to one another in the practical affairs of life. Practicing law also gave me many opportunities to help people and organizations along the way.

This book is about the current state of the legal profession. It is, overall, not a happy state. During the past several years stress and dissatisfaction among lawyers have reached epidemic proportions. At the same time, public esteem for the legal profession has fallen to an all-time low.

The current state of affairs can be attributed to a number of developments affecting the legal profession and the practice of law that began in 1969 when the American Bar Association published its Model Code of Professional Responsibility. The Model Code established the professional ideal of zealous representation, encouraging lawyers to be fervent partisans on behalf of their clients. A few years later, widespread publicity about the Watergate conspiracy exposed a number of lawyers breaking the law and engaging in behavior that was not constrained by ethical or moral principles. In the late 1970s a decision by the Supreme Court ended bans on advertising by lawyers. During the 1980s larger and larger law firms began to enter the scene. In the aftermath of these developments the practice of law has become less about pursuing justice and serving the best interests of clients, and more about making money and winning for the sake of winning. So long as the profession stays on its current path, we can expect lawyers to continue to suffer from the manifestations of stress and become disillusioned about the practice of law. We can also expect the reputation of the profession to continue its decline until, at some point, clients and the public we serve no longer allow us to enjoy the privileges we have claimed for ourselves.

As lawyers we can choose a different future, one that is better for our profession, better for our clients, and better for the society we serve. That is why I wrote this book.

John Allison
November 2015

Part One

THE LEGAL PROFESSION IN CRISIS

When written in Chinese, the word 'crisis'
is composed of two characters —
one represents danger
and one represents opportunity.

JOHN F. KENNEDY [1]

Part One

One

Lawyers in the United States

The United States has a reputation for having a lot of lawyers. Compared to other countries, that reputation is well deserved. According to a European Union study there are more than twice as many lawyers per capita in the United States as there are in Europe.[2]

A brief look at some statistics will provide a foundation for our discussion about the legal profession in the United States today. According to a data summary published by the American Bar Association, in 2012 there were more than 1,268,000 licensed lawyers in the United States.[3] Roughly eight percent of those lawyers were inactive or retired, or were working as judges or teachers. The remaining ninety-two percent, or roughly 1,166,500 lawyers, were actively practicing law. With a total population in 2012 of approximately 315 million people, including children,[4] the United States had one practicing lawyer for every 270 people. For the sake of comparison, in the same year there was one doctor for every 377 people in the United States.[5]

Of the roughly 1,166,500 lawyers who were actively practicing law in 2012, nearly twenty percent worked for a government agency, a business organization, a public defender, a legal aid organization or a non-profit group. The remaining 938,300 lawyers were in private practice.[6] Most of the lawyers in private practice are solo practitioners or members of small law firms with up to ten lawyers. Solo practitioners may set up their own law office or they may enter into office sharing arrangements with other lawyers. About sixteen percent of the lawyers in private practice work in much larger law firms that have more than one hundred lawyers, including some firms that have more than a thousand lawyers. The remaining fourteen or fifteen percent of lawyers in private practice work in mid-size law firms.[7]

One may wonder why so many people in the United States choose the practice of law for their career. There are, of course, a number of different reasons. Some of those reasons are personal. A person may choose the practice of law to follow a family tradition. Some people knew or read stories about lawyers and the idea of being a lawyer captured their imagination. Others may believe the practice of law will give them the chance to use their intellectual gifts while earning a comfortable living. Some may want the status of being a member of a profession and feel that the legal profession is the one most closely aligned with their talents and interests.

Others choose the practice of law as a stepping stone to achieve their perception of worldly success. They may have political ambitions and realize that many elected officials in the United States are lawyers. Or they may want to own their own business and think that earning a law degree and practicing law for a few years will give them a good background for success in the business world. Others heard or read stories about some lawyers who achieved considerable financial success from practicing law, and they simply want the chance to make a great deal of money.

A number of lawyers choose the profession because they hope it will give them a chance to make a difference in the world. Some may want to advance a social action or public policy agenda and feel that practicing law will give them the chance to work through the legal system to advance their ideas about positive social change. Others are drawn to the criminal justice system and want to devote their career to prosecuting criminal offenses or to defending people accused of crime. And some may feel that working as a lawyer in the international arena will give them the chance to travel and experience different cultures, and perhaps even help bring peace to the world.

Many lawyers are motivated to join the profession by a simple desire to help people. From stories they heard or books they read or movies they watched, they understand that lawyers are in a unique position to help people with some of the most difficult and challenging practical issues they may face in life. Lawyers can protect the weak from abuse by the powerful. Lawyers can help achieve justice and prevent injustice. Lawyers can help people resolve their disputes without resorting to violence. Lawyers can help inventors and entrepreneurs protect their intellectual property and create a successful business. Lawyers can guide people and organizations through the complexities of the many laws and regulations that affect our daily lives and our businesses. Lawyers can help people navigate some of life's most difficult transitions such as death, disability and divorce.

Yet with so much hope and potential, the legal profession is currently in a state of crisis. In the next two chapters we will examine the decline in public esteem for the legal profession as a whole and the epidemic of distress among lawyers today.

Two

The Decline in Public Esteem

Lawyers have been the subject of jokes, satire and derisive comments since even before William Shakespeare wrote the famous line, "The first thing we do, let's kill all the lawyers."[8] There are probably many reasons why people have enjoyed poking fun at lawyers. They seem to have an odd language of their own, using words and phrases like "whereas," "wherefore," "aforesaid," and "party of the first part," when plain English would be easier to understand. Lawyers essentially have a monopoly on representing people in a legal system that lawyers helped create. Lawyers are often prosperous members of society even though they do not produce anything that can be used for the basic necessities of life such as food, clothing, shelter or transportation. Much of a lawyer's work is not visible to clients. Lawyers may act as advocates for unpopular causes and represent people accused of heinous crimes. Lawyers make hair-splitting arguments and interpret words in ways that can seem to defy common sense. They often appear to be helping people evade the law. And a lawyer's fees can be very expensive.

Yet lawyers have served critical functions in our society. They had major roles in the founding of the United States. Lawyers were relied on to create our unique system of government that protects our basic freedoms and establishes a social order based on the rule of law. We can find a number of examples of lawyers who, throughout our history, made profound and positive contributions to society and to our enjoyment of life.

The Declaration of Independence was drafted by Thomas Jefferson, a practicing lawyer in Virginia.[9] After the colonies won their independence from Great Britain they ratified the Articles of Confederation which established a loose confederation of sovereign states with a relatively weak central government. Over the next few years the need for a stronger central government became apparent. The first person to propose a Constitutional Convention for the purpose of revising the Articles of Confederation was Alexander Hamilton, a lawyer who felt that a new relationship among the states with a stronger national government needed to be created.[10]

Alexander Hamilton had been born out of wedlock in the British West Indies in 1755 and came to North America in his late teens. After beginning collegiate studies at King's College, Hamilton joined the Continental Army where he rose to the rank of Colonel and served as aide to General George Washington. After the Revolutionary War ended, Hamilton completed his legal education and was admitted to practice law in the State of New York. He opened a law office in Albany and built a successful law practice.[11]

In 1787 the Constitutional Convention was held in Philadelphia. Hamilton was one of the delegates from the State of New York. Thirty-four of the fifty-five delegates to the Constitutional Convention were lawyers.[12] After considerable debate a compromise was reached. A new Constitution that would replace the Articles of Confederation was signed by thirty-nine of the delegates. The delegates decided that the Constitution would take effect once it was ratified by nine state conventions.[13]

Ratification of the Constitution was in serious doubt. There were deep divisions within the states between people who favored a strong central government and people who feared that a strong central government would encroach on the prerogatives of the states that had only recently won their independence from Great Britain. Alexander Hamilton began a project to write and publish essays promoting ratification of the new Constitution. He recruited John Jay and James Madison to write some of the essays, though he wrote most of them himself. A total of eighty-five essays were written and initially published in newspapers. In 1788 the essays were collected and republished in a bound volume as *The Federalist Papers*. Later that year the new Constitution was ratified, having been approved by eleven states.[14]

During the intense ratification debates a number of delegates expressed concerns that a strong central government would threaten individual rights.[15] James Madison, who had studied law but chose a career as a statesman and politician rather than as a practicing lawyer,[16] had a key role in framing the Constitution. He initially questioned the need for amendments to protect individual rights, though he had long been an advocate for the right of individuals to freely exercise their religion. Thomas Jefferson, and others, convinced Madison that amendments protecting individual rights from abuse by the new central government were needed.[17] After the Constitution was ratified, Madison served in the First Congress and drafted a set of proposed amendments to the Constitution. The language of his proposed amendments was revised during the legislative process in the House and Senate. On September 25, 1789 the First Congress submitted twelve Constitutional amendments to the states for ratification. Ten of the amendments were ratified by the states in 1791 and became known as the "Bill of Rights," placing specific limitations on the power of the federal government.[18] The Bill of Rights as ratified in 1791 did not impose limitations on the power of the states. It was not until the twentieth century that the Supreme Court decided a series of cases making certain provisions in the Bill of Rights applicable to the states through the due process clause of the Fourteenth Amendment that had become part of the Constitution in 1868.[19]

The United States Constitution created a unique system of checks and balances among the three branches of the federal government – the executive, the legislative and the judicial. The Constitutional role and importance of the judicial branch was established in 1803 when the Supreme Court decided the landmark case of *Marbury v. Madison* in an opinion written by Chief Justice John Marshall.[20]

John Marshall had become a lawyer after serving with distinction in the Revolutionary War. He built a successful law practice, concentrating on appellate cases, and was George Washington's personal lawyer. Marshall was a Federalist who served as Secretary of State in John Adams' Cabinet. President Adams, near the end of his term, nominated John Marshall to be the Chief Justice of the Supreme Court. Marshall's appointment was confirmed by the Senate shortly before Thomas Jefferson took office as President and power shifted from the Federalists to the anti-Federalist Democratic-Republicans as a result of the election in 1800.[21]

William Marbury's appointment as a Justice of the Peace was part of John Adams' plan near the end of his presidency to pack the federal judiciary with Federalists before control of the legislative and executive branches of the federal government shifted to the Democratic-Republicans. The commission confirming Marbury's appointment was signed by President Adams and countersigned by John Marshall, who was still acting as Secretary of State. However, until the commission was delivered to Marbury he could not serve as a Justice of the Peace. In the frantic final moments of John Adams' presidency, some of the commissions, including Marbury's, were not delivered. The incoming President, Thomas Jefferson, refused to honor Marbury's appointment.[22]

William Marbury filed a lawsuit to obtain a writ of mandamus compelling James Madison, who had succeeded John Marshall as Secretary of State, to deliver the commission confirming Marbury's appointment as a Justice of the Peace. The suit was filed originally in the Supreme Court pursuant to the Judiciary Act of 1789 which authorized the Supreme Court "to issue writs of mandamus in cases warranted by the principles and usages of law, to any courts appointed, or persons holding office, under the authority of the United States."[23] The Supreme Court declined to issue the writ of mandamus that William Marbury sought. Chief Justice John Marshall wrote the Court's opinion. He acknowledged that Marbury was entitled to a writ of mandamus requiring James Madison to deliver his commission. However, Marshall decided that the Supreme Court did not have the power to issue the writ of mandamus because the Judiciary Act of 1789 expanded the Supreme Court's original jurisdiction beyond what Article III of the Constitution allowed.

Chief Justice Marshall's opinion described the function of the Court in words that firmly defined the role of the judicial branch in our system of government: "It is emphatically the province and duty of the judicial department to say what the law is."[24] Marshall also interpreted the Constitution in a way that enabled him to use Marbury's lawsuit as an opportunity to establish the principle of judicial review. That principle has been used by courts ever since as the basis for declaring laws to be unconstitutional:

> [T]he particular phraseology of the Constitution of the United States confirms and strengthens the principle, supposed to be essential to all written constitutions, that a law repugnant to the Constitution is void.[25]

It is worth noting that nothing in "the particular phraseology of the Constitution" expressly gives the judicial branch the power to determine whether laws passed by the legislative branch are constitutional.

Marshall interpreted Article III of the Constitution to make a clear distinction between the Supreme Court's original jurisdiction and its appellate jurisdiction. His opinion quotes the portion of Article III which provides that "the Supreme Court shall have original jurisdiction in all cases affecting ambassadors, other public ministers and consuls, and those in which a state shall be a party. In all other cases, the Supreme Court shall have appellate jurisdiction."[26] Based on that language in Article III, it seems fairly clear that Marbury's lawsuit did not fit within any of the categories of cases for which the Supreme Court has original jurisdiction. However, Article III also contains the "Exceptions clause," which adds to the second quoted sentence the language "with such Exceptions and under such Regulations as the Congress shall make." A respectable argument can be made that the Judiciary Act of 1789, which allowed Marbury to file his lawsuit originally in the Supreme Court, was authorized by the Exceptions clause in Article III of the Constitution.[27] Marshall's opinion does not even mention, let alone discuss, the Exceptions clause. Chief Justice Marshall seems to have gone out of his way to use Marbury's case as an opportunity to firmly establish the role of the judicial branch as the ultimate arbiter of the constitutionality of laws passed by the legislature.

A few decades later another lawyer, Abraham Lincoln, led the country through one of its most challenging periods and our nation survived. Lincoln became a self-taught lawyer after working as a surveyor and co-owning a general store. He became active in state and local politics. Lincoln built a thriving law practice in Springfield, Illinois and "rode the circuit" twice a year to handle cases in neighboring courts. During the course of his legal career he became known as "Honest Abe" because he had a reputation for absolute truthfulness. He was also known for treating his opponents fairly. In the 1850s Lincoln handled a number of railroad cases and established a reputation as a successful railroad lawyer. Lincoln's interest in railroad cases was inspired by his belief that expansion of the rail network, particularly the rail lines running east and west, was important to the economic growth of the United States. As Lincoln celebrated his forty-eighth birthday in February of 1857 he was devoting most of his time to a very successful law practice.[28]

On March 6, 1857 the United States Supreme Court handed down its decision in *Dred Scott v. Sandford*.[29] Dred Scott, whose ancestors were brought to this country from Africa and sold as slaves, was a slave owned by an army surgeon named Dr. Emerson who lived in Missouri. Dr. Emerson took Dred Scott with him to a military post in Illinois and later to Fort Snelling in the part of the Upper Louisiana Territory that later became the State of Minnesota. At the time, Illinois was a free state and slavery was not allowed in the Upper Louisiana Territory. Dred Scott married Harriet, another slave, at Fort Snelling which was located in a free territory. Their eldest daughter, Eliza, was born on a river boat within the State of Illinois, a free state. When Dr. Emerson left Fort Snelling he returned to Missouri with Dred Scott, Harriet and Eliza. The Scotts' second daughter, Lizzie, was born in Missouri.[30]

A few years later Dr. Emerson sold Dred, Harriet, Eliza and Lizzie Scott to John Sandford as slaves. Scott filed a lawsuit against Sandford in federal court in Missouri, seeking his freedom and the freedom of his family based on the fact that he had lived in a free state and in a territory that prohibited slavery. Under the Constitution, the jurisdiction of federal courts extends to controversies between citizens of different states.[31] Sandford was a citizen of New York and Scott claimed that he and the members of his family were citizens of Missouri. The Supreme Court, in an opinion written by Chief Justice Roger Taney, ruled that the federal courts did not have jurisdiction to hear the Scotts' case. The Court's ruling was based on Taney's conclusion that descendents of African slaves were not "citizens" of the United States within the meaning of the Constitution. As they were not citizens of the United States, they could not be deemed to be citizens of Missouri.[32]

Stephen Douglas, the senior Senator from Illinois, publicly supported the *Dred Scott* decision even though it was widely criticized. Lincoln disagreed with the decision and thought that Chief Justice Taney had grossly misinterpreted the Declaration of Independence and the Constitution. Lincoln accused both Taney and Douglas of working to make slavery a permanent institution in at least some of the states.[33] Lincoln, a Republican, ultimately agreed to challenge Douglas, a Democrat, for Douglas' Senate seat in the 1858 election. The famous Lincoln-Douglas debates ensued. Although Lincoln won the popular vote, the Republicans failed to gain control of the Illinois State Legislature which at the time chose the United States Senator. As a result, Douglas retained his Senate seat.[34]

Two years later, Lincoln and Douglas met again as political opponents in the Presidential election of 1860. Abraham Lincoln won that election and became our sixteenth President. His first challenge was to preserve the Union that was threatened by the secession of Southern states. Lincoln led the country through the Civil War, which he viewed as a struggle to save the Union from an insurrection and rebellion. Although Lincoln had long been opposed to slavery, he did not initially consider the abolition of slavery to be an objective of the Civil War.[35]

A year into Abraham Lincoln's presidency the situation was grim. The Union forces had achieved only limited military success. The government was no longer able to borrow money and had to print "greenbacks" in order to pay its bills. Cotton shortages were causing serious unemployment in European textile mills, leading some countries to at least consider granting diplomatic recognition to the Confederacy. By the fall of 1862, after considerable debate and soul-searching, President Lincoln decided it was necessary to expand the focus of the Civil War by emancipating the slaves in order to preserve the Union.[36] Acting pursuant to his war powers under the Constitution, Lincoln issued his final Emancipation Proclamation on January 1, 1863 declaring that the slaves in the States then in rebellion against the United States would be free.[37] He believed that issuing the Emancipation Proclamation would be the most memorable act of his presidency.[38]

Forty-five years later, Thurgood Marshall was born in Baltimore. He became a brilliant lawyer who devoted much of his career practicing law to the abolition of racial segregation in public education. Thurgood's paternal grandfather and maternal great-grandfather were slaves who had been brought to this country from Africa.[39] His father, William Marshall, taught him about the history of the Constitution and about the Supreme Court's 1896 decision in *Plessy v. Ferguson*,[40] which established the "separate but equal" doctrine that sanctioned separate facilities for blacks so long as they were "equal" to the facilities made available to whites. Thurgood Marshall learned from his father how the Supreme Court's decision in *Plessy v. Ferguson* enabled states to replace slavery with racial segregation and discrimination.[41]

When Thurgood Marshall decided to become a lawyer he applied for admission to the University of Maryland's law school which was a ten minute trolley ride away from his home. His application was rejected because he was black.[42] He applied to Howard University's law school in Washington, D. C. and was admitted there. One of his law school professors, Charles Houston, ultimately became Marshall's mentor and lifelong friend. Houston was committed to training black law students to become capable lawyers who could use their legal skills to secure equal rights for African Americans. The law school became an important resource for the NAACP's civil rights litigation.[43]

In 1933 Thurgood Marshall graduated from law school, first in his class, and was admitted to practice law. He opened a law office in Baltimore in the midst of the Great Depression. It was difficult to find paying clients. His interest in civil rights led him to become active in the Baltimore chapter of the NAACP.[44] In his first major civil rights case Marshall represented Donald Murray, an African American who had been refused admission to the University of Maryland's law school because of his race. Marshall won the case by arguing that the separate but equal requirement established by the Supreme Court in *Plessy v. Ferguson* was not satisfied because, as a factual matter, the only school in Maryland that Murray could attend for a legal education was not equal to the University of Maryland's law school.[45]

Three years later, Thurgood Marshall and Charles Houston made a similar argument to the United States Supreme Court in *Missouri ex rel. Gaines v. Canada*[46] on behalf of an African American client, Lloyd Gaines, whose application for admission to the University of Missouri's law school had been rejected based on his race.[47] The Supreme Court decided that Gaines' law school application could not lawfully be rejected because the State of Missouri did not offer separate but equal legal education to African Americans inside the state.[48]

It was not until the late 1940s that Charles Houston and Thurgood Marshall decided it was time to make a direct legal challenge to the separate but equal doctrine of *Plessy v. Ferguson*. Marshall had become the NAACP's chief legal counsel and director of its Legal Defense Fund in New York.[49] He led the legal team litigating the group of consolidated cases that became known as *Brown v. Board of Education*.[50] Marshall's goal in those cases was to end the practice of racial segregation in public education. To achieve that result he needed to persuade the Supreme Court that *Plessy v. Ferguson* should not be applied to cases involving access to public education. He presented sociological and psychological evidence to challenge the underlying premise of the separate but equal doctrine and to place that doctrine in its historical context. He also argued that no rational basis could be found for treating people differently based solely on their race.[51] In a unanimous opinion which Chief Justice Earl Warren read aloud from the bench on May 17, 1954,[52] the Supreme Court adopted Thurgood Marshall's arguments and decided that "in the field of public education the doctrine of 'separate but equal' has no place.

Separate educational facilities are inherently unequal" in violation of the equal protection clause of the Fourteenth Amendment to the Constitution.[53]

Several years after the Supreme Court's decision in *Brown v. Board of Education*, President Kennedy nominated Thurgood Marshall to fill a vacancy on the U. S. Court of Appeals for the Second Circuit. Marshall was confirmed by the Senate and he began serving as a federal appellate court judge in 1962. During his tenure on the Court of Appeals, Judge Marshall wrote ninety-eight majority opinions. At President Johnson's request Marshall left the bench in 1965 to become the first African American Solicitor General of the United States, who is the lawyer responsible for representing the United States in cases before the Supreme Court. Two years later Thurgood Marshall became the first African American Justice of the United States Supreme Court, a position he held until his retirement in 1991.[54] Justice Thurgood Marshall was also the first member of the Supreme Court born and raised in Maryland since Chief Justice Roger Taney. In 1857 Taney wrote the notorious opinion in the *Dred Scott* case in which the Supreme Court decided that descendants of African slaves were not citizens of the United States within the meaning of the Constitution.[55]

These are only a few examples of lawyers who were committed to public service and who helped shape our national institutions and culture. Lawyers continue to make positive contributions to society and to our quality of life every day. Many lawyers are considered to be pillars of their communities.[56] They are respected for their practical wisdom and sound judgment. Lawyers are frequently asked to sit on the governing boards of charities and other non-profit organizations. They may serve their communities in leadership roles as mayors and other elected officials. Supreme Court Justice Lewis Powell emphasized the historical role of lawyers as active participants in civic affairs:

> Members of the legal profession customarily are leaders in the civic, charitable, cutural and political life of most communities. Indeed, the professional responsibility of lawyers is thought to include the duty of civic and public participation.[57]

Despite the positive contributions many lawyers make to our society, the reputation of the legal profession as a whole in the United States began to deteriorate in the 1970s for reasons that will be discussed later in chapters five through nine. By the 1990s, the results of public opinion polls indicated that only twenty percent of the people believed lawyers to be honest and ethical.[58] In subsequent years public esteem for lawyers has continued to decline. The extent of the decline was measured and quantified by the Pew Research Center which conducted statistically valid public opinion surveys in 2009 and in 2013.[59]

The Pew Research surveys were designed to measure public esteem for ten occupational groups: artists, business executives, clergy, engineers, journalists, lawyers, medical doctors, military personnel, scientists and teachers. Based on the percentage of respondents saying that a group contributes "a lot" to society's well being, lawyers were rated in ninth place in 2009, barely ahead of business executives who were ranked in last place. By 2013, lawyers had fallen to last place, with only eighteen percent of respondents saying that lawyers contribute "a lot" to the well being of society.

Further analysis of the survey results for 2013, when lawyers were ranked in last place, is even more disturbing. While the lowest percentage of respondents (eighteen percent) said that lawyers contribute "a lot" to society's well being, only forty-three percent said that lawyers make "some contribution." An astonishing thirty-four percent of the respondents said that lawyers contribute "not very much" or "nothing" to the well being of society. That was the highest negative percentage for any of the ten occupational groups by a significant margin.

These results do not bode well for the future of the legal profession. They indicate that the profession is losing the respect, and may ultimately lose the support, of the society it serves. Lawyers may gradually lose their exclusive right to perform services that have traditionally been considered to be the practice of law. Their broad authority and discretion to operate our system of justice in various roles may be curtailed in ways that could undermine our basic freedoms and the rule of law. The legal profession may lose its status as a self-policing profession in which the formulation of ethical rules and discipline for ethical lapses is entrusted to lawyers.[60] Yet the survey results suggest a question that is even more fundamental: How gratifying can it be to work in a profession that is perceived by a third of the people to add little or nothing to the well being of society?

Three

An Epidemic of Distress

A dictionary definition of an epidemic is a disease or condition "affecting or tending to affect a disproportionately large number of individuals within a population, community, or region at the same time."[61] While a number of lawyers find meaning and personal fulfillment in their professional lives, there is an epidemic of distress within the legal profession as a whole. The distress manifests itself in a number of different ways.

Lawyers are significantly more likely than members of the general population to suffer from clinical depression. Four researchers at Johns Hopkins University studied the incidence of major depressive disorder in a statistical sample of nearly 12,000 people who were members of 105 different occupations and occupational groups.[62] The raw data were adjusted to account for sociodemographic factors and employment status in order to make the study results statistically valid.[63] After making those adjustments the researchers concluded that lawyers currently employed in the profession are 3.6 times more likely than the general population to suffer from major depressive disorder.[64] The researchers point out that "[d]epression is produced by stresses of various sorts."[65]

Lawyers are twice as likely as the general population to abuse alcohol on a regular basis,[66] in an apparent effort to reduce stress or to dull some form of emotional pain so they can keep on going. Some lawyers choose not to keep on going. The suicide rate among lawyers has been estimated to be nearly twice the suicide rate in the general population.[67]

Membership surveys conducted by some state bar associations reveal that significant numbers of lawyers experience symptoms of clinical depression, anxiety or other manifestations of stress on a regular basis. Roughly one-quarter of the lawyers responding to a survey in North Carolina reported symptoms of depression or anxiety.[68] In the State of Washington nineteen percent of the lawyers participating in a research study reported that they suffered from depression.[69] A study of law students and practicing lawyers in Arizona produced results consistent with the findings in North Carolina and Washington.[70] According to estimates by Benjamin Sells, a lawyer who became a psychotherapist, at least twenty-five percent of the members of the legal profession suffer from depression, anxiety, social isolation or feelings of inadequacy in personal relationships.[71]

These statistics, as troubling as they are, only tell part of the story. Other information suggests that increasing numbers of lawyers are profoundly dissatisfied with their professional lives.[72] In a speech given in 1999, Supreme Court Justice Sandra Day O'Connor said that "many lawyers today are dissatisfied with their professional lives" and described practicing lawyers, as a group, as "a profoundly unhappy lot."[73] According to a RAND study commissioned by the State Bar of California, lawyers in California expected large numbers of their colleagues to leave the profession due to dissatisfaction with the practice of law. Only half of the lawyers responding to the survey said they would choose to be lawyers if they had another chance to pick a career. Seventy-eight percent expected the practice of law to become increasingly stressful.[74] In a membership survey conducted by the North Carolina Bar Association, only 53.9 percent of the lawyers responding to the survey expressed an interest in continuing to practice law for the rest of their careers.[75] A survey conducted by the University of Michigan Law School found that, five years after graduation, only thirty-two percent of the lawyers in private practice were "quite satisfied" with their careers overall, *and only fourteen percent were "quite satisfied" with the value of their work to society.*[76] More recently, in April of 2014 the

American Bar Association reported the results of a multi-year study that was designed to track the careers of a nationally representative cohort of lawyers newly admitted to the practice. The study found that twenty-four percent of the survey participants admitted to practice in 2000 were no longer practicing law twelve years later.[77]

There clearly is an epidemic of distress within the legal profession, whether the distress becomes manifest as clinical depression, anxiety, alcohol abuse, suicide or profound feelings of dissatisfaction. The practice of law can surely be very demanding and stressful. Yet work in other professions can be very demanding and stressful as well. To see whether there seems to be something unique about the nature of the stress within the legal profession, let's take another look at the Johns Hopkins study that found lawyers 3.6 times more likely than the general population to suffer from clinical depression.

The Hopkins study examined the incidence of major depressive disorder among the members of 105 different occupations and occupational groups. The relatively high odds ratio for lawyers can be compared to the odds ratios for two other professional occupational groups in the Johns Hopkins study. The researchers calculated an odds ratio of 0.685 for members of "other professional specialty occupations" such as economists, psychologists, sociologists, clergy and religious workers.[78] An odds ratio of 0.685 means members of that group of professional occupations are nearly one-third *less likely* than the general population to suffer from major depressive disorder, and 5.25 times *less likely* than lawyers to suffer from that condition. The results of the study are even more striking for the members of "health diagnosing occupations," an occupational group consisting of physicians, dentists, pharmacists, physical therapists and similar medical professionals.[79] The researchers found no incidence of major depressive disorder among the members of the "health diagnosing" occupational group who were included in the study sample of 12,000 people. That result does not mean members of health diagnosing occupations do not suffer from clinical depression. It is well known that some physicians, dentists and other medical professionals suffer from that condition. The study result simply means that the incidence of clinical depression among members of health diagnosing occupations is so small that it could not be detected in the study sample of 12,000 people. In sharp contrast, with an odds ratio of 3.6 lawyers are many times more likely than members of the health diagnosing occupations to suffer from clinical depression.

Members of health diagnosing occupations and other professional specialty occupations may need to work hard and put in long hours. They can have very stressful jobs. Many physicians and members of the clergy are "on call" much of the time to deal with crises or other emergency situations, and they often need to help people cope with suffering and death. The work of psychologists, sociologists and medical professionals can be very intense. Economists can be under enormous pressure to make accurate predictions about economic trends and results. Physicians and other medical professionals make life-and-death decisions on a regular basis. According to the Johns Hopkins study, members of those occupational groups are less likely than the general population to suffer from clinical depression, and many times less likely than lawyers. The results of the Johns Hopkins study suggest there is something unique about the nature of the stress within the legal profession that is different from the stress experienced by other professionals. We will examine the nature and the causes of the particular stress experienced by lawyers in chapters four through nine.

Part Two

How We Lost Our Way

*A people that values its privileges
above its values soon loses both.*

Dwight D. Eisenhower[80]

PART TWO

Four

THE NATURE OF LEGAL EDUCATION

I t begins in law school.

Students come to law school with many different undergraduate backgrounds. Some law students have college degrees in the social sciences, such as political science, psychology or sociology. Others earned degrees in economics, business administration or accounting. Some law students majored in the humanities, such as history, philosophy, art or English. Others majored in engineering, mathematics or one of the natural sciences such as chemistry, physics or biology. The primary mission of the law school experience is to teach students from all of these various academic backgrounds to think like lawyers.[81]

Law students quickly learn that, in the words of Aristotle, "The law is reason free from passion."[82] They also learn that legal reasoning is a logical exercise. As former Supreme Court Justice Oliver Wendell Holmes, Jr. once said, "The training of lawyers is a training in logic."[83] Yet legal reasoning is a form of logic that teaches lawyers to think differently than most other people.[84]

A legal scholar who had a profound impact on the nature of legal education was Christopher Columbus Langdell, Dean of the Harvard Law School from 1870 to 1895.[85] He is credited with introducing the case method of instruction which is still being used in law schools today. Dean Langdell believed that the study of law needs to be rigorously scientific so that law schools have intellectual respectability within the academic community. He conceived of legal analysis as a science, similar in nature to geometry, with elementary and subordinate legal principles that can be understood and developed through logical analysis without regard for worldly experience. He was motivated at least in part by a desire to replace apprenticeship training by practicing lawyers with a university-based legal education.[86] While Dean Langdell's geometrical model of the law was later criticized by other legal scholars, his scientific approach to legal analysis has continued to influence legal education.[87] The law is taught as an academic and intellectual exercise that is detached in many ways from real life. The law school experience trains lawyers to suppress important aspects of their humanity in order to refine their skills in a unique form of logical analysis.

Most law school courses use the case method of instruction. A law school textbook will typically contain many appellate court decisions relevant to the subject of the course with some analysis and discussion by the author of the textbook. For example, a textbook on constitutional law will contain judicial opinions in cases decided by the Supreme Court and other appellate courts on issues involving specific constitutional provisions, such as the Commerce Clause, the Due Process Clause or the First Amendment. A contract law textbook will include appellate court decisions addressing issues relating to the existence of an enforceable contract, such as whether the parties mutually agreed to the contract terms, or whether the promises the parties made in the contract were supported by adequate consideration. A textbook on tort law will include cases dealing with issues such as the existence of a duty to the injured party, whether the harm to the injured party was reasonably foreseeable, and whether the injured party assumed the risk of the harm that occurred. By studying the appellate court decisions and discussing them in class, law students will learn many of the basic legal principles associated with the subject of the course. More important, however, they will be taught to think like lawyers as an intellectual exercise from an academic perspective.

The law school experience involves a great deal of reading. During their three or four years in law school, students are expected to read and analyze hundreds of appellate court opinions and be prepared to discuss them in class. The way the cases are studied and discussed is a rational exercise focused on the facts of the particular case and the legal issues addressed by the court. If a student is called on by the law professor to discuss a case in class, he or she is expected to be prepared to recite the facts of the case, the legal issues presented, the court's holding and the court's rationale. The facts are limited to those which are legally relevant to the issues raised by the parties. The legal issues the student is expected to identify are the legal issues that were presented to the court. The holding is the court's decision on the precise legal issue or issues the court addressed. The rationale is a brief summary of the court's reasoning process with reference to the legal issues the court decided. The student is expected to distinguish the court's holding and rationale from surplus language in the court's opinion, referred to as *dicta*, which is not relevant to the outcome of the case and which may or may not suggest how the court would decide a somewhat different case in the future.

Many law professors continue to use the Socratic method in class,[88] which is a way of questioning and challenging students that was illustrated by John Houseman's performance as Professor Charles Kingsfield in the 1973 film, *The Paper Chase*.[89] A student's explanation of a case may be challenged by the professor with a question. The professor may then call on another student in the class to ask whether the other student agrees or disagrees with the first student. The professor may ask one of the students whether the outcome of the case would be different if the facts were a little different, and why there would or would not be a difference in the outcome. The analysis and discussion of appellate court decisions using the Socratic method is supposed to teach law students critical thinking and help them learn how the common law gradually evolves from one case to the next. Students learn how to make arguments based on analogies to earlier decisions and factual distinctions from controlling precedent rather than on the application of abstract principles.[90] The Socratic method is also intended to develop the ability of law students to think on their feet and to argue conflicting legal positions.[91] For law students who are subjected to the Socratic method, the experience can be quite unnerving.

A hypothetical example of the Socratic method, based on a First Amendment case decided by the Supreme Court in 2009, illustrates the teaching process. *Pleasant Grove City v. Summum*[92] involved a challenge by the Summum church to a decision by Pleasant Grove City, Utah that refused to allow the church to place a permanent monument in a city park. Summum, a religious organization founded in 1975 and headquartered in Salt Lake City, incorporates elements of Gnostic Christianity and subscribes to Seven Principles of Creation known as the "Seven Aphorisms."[93] Summum wanted to donate and place a stone monument displaying the Seven Aphorisms in Pioneer Park, which already contained a stone monument displaying the Ten Commandments as well as fourteen other permanent monuments or displays. Eleven of the existing monuments and displays, including the Ten Commandments monument, had been donated by private groups or individuals. Pleasant Grove City denied Summum's request, explaining that its practice was to limit monuments in the park to those relating to the history of the city or those donated by groups with long-standing ties to the Pleasant Grove community. Summum filed suit in U. S. District Court seeking an injunction requiring the city to allow Summum to place its monument in Pioneer Park, asserting that the city "had violated the Free Speech Clause of the First Amendment by accepting the Ten Commandments monument but rejecting the proposed Seven Aphorisms monument."[94] After losing its case in District Court, Summum appealed to the U. S. Court of Appeals for the Tenth Circuit which reversed the District Court and ruled that the city "could not reject the Seven Aphorisms monument unless it had a compelling justification that could not be served by more narrowly tailored means."[95] After agreeing to hear the case, the Supreme Court reversed the Tenth Circuit and ruled that Summum was not entitled under the Free Speech Clause of the First Amendment to place its Seven Aphorisms monument in Pioneer Park. All nine Supreme Court Justices agreed on the result, although four of the Justices filed concurring opinions to express somewhat different reasons for the outcome.

With *Pleasant Grove City v. Summum* in mind, let's drop by Professor Melrose Stern's Constitutional Law class where the case is being discussed. We may see something like this:

Professor Stern, calling on Tom Cooper: "Mr. Cooper, can you tell us the facts of the case and the issue presented to the Court?"

Tom Cooper: "The Summum church wanted to donate and erect a monument to the Seven Aphorisms in a city park which already had a monument to the Ten Commandments. The city rejected the donation and refused to allow Summum to build its monument in the park. Summum sued, believing the city had violated its free speech rights under the First Amendment."

Professor Stern: "Mr. Cooper, have you forgotten to tell us about some of the facts?"

Tom Cooper: "Well, there were already fifteen permanent monuments or displays in the park, including the Ten Commandments monument, and the city seemed concerned that the park could become cluttered with monuments."

Professor Stern: "Where would you draw the line, Mr. Cooper? Should the city not be concerned if there were only three monuments instead of fifteen?"

Tom Cooper: "I don't think there is a bright line. It should be left up to the city. The city owns the park."

Professor Stern: "Wouldn't you be concerned, Mr. Cooper, if there was only one existing monument in the park, the monument to the Ten Commandments?"

Tom Cooper, noticing that the palms of his hands are becoming sweaty because he does not see a good way to get off the hook: "Well, I suppose I would be concerned because it wouldn't seem fair to Summum and its followers to have the Ten Commandments on display in a public park when Summum subscribes to the Seven Aphorisms instead."

Professor Stern: "Fair, Mr. Cooper? Fair? Where does the word 'fair' appear in the First Amendment?"

Professor Stern, as he turns to call on Mary Nichols: "Ms. Nichols, what was the Court's holding in the case?"

Mary Nichols, who has not read the case because she went out to dinner with her fiancée and his parents the night before, simply says: "I'm sorry, Professor. I'm not prepared."

Professor Stern: "What a shame, Ms. Nichols. Perhaps you can manage to come prepared to class tomorrow."

Professor Stern, calling on Sally Smith: "Ms. Smith, what was the Court's holding in the case?"

Sally Smith : "The Supreme Court held that a private organization does not have a free speech right under the First Amendment to place a permanent monument in a public park."

Professor Stern: "Don't words on a monument constitute speech, Ms. Smith?"

Sally Smith: "Yes, they do, but that was not relevant to the Court's decision."

Professor Stern: "Why not?"

Sally Smith: "Because the rationale for the Court's decision was that the placement of a permanent monument in a public park is a form of government speech which is not subject to scrutiny under the Free Speech Clause of the First Amendment. The Court made a distinction between the placement of a permanent monument and transitory expressive acts by private citizens such as speeches which are given protection under the Free Speech Clause."

Professor Stern: "Ms. Smith, where in the First Amendment is there an exception for government speech?"

Sally Smith: "There isn't. However, the Supreme Court has held in other cases that the Free Speech Clause is intended to protect private speech; it does not regulate government speech."

Professor Stern, calling on Kevin Green: "Mr. Green, why should the government speech doctrine not have been applied in this case?"

Kevin Green: "As Summum argued, applying the government speech doctrine in this case has the effect of favoring a public display of the Ten Commandments over the Seven Aphorisms. The government speech doctrine was developed in judicial opinions without standards or criteria governing its application. Particularly when public expressions of religious beliefs are involved, a government should not be entitled to choose one set of beliefs over another for public display."

Professor Stern: "Mr. Green, wasn't the Ten Commandments monument placed in Pioneer Park nearly forty years earlier by the Fraternal Order of Eagles as part of their national campaign to combat juvenile delinquency?"

Kevin Green: "Yes it was, although the purpose of the Eagles' national campaign should not be a factor in the outcome of the case. There is no evidence in the record to demonstrate that the Ten Commandments would be any more effective than the Seven Aphorisms in combating juvenile delinquency. I recognize, though, that Summum would have a stronger argument if the Ten Commandments monument had been placed in Pioneer Park more recently. I think Summum would have a really compelling argument if its Seven Aphorisms monument and the Eagles' Ten Commandments monument were being proposed to the city at the same time."

Professor Stern continues to question his students about this case and about the other cases that were included in the reading assignment for the day. As the class ends and the students gather their books and notes, they have various thoughts and feelings about what happened in class. Many of the students feel some sympathy for Tom Cooper, perhaps because they experienced a similar embarrassment in class on another occasion or because they dread the possibility of personally having such an experience in front of their peers. All of the students have been reminded about the importance of coming to class prepared. Their perception that an answer to a question generally leads to another question was reinforced. They may be starting to think that the law is not necessarily supposed to be fair. Sally Smith and Kevin Green might be feeling pleased with themselves, believing they held their own with Professor Stern and demonstrated their analytical skills to their peers. All the students are likely to leave the class feeling somewhat bewildered, since the experienced legal scholar in the room, Professor Stern, never expressed his view of the Court's decision or his opinion about how the government speech doctrine might evolve and be applied in future cases.

Continued exposure to the Socratic method of instruction has profound effects on many law students that will stay with them throughout their legal careers. They may learn to be skeptical and suspicious, questioning nearly everything. They may develop a style of communication that comes across to most people as argumentative. They may use the skills they developed in making distinctions based on factual differences to marginalize other people in order to gain a competitive advantage. They may develop an unconscious habit of answering a question with another question, or asking a series of questions to probe every possibility, which tends to put other people on the defensive. At the extreme, students who become enamored with the "sport" of the Socratic method may start using hard-edged questions with a touch of sarcasm to try to put other people down.

The practice of law, and life in general, are based on relationships among people. Law students who consciously or unconsciously allow the Socratic method to become part of their way of being may have difficulty establishing meaningful professional and personal relationships. Habits developed as a result of continued exposure to the Socratic method can become barriers to intimacy. Many lawyers express feelings of inadequacy and inferiority in their personal relationships.[96] It is not uncommon for the partner of a lawyer to say, in the midst of an argument, "Stop cross-examining me!"[97]

The academic study of appellate court decisions also isolates law students from the context and the emotional content of a dispute. When the outcome of a case is appealed, the information presented to the appellate court is an abbreviated version of what happened in the trial court. In an appeal, the parties are required to identify the legal issues they want the appellate court to consider. The parties are also required to cite references to specific parts of the trial court record in support of their arguments. Appellate court briefs are limited in length, so the parties need to confine their legal arguments and their references to factual information in the trial court record to the issues that really matter. As a result of this process, the case presented to the appellate court is a distilled and legalistic version of the case that was litigated in the trial court. After an appeal has been briefed and argued, the appellate court decides the case and issues a written opinion explaining its decision. Law students study the appellate court's opinion. They do not study the trial court record. Even in a trial court, evidence is admissible only if it has a tendency to prove or disprove a fact that is of consequence to the outcome of the case.[98] Information that is not relevant to the legal issues involved in the case will be excluded from evidence at trial and will not become part of the record for the appeal.

The Supreme Court's majority opinion in *Indiana v. Edwards*[99] illustrates how an appellate court's discussion of the legal issues raised on appeal can present law students with an incomplete and even distorted picture of the underlying dispute. Ahmad Edwards, the defendant in a criminal case, tried to steal a pair of shoes from a department store in Indiana. When he was caught in the act, he drew a gun and fired at a security guard, missing the guard and wounding a bystander. He was arrested and charged in state court with theft, criminal recklessness, battery with a deadly weapon and attempted murder. He was also suffering from schizophrenia, a serious mental illness.

Five months after his arrest, Edwards was found incompetent to stand trial and was committed to a state mental hospital for further evaluation and treatment. Based on earlier Supreme Court decisions under the Sixth Amendment to the Constitution, it "has long been accepted that a person whose mental condition is such that he lacks the capacity to understand the nature and object of the proceedings against him, *to consult with counsel, and to assist in preparing his defense* may not be subjected to a trial."[100] Several months after Edwards was released from the state mental hospital the trial court found that "Edwards, while 'suffer[ing] from mental illness,' was 'competent to assist his attorneys in his defense and stand trial for the charged crimes.'"[101] Later on, the trial court conducted a third mental competency hearing and concluded, based on additional psychiatric evidence, that Edwards was not then competent to stand trial. He was committed again to the state mental hospital. Eight months after that commitment, the hospital reported that Edwards' condition had improved to the point that he was then competent to stand trial.

Nearly a year later, shortly before his trial, Edwards told the trial court that he wanted to represent himself and asked for a continuance of the trial date so he could prepare his defense. The court denied the request for a continuance. The case proceeded to trial with Edwards represented by legal counsel. The jury convicted him of criminal recklessness and theft, but failed to reach a verdict on the two more serious charges.

The state decided to retry Edwards on the battery with a deadly weapon and attempted murder charges, which it was able to do since he had not been acquitted of those charges in the first trial. Edwards again asked the trial court for permission to represent himself. The trial court denied his request, noting that "Edwards still suffered from schizophrenia" and concluding that "[w]ith these findings, he's competent to stand trial but I'm not going to find he's competent to defend himself."[102] Edwards was represented by a court-appointed lawyer at his retrial. He was convicted on the battery with a deadly weapon and attempted murder charges. Edwards appealed his conviction and the Supreme Court ultimately agreed to hear his case.

The issue for the Supreme Court to decide was whether Edwards, with his confirmed mental illness, could be found competent to stand trial but not competent to represent himself. The Supreme Court had decided earlier that a defendant in a criminal case has a constitutional right under the Sixth Amendment to waive the right to be represented by legal counsel and to proceed *pro se* if the defendant knowingly and voluntarily chooses to do so.[103] A defendant has that constitutional right of self-representation without needing to demonstrate any particular level of intelligence, legal knowledge, ability to communicate or ability to persuade other people. Some defendants in criminal cases are capable of representing themselves and do not need to be represented by a lawyer in order to receive a fair trial. The results of a research study indicate that the very small percentage of defendants who choose to represent themselves in felony trials are somewhat less likely to be convicted than defendants who are represented by legal counsel.[104]

In an opinion joined by seven of the Justices, the Supreme Court decided that Edwards, due to his mental illness, did not have a constitutional right to represent himself in his criminal trial. The majority opinion appears to be a well-reasoned, logical discussion of earlier decisions by the Court, carefully explaining how the earlier decisions seem to lead to the Court's result in this case. The opinion cites an *amicus* brief filed by the American Psychiatric Association expressing the view that "common symptoms of severe mental illness can impair the defendant's ability to play the significantly expanded role required for self-representation even if he can play the lesser role of represented defendant."[105] An appendix to the majority opinion contains a rambling and disjointed statement which Edwards attached to his presentence investigation report.[106] A law student reading the majority opinion can readily conclude that the Court reached a common sense result and prevented Edwards' mental illness from depriving him of a fair trial.

However, the majority opinion does not contain a clue about why Ahmad Edwards wanted to represent himself. The opinion also omits any discussion about the nature of Edwards' mental illness. All we are told is that he had a diagnosis of schizophrenia and that he was committed to the state mental hospital for several months on two different occasions.

Justice Scalia wrote a dissenting opinion in which Justice Thomas joined. The dissenting opinion begins with a sharp criticism of the majority:

> The Constitution guarantees a defendant who knowingly and volun-
> tarily waives the right to counsel the right to proceed *pro se* at his trial.
> [Citation omitted.] A mentally ill defendant who knowingly and vol-
> untarily elects to proceed *pro se* instead of through counsel receives a
> fair trial that comports with the Fourteenth Amendment. [Citation
> omitted.] The Court today concludes that a State may nonetheless
> strip a mentally ill defendant of the right to represent himself when
> that would be fairer. In my view the Constitution does not permit a
> State to substitute its own perception of fairness for the defendant's
> right to make his own case before the jury – a specific right long un-
> derstood as essential to a fair trial.[107]

Justice Scalia then went on to provide some of the factual information that was missing from the majority opinion. Edwards was found competent to stand trial based on the report of a psychiatrist who described his thought processes as coherent and who found that he communicated very well, was easy to understand, displayed a cooperative attitude and had good cognitive functioning with average intelligence. The psychiatrist noted that Edwards "had the capacity to challenge prosecution witnesses realistically and to testify relevant-ly."[108] While Edwards filed a number of unintelligible pleadings with the trial court, he also filed several intelligible pleadings and "made arguments in the courtroom that were more coherent than his written pleadings."[109] Perhaps most important, Edwards told the trial judge why he wanted to represent himself. He disagreed with his court-appointed lawyer about the best defense to the attempted murder charge. Edwards' lawyer thought that establishing a lack of intent to kill would be the best defense to that charge. Edwards wanted, instead, to argue self-defense. The trial court rejected Edwards' request to be allowed to represent himself. His court-appointed lawyer defended the attempted murder charge by arguing that Edwards lacked the intent to kill. Edwards was convicted of attempted murder.[110] The unfairness of that result is highlighted in the dissenting opinion:

> Edwards wished to take a self-defense case to the jury. His counsel preferred a defense that focused on lack of intent. Having been denied the right to conduct his own defense, Edwards was convicted without having had the opportunity to present to the jury the grounds he believed supported his innocence.[111]

Yet even with the dissenting opinion, law students studying this case will not have a complete picture of what happened to Ahmad Edwards. Neither the majority opinion nor the dissent discusses the nature of schizophrenia. Diagnostic criteria for schizophrenia include delusions and hallucinations.[112] A diagnosis of schizophrenia can be based on any one of three different disorders. We are not told anything about Edwards' specific mental illness. If he was suffering from paranoid schizophrenia, he may have hallucinated, heard voices and had delusions that he was being hunted or attacked.[113] Given his mental illness, Edwards may have reasonably believed that he was acting in self defense when he drew a gun and fired at the security guard. He never had a chance to present that argument to the jury.

Legal issues and disputes do not arise in a vacuum. They arise in the context of human relationships and human experience. Law students are taught how to rationally analyze appellate court decisions based on the legally relevant facts described in the court's written opinion. They are unlikely to know the broader interests, objectives and motivations of the litigants, since those matters are generally not relevant to the legal issues presented to a court.

Two authors, Chris Goodrich and Scott Turow, have written books describing their experiences in the first year of law school, one at Yale[114] and the other at Harvard.[115] Both authors recount examples of law students struggling with the concept that emotions are irrational and should be excluded from legal analysis.[116] Unfortunately, some students internalize that concept and develop a habit of suppressing their own emotions which is a habit that may stay with them for the rest of their lives. Lawyers who suppress their emotions create stress within themselves and may find it difficult to have meaningful personal relationships. The internal stress they create by suppressing their emotions not only makes them more likely to experience the psychological manifestations of stress, but also makes them more susceptible to chronic physical disease.[117]

Law students are trained to accept the idea that emotional, moral and spiritual considerations are simply not relevant to proper legal analysis. Students who embrace that idea and allow it to become part of their way of being in the world set themselves apart from most other people and cut themselves off from the spiritual and emotional aspects of human experience.[118] As expressed by Anthony Kronman, former Dean of Yale Law School, law students sometimes complain that they feel the process of legal education threatens to rob them of their souls.[119]

There is also a lot missing from the law school curriculum. Students will not find a class or a seminar devoted to the meaning of justice, even though "Equal Justice Under Law" is a primary goal of our legal system carved in stone above the main entrance to the United States Supreme Court. They are taught the ethical rules of professional conduct, but they are not really taught how to be ethical professionals.[120] They are also not taught how to claim and assert their personal integrity in situations that invite them to compromise their ethical and moral principles.[121] Law students are not taught skills of leadership, collaboration, effective communication or creative problem solving. They are not taught how to understand the context in which a client is experiencing a legal problem so they can give wise and practical counsel that addresses the client's broader interests. They are not taught how to deal with difficult people without becoming adversarial. While some law schools offer elective clinical programs, students are not really taught how to practice law.

Unlike doctors, therapists and members of certain skilled trades, an internship or apprenticeship is not required for lawyers. Law students graduate from law school and quickly start studying for the bar examination. If they pass the bar examination and obtain a license to practice law, they become members of the legal profession and can start representing clients right away. They begin their legal careers with little, if any, practical guidance about ways to deal with the challenges and the external sources of stress they will surely encounter as practicing lawyers.

Five

Publicity About the Lawyers of Watergate

Widespread publicity about the Watergate conspiracy during the early 1970s tarnished the reputation of the legal profession because so many of the active participants in the conspiracy were lawyers.[122] As the truth about the conspiracy came to light in 1973 and 1974, the American people learned that a number of lawyers had engaged in clandestine and illegal activities to affect the outcome of the 1972 presidential election. The lawyers engaging in those activities were driven by personal ambition and by President Nixon's desire to win reelection in a landslide. They acted without regard for ethical rules or moral principles. The public also learned that several lawyers orchestrated and actively participated in a conspiracy to cover up what they had done. All of those lawyers were licensed attorneys who had practiced law after graduating from first-rate law schools.

The publicity was triggered by the arrest in the early morning hours on Saturday June 17, 1972 of five burglars who had broken into the headquarters of the Democratic National Committee on the sixth floor of the Watergate Office Building in Washington, D. C. The burglars were arrested at the scene wearing latex gloves and carrying electronic and photographic equipment. Four of the burglars had in their possession $4,500 in new one hundred dollar bills. Within hours of the arrest one of the burglars, James W. McCord, Jr., was identified by the news media as the security chief for President Nixon's re-election committee.[123]

The *Washington Post* assigned two young reporters, Bob Woodward and Carl Bernstein, to cover the story. The results of their investigation were published in a series of articles in the *Washington Post* over many months beginning shortly after the Watergate break-in. Other media outlets took an interest in the story and published more articles about Watergate.[124] As the investigation continued and the conspiracy began to unravel, it became apparent that the Watergate break-in was only the tip of an iceberg. After President Nixon's re-election in November of 1972, the public began to learn about the Plumbers, a "dirty tricks" operation, illegal campaign contributions, money laundering, a secret fund of campaign cash, and the burglary of a psychiatrist's office. The public also learned about an orchestrated cover-up that was calculated to make the participants in the Watergate break-in appear to be a group of renegades out on a lark of their own.[125]

Significant developments in 1973 and 1974 increased public awareness about Watergate. On February 7, 1973 the United States Senate established the Select Committee on Presidential Campaign Activities to investigate whether any illegal or unethical acts had been committed during the 1972 presidential election campaign and whether there had been a subsequent cover-up. That Committee, which soon became known as the Senate Watergate Committee, was chaired by Senator Sam Ervin, Jr. who had a long and distinguished career in the Senate after practicing law as a trial lawyer and serving as a state trial court judge in North Carolina. The Senate Watergate Committee consisted of four Democrats, including Senator Ervin, and three Republicans. The Committee had a staff of roughly seventy-five lawyers, investigators and assistants.[126]

The Senate Watergate Committee conducted an investigation and began holding public hearings on May 17, 1973. The public hearings took place over a period of six months and were broadcast live on television. The television audience had the opportunity to watch 63 witnesses testify and answer questions about various aspects of Watergate. A Gallup survey found that around 90 percent of Americans had watched at least some of the televised broadcasts.[127]

In May of 1973 the Senate passed a unanimous resolution calling for the appointment of a Special Prosecutor to investigate the Watergate conspiracy and determine whether criminal charges should be brought against any of the participants. Later that month the Office of Special Prosecutor was established and a Special Prosecutor was appointed.[128] The criminal investigation began. In October 1973 President Nixon, determined to avoid disclosing certain White House materials that had been subpoenaed, fired the Special Prosecutor who would not withdraw the subpoena. Nixon's action was widely publicized and generated significant public outrage. He soon relented and agreed to the appointment of a new Special Prosecutor who continued the criminal investigation.[129]

Grand juries were convened and indictments were handed down. A number of participants in the Watergate conspiracy pled guilty to criminal charges. Criminal trials of indicted participants who did not plead guilty took place in 1973 and 1974 and received widespread publicity.[130] Many of the criminal defendants who pled guilty or who were convicted at trial were lawyers.

On February 6, 1974 the House of Representatives decided, by a vote of 410 to 4, to begin a formal inquiry to consider whether President Nixon should be impeached. The House Judiciary Committee began its impeachment hearings on May 9, 1974 behind closed doors. The Judiciary Committee later decided to allow live radio and television coverage of the impeachment debates which occurred over six days at the end of July. Millions of Americans watched the televised debates on the Articles of Impeachment and saw the House Judiciary Committee approve three Articles calling for President Nixon's impeachment by the House of Representatives, trial by the Senate, and removal from office.[131]

Before the House of Representatives could act on the Judiciary Committee's impeachment recommendation, President Nixon decided to resign. On August 9, 1974 Nixon became the first President of the United States to resign from office. By the time he resigned, the American people had been hearing and reading about the Watergate conspiracy for two years. According to a

Gallup Poll 98 percent of Americans had heard or read about Watergate.[132] They learned an incredible story about the misconduct and criminal behavior of a number of lawyers.

Richard Nixon was a lawyer. He graduated with honors from the Duke University School of Law in 1938. He then returned to his home in the Los Angeles area to practice law.[133] World War II intervened. After completing military service in the Navy, Nixon returned to California and entered politics. He was elected to the U. S. House of Representatives in 1946 and re-elected in 1948. In 1950 Nixon was elected to the U. S. Senate. He was chosen to be Dwight Eisenhower's running mate in the 1952 presidential election. Eisenhower won the election in 1952 and was re-elected in 1956. As a result, Nixon served as President Eisenhower's Vice-President for eight years.

In 1960 Vice-President Nixon was nominated as the Republican Party's candidate for President. He ran against Senator John Kennedy of Massachusetts who was the Democratic Party's nominee. John Kennedy defeated Richard Nixon in an election that was incredibly close. Kennedy won the popular vote by only 113,057 votes out of nearly 69 million votes cast.[134] After losing the 1960 presidential election, Richard Nixon resumed practicing law in Los Angeles and earned roughly $350,000 in 1961.[135]

In 1962 Richard Nixon tried to make a political comeback by running for Governor of California against the popular Democratic incumbent, Edmund G. ("Pat") Brown. Nixon lost that election and decided to return to the private practice of law. In June of 1963 he moved with his family to New York and became a senior partner in a Manhattan law firm that was re-named Nixon, Mudge, Rose, Guthrie and Alexander. While practicing law in New York, Nixon established a close professional relationship and friendship with John Mitchell. A graduate of Fordham University School of Law, Mitchell was a highly successful lawyer in private practice at another Manhattan firm. When the two law firms merged, Richard Nixon and John Mitchell became law partners. Their firm had a very lucrative law practice.[136]

After a few years of practicing law, Nixon decided to run for office again in the presidential election of 1968. His law partner John Mitchell became his campaign manager. The 1968 presidential election was a cliff-hanger for Nixon. The results of a Harris poll shortly before the election showed the Democratic candidate, Senator Hubert Humphrey, ahead by three percentage points. When the votes were counted Nixon won by a narrow margin. He did not win with a majority of the popular vote due to the presence of a third-party candidate, George Wallace. Richard Nixon received 43.40 percent of the popular vote while Hubert Humphrey received 42.72 percent.[137] Nixon's narrow victory in 1968, as well as his narrow defeat in 1960, would set the stage for Watergate.

When Richard Nixon took office as our thirty-seventh President in January of 1969 he had an inner circle of four close advisers – John Mitchell, John Ehrlichman, Herbert Kalmbach and H. R. ("Bob") Haldeman. They would later play key roles in the Watergate conspiracy. Three members of Nixon's inner circle were lawyers. John Mitchell, Nixon's former law partner and campaign manager, became Attorney General of the United States and head of the Department of Justice. John Ehrlichman became White House Counsel, essentially serving as President Nixon's in-house lawyer. Ehrlichman, who graduated from Stanford Law School, was a successful lawyer in private practice in Seattle, Washington with extensive courtroom experience. Herbert Kalmbach, a graduate of the University of Southern California Law School, was Nixon's personal lawyer and one of his principal fund-raisers. Bob Haldeman, a former advertising agency executive, was the only non-lawyer in the group. He became President Nixon's Chief of Staff.[138]

Other future participants in the Watergate conspiracy were soon added to the White House team. Charles Colson, a former Marine who graduated with honors from George Washington University Law School and founded a successful private law firm, joined the White House as Special Counsel to the President. Colson reported directly to Nixon. Egil ("Bud") Krogh, Jr., a graduate of the University of Washington School of Law and a young lawyer in John Erhlichman's Seattle law firm, followed Ehrlichman to the White House and became one of his principal deputies. Jeb Stuart Magruder, a businessman who was not a lawyer, was hired by Bob Haldeman to be his special assistant at the White House. Dwight Chapin, who also was not a lawyer, had worked in Haldeman's advertising agency and became President Nixon's appointments secretary.[139]

In 1970 President Nixon moved John Ehrlichman from his position as White House Counsel to a new position as the Chief of Domestic Policy. On Bud Krogh's recommendation, John Dean was hired to replace Ehrlichman as White House Counsel. Dean was a lawyer who had worked for a private law firm for a few months after his graduation from the Georgetown University Law Center. He then served as Chief Republican Counsel for the House Judiciary Committee. He left that position for the Department of Justice where he became Associate Deputy Attorney General. When John Dean joined the White House staff on July 27, 1970 he became President Nixon's in-house lawyer.[140] He would later play a central role in the Watergate conspiracy.[141]

Two more lawyers who would become involved in Watergate were added to the White House staff the following year. Gordon Strachan, who graduated from law school at the University of California, Berkeley, was a young lawyer practicing at the firm in which Nixon and Mitchell had been law partners. Strachan was hired to be Bob Haldeman's personal assistant. G. Gordon Liddy, a graduate of Fordham University School of Law, was brought to the White House from the Treasury Department on Bud Krogh's recommendation. Liddy was a lawyer who had joined the FBI and had also served as an Assistant District Attorney in upstate New York.[142]

Charles Colson, President Nixon's Special Counsel, recruited E. Howard Hunt to join the White House staff as a consultant. Howard Hunt was not a lawyer. He had retired from the CIA as a covert intelligence officer. He was given an office in the Executive Office Building where Nixon also had an office across the street from the White House.[143]

In 1971 President Nixon became concerned about his prospects for re-election. Registered Democratic voters outnumbered registered Republicans. The Democrats controlled both houses of Congress. The Republicans had not done well in the 1970 mid-term elections in populous states that would account for large numbers of electoral votes in the presidential election. The ongoing War in Vietnam was diminishing President Nixon's popularity. One of the candidates for the Democratic Party's nomination, Senator Edmund Muskie of Maine, was pulling ahead of Nixon in the polls. The 1960 and 1968 presidential elections had been very close. Nixon did not want to be a one-term President. He also did not want the 1972 election to be another cliff-hanger. To the contrary, President Nixon wanted to win re-election in a landslide that would give him a mandate for his second term.[144]

Nixon decided to set up an organization for his re-election campaign that was separate from the Republican National Committee. In the spring of 1971 the Committee to Re-Elect the President was established. The Committee to Re-elect became known as CREEP. Jeb Magruder was transferred from the White House to CREEP to serve as its initial Director. John Mitchell was going to be Nixon's campaign manager again, and he planned to resign as Attorney General and take over as Director of CREEP early in 1972.[145] Gordon Strachan, a lawyer on Bob Haldeman's staff, was transferred from the White House to CREEP. Strachan's assignment was to be the liaison between CREEP and the White House.[146]

President Nixon's nomination as the Republican Party's candidate was secure. He realized that his chances for re-election could be improved if the weakest Democratic candidate received the Democratic Party's nomination. He felt that Senator George McGovern, who was perceived to be far to the left of center politically, would be the most vulnerable opponent.[147]

In June 1971 Dwight Chapin and Gordon Strachan hired Donald Segretti to engage in political espionage and sabotage to disrupt the Democratic primaries and undermine the campaigns of candidates for the Democratic Party's nomination, particularly the campaign of Senator Edmund Muskie who was leading Nixon in the polls. Segretti was a lawyer who had graduated from law school at the University of California, Berkeley, and was completing his tour of duty as a Captain in the Army's Judge Advocate General Corps. Arrangements were made for Segretti to be paid for his services and expenses by Herbert Kalmbach, Nixon's personal lawyer, out of unreported surplus campaign contributions. At least some of the payments to Segretti were made in cash from campaign funds that Kalmbach kept in two safe deposit boxes. The activities of Donald Segretti and his staff, which will be described later in this chapter, would become known as the "dirty tricks" operation.[148]

In addition to being concerned about his re-election, Nixon was frustrated by what he perceived to be leaks of national security information. He was particularly upset by Daniel Ellsberg's leak of the Pentagon Papers. Daniel Ellsberg had worked for Henry Kissinger, Nixon's National Security Adviser. Ellsberg became disillusioned about the Vietnam War and leaked the Pentagon Papers to a reporter at the *New York Times*. The initial story about the Pentagon Papers appeared in the *New York Times* on June 13, 1971. Though Ellsberg was indicted by a federal grand jury and would stand trial for the unauthorized possession of defense information and theft of government property, Nixon wanted him publicly discredited. He also wanted leaks of sensitive information to stop.[149]

In July of 1971 the White House created a secret Special Investigations Unit under the direction of John Ehrlichman. The Unit became known as the Plumbers because its mission was to investigate and stop leaks. Ehrlichman's deputy, Bud Krogh, was put in charge of the Plumbers and another lawyer, David Young, served as the staff director. David Young was a graduate of Cornell Law School who practiced law in a large New York law firm before joining Henry Kissinger's staff. He was transferred to the White House staff when he was given the Plumbers assignment. Bud Krogh recruited Gordon Liddy for the Plumbers, and Howard Hunt also joined the team. The Plumbers were given an office in the Executive Office Building across the street from the White House. To help maintain secrecy their outside telephone line was set up in the name and home address of Kathleen Chenow, the Plumbers' secretary who lived in Alexandria, Virginia.[150]

On July 20, 1971 FBI agents tried to interview Daniel Ellsberg's psychiatrist, Dr. Lewis Fielding, who refused to be interviewed about one of his patients. A week later Howard Hunt sent a memo to Charles Colson, Nixon's Special Counsel, suggesting that Dr. Fielding's psychiatric records for Daniel Ellsberg be obtained as part of a plan to destroy Ellsberg's credibility. Colson and Hunt then persuaded the Plumbers to come up with a plan. On August 11 Bud Krogh and David Young sent a memo to John Ehrlichman recommending a covert operation to gain access to Dr. Fielding's psychiatric records on Daniel Ellsberg. Ehrlichman approved the covert operation so long as it would not be traceable to the White House. He would later claim that he did not expect the covert operation to involve a burglary.[151]

In late August, Gordon Liddy and Howard Hunt cased Dr. Fielding's office and apartment in order to satisfy Krogh and Young that the operation would not be traceable. With the approval of Krogh and Young, Hunt recruited three anti-Castro men living in Miami whom he knew from his time in the CIA. To finance the operation Bud Krogh gave Gordon Liddy $5,000 which Krogh had obtained from Charles Colson. On September 3, 1971 the three men from Miami burglarized Dr. Fielding's office. Gordon Liddy and Howard Hunt supervised the burglary. The burglars were not able to find any damaging information about Daniel Ellsberg in Dr. Fielding's office.[152] Within a few weeks after the failure of that operation, the Plumbers were disbanded.[153]

Charles Colson and Howard Hunt were not dissuaded from continuing to try to discredit Daniel Ellsberg. Hunt wrote a disparaging article about Ellsberg's leading criminal defense lawyer, characterizing the lawyer as a champion of leftist causes and pointing out that the lawyer's daughter had been involved in the Weather Underground. Colson gave the article to journalists in an effort to discredit Ellsberg and undermine his defense to the criminal charges against him.[154]

During the course of Ellsberg's criminal trial the presiding judge learned about the burglary of Dr. Fielding's office. The judge was also informed that the FBI had wiretapped some of Ellsberg's conversations, but was unable to locate the records of those wiretaps. As a result of these disclosures the judge declared a mistrial and permanently dismissed all charges against Daniel Ellsberg on grounds of government misconduct.[155] After the case was dismissed, the wiretap records which the FBI had been unable to find were discovered in John Ehrlichman's safe at the White House.[156]

Towards the end of 1971 Nixon's re-election campaign started to shift into high gear. John Mitchell, who was still Attorney General, asked John Dean to find a lawyer to serve as CREEP's General Counsel who would also be responsible for gathering intelligence. Dean consulted with Bud Krogh about the possibility of recommending David Young for the job. Krogh recommended Gordon Liddy instead. John Mitchell, while still Attorney General, interviewed Liddy and approved Krogh's recommendation. Ehrlichman, Haldeman and Magruder agreed. They were impressed by Liddy's background as a lawyer, FBI agent and Plumber. Liddy became General Counsel of CREEP on December 6, 1971.[157]

Gordon Liddy did not waste time developing a proposed intelligence plan. As General Counsel of CREEP, Liddy presented his initial plan to Attorney General John Mitchell at a meeting in Mitchell's office at the Department of Justice on January 27, 1972. Jeb Magruder and White House Counsel John Dean were also present. The intelligence plan had the code name "GEMSTONE." The initial GEMSTONE plan had a proposed budget of $1 million to finance kidnappings, sabotage, hiring prostitutes to obtain campaign information, wiretapping, and planting spies in the campaigns of potential Democratic nominees. Mitchell said that was not quite what he had in mind and the proposed budget was out of the question. Mitchell suggested that Liddy revise his plan. The group met again in Mitchell's office at the Department of Justice on February 4 when Liddy presented a revised plan with a proposed budget of $500,000. Liddy's revised GEMSTONE plan was not approved at the February 4 meeting.[158] On March 1, a few weeks after that meeting, John Mitchell resigned as Attorney General and became the full time director of CREEP. Mitchell's successor as Attorney General was Richard Kleindeist, a graduate of Harvard Law School who had been serving as Deputy Attorney General since 1969.[159]

When approval for Liddy's GEMSTONE plan appeared to be stalled, Charles Colson and Gordon Strachan urged Jeb Magruder to take action to get an intelligence plan approved. On March 30, 1972 Magruder met with John Mitchell in Key Biscayne, Florida and presented a scaled down Liddy plan that had a proposed budget of $250,000. Liddy's scaled down plan was sometimes referred to as GEMSTONE III. The plan provided for bugging the Democratic National Committee offices in the Watergate Office Building and in a Miami hotel, and bugging Senator McGovern's headquarters in Washington. Liddy's GEMSTONE III plan was approved.[160]

Meanwhile, Donald Segretti was carrying out his dirty tricks operation. He caused political meetings and fundraising events to be disrupted with stink bombs and with people he hired to attend and engage in unruly behavior. In his efforts to sabotage Senator Muskie's campaign for the Democratic Party's nomination, Segretti stole Muskie's campaign stationary and wrote spurious letters to potential voters on which he forged Muskie's signature. One of Segretti's counterfeit letters, written on Citizens for Muskie stationary, falsely claimed that Senator Henry Jackson, one of Muskie's opponents in the Florida primary, had fathered an illegitimate child while in high school and had been arrested on sexual charges in Washington, D. C. The letter also falsely claimed that Hubert Humphrey had been arrested for drunk driving in the company of a prostitute. Segretti mailed the letter to Florida voters three days before the Democratic primary. The letter was intended to make Democratic voters want to distance themselves from Senator Muskie. Another Segretti letter that became known as the "Canuck letter" was written on Muskie letterhead and contained derogatory comments about French Canadians. That letter was designed to alienate Senator Muskie from voters in the New Hampshire Democratic primary who had relatives in Canada. By April of 1972 Muskie was effectively eliminated as a contender for the Democratic Party's nomination. Senator George McGovern, Nixon's ideal opponent in the presidential election, became the front-runner. Muskie formally withdrew from the race on April 27, 1972. The dirty tricks operation helped achieve that result.[161]

On May 28, 1972 five men broke into the headquarters of the Democratic National Committee in the Watergate Office Building in Washington, D. C. One of the burglars was James McCord, a retired chief of physical security for the CIA who had been hired full time by CREEP at the beginning of the year. The other four burglars were from Miami, including the three men from

Miami who had broken into Dr. Lewis Fielding's office the previous year. Acting on directions from Gordon Liddy and Howard Hunt, the burglars photographed documents and planted bugging devices on the telephones of Lawrence O'Brien, Chairman of the Democratic National Committee, and R. Spencer Olner, another Democratic Party official. The costs of the Watergate operation were paid in cash with campaign funds taken from a safe in CREEP's office and given to Gordon Liddy. By that time, Liddy had become General Counsel of the Finance Committee of CREEP.[162]

After the burglars left the building, another man hired by James McCord began monitoring the wiretaps from a room at the Howard Johnson Motel across the street from the Watergate. He gave McCord logs of the intercepted conversations. McCord in turn gave the logs to Gordon Liddy. Copies of the logs were attached to cover memos captioned "GEMSTONE" and distributed to Jeb Magruder and Gordon Strachan. Magruder gave copies to John Mitchell. The information had little value. Mitchell called Liddy into his office to express his dissatisfaction. One of the main problems with the quality of the information was that the bugging device installed on Lawrence O'Brien's telephone was malfunctioning.[163]

James McCord and the four men from Miami broke into the Democratic National Committee's headquarters at the Watergate again on June 17, 1972. Their main objective was to replace the malfunctioning bugging device on Lawrence O'Brien's telephone. This time the burglars were caught and arrested at the scene. Gordon Liddy and Howard Hunt, who had set up a command post in a room at the adjacent Watergate Hotel, learned about the arrests when they occurred. The four men from Miami had $4,500 in new one hundred dollar bills in their collective possession at the time of their arrest. They had received that cash from Gordon Liddy. It came from CREEP.[164]

The cover-up began immediately. Within hours of the burglars' arrest early on Saturday morning, Gordon Liddy went to CREEP's office and shredded his GEMSTONE files and other incriminating documents. Sometime later he instructed his secretary to shred her stenographic notebooks as well as any of her documents that mentioned Gordon Liddy.[165] Over the weekend Gordon Strachan went through his files and Bob Haldeman's files, shredding documents relating to Liddy's intelligence plan, Segretti's activities, results of the Watergate wiretaps and notes of Strachan's meetings with Haldeman.[166] Both Gordon Liddy and Gordon Strachan were lawyers. Before the work week began on Monday June 19, they were already destroying incriminating evidence.

A formal cover-up plan evolved in a series of meetings over the next few days in John Mitchell's office and in his apartment. The participants in those meetings, in addition to Mitchell, were John Dean, Jeb Magruder, Robert Mardian and Fred LaRue. Robert Mardian became CREEP's in-house lawyer after serving as Assistant Attorney General in John Mitchell's Department of Justice. He was a graduate of the University of Southern California Law School. Fred LaRue was a wealthy businessman who became John Mitchell's chief lieutenant. Mitchell's overriding goal was to prevent Watergate from becoming an issue in President Nixon's campaign for re-election. To achieve that goal the group decided to do everything possible to keep the connection between the Watergate break-in and CREEP a secret.[167]

In one of the initial meetings of the group on June 19, Jeb Magruder asked John Mitchell what he should do with some GEMSTONE files he had in his briefcase. The GEMSTONE documents would have tied the Watergate break-in to CREEP. Mitchell replied that it might be a good idea for Magruder to have a little fire at home. Magruder burned his copies of the GEMSTONE documents in his fireplace at home that night.[168]

A key element of the initial cover-up strategy was to confine any criminal investigation to the Watergate break-in and the five burglars who had been arrested. The cover-up strategy was soon modified when the FBI learned that Gordon Liddy and Howard Hunt were also involved in the Watergate operation. The revised cover-up strategy would focus on confining any criminal investigation to the Watergate break-in and taking the position that Liddy, Hunt and the five burglars were acting independently for their own illegitimate purposes. The goal was to avoid having a criminal investigation uncover other issues such as the existence of the Plumbers, the campaign's connection with the burglary of Dr. Fielding's office, Segretti's dirty tricks operation, unreported campaign contributions, illegal corporate campaign contributions, money laundering, and certain activities of Howard Hunt.[169]

John Ehrlichman was another participant in some of the early meetings to plan the Watergate cover-up. Late in the afternoon of June 19, two days after the Watergate burglars were arrested, John Dean and Charles Colson met with John Ehrlichman in Ehrlichman's office. At the meeting the three lawyers decided it would be a good idea for the contents of Howard Hunt's safe in the Executive Office Building to be removed and placed in the custody of White House Counsel John Dean. The next day the contents of Howard Hunt's safe were delivered to John Dean's office in the White House. Dean and his assistant, Fred Fielding, went through the contents of the safe wearing latex gloves. They found a revolver, a stack of documents nearly a foot high, some classified State Department cables and a black suitcase full of bugging equipment. Dean locked the gun and the bugging equipment in his closet, sent some of the State Department cables to David Young, and put several folders of documents he considered to be politically embarrassing in his safe. Those documents included a psychological profile of Daniel Ellsberg and a phony State Department cable doctored to make it appear that President John Kennedy had ordered the assassination of South Vietnam President Diem.[170] The phony State Department cable was part of a project that Howard Hunt and Charles Colson had been working on to discredit the Kennedys in case Senator Edward Kennedy of Massachusetts sought or received the Democratic Party's nomination.[171]

After discussing the contents of Howard Hunt's safe with John Ehrlichman, John Dean came up with the idea of giving the materials that were not politically sensitive to FBI agents and giving the politically embarrassing documents to the Acting Director of the FBI, L. Patrick ("Pat") Gray.[172] Pat Gray was a lawyer who became Acting Director of the FBI on May 3, 1972 following the death of the original FBI Director, J. Edgar Hoover. Gray served as Acting Director until he resigned on April 27, 1973. He came to the FBI from the Department of Justice where he had been designated to be Deputy Attorney

General. He was a graduate of the U. S. Naval Academy who served as a sub-marine commander in World War II and in the Korean War. After graduating from George Washington University Law School, where he was an editor of the Law Review and a top student elected to the Order of the Coif, Gray began practicing law with a firm in New London, Connecticut. After he resigned as Acting Director of the FBI Pat Gray returned to the private practice of law.[173]

Ehrlichman approved John Dean's plan to give the politically embarrassing documents to Pat Gray. Dean's plan gave the White House the opportunity to claim later on that virtually everything found in Howard Hunt's safe had been turned over to the FBI. During the next few days Dean put a number of politically sensitive documents, including the phony State Department cable, into two envelopes. He set aside two Hermes notebooks containing information relating to the GEMSTONE project. He delivered the remaining contents of Howard Hunt's safe to FBI agents. At a meeting in John Ehrlichman's office on June 28, John Dean handed the two envelopes to Pat Gray. Gray was told the envelopes contained politically sensitive documents unrelated to Watergate that should never see the light of day. Six months later, Pat Gray opened the envelopes at home and glanced at the contents. He tossed both envelopes with all the documents they contained into the fireplace to burn up along with his Christmas trash.[174]

While Gray was serving as Acting Director of the FBI the White House put pressure on him to confine the scope of the FBI's investigation. Soon after the Watergate burglars were arrested, the FBI traced the forty-five one hundred dollar bills found in the burglars' possession to the Republic National Bank of Miami where Bernard Barker had an account. Bernard Barker was one of the Watergate burglars who had also broken into Dr. Fielding's office. John Dean learned about the results of the FBI's investigation from Pat Gray. The White House became concerned that further investigation by the FBI about the source of the CREEP funds used to finance the Watergate operation would uncover a scheme that had laundered secret contributions to President Nixon's re-election campaign through a bank in Mexico.[175]

On June 23 Bob Haldeman and John Ehrlichman summoned Richard Helms and Vernon Walters to a meeting in the White House. Helms was the

Director of the CIA and Walters was the Deputy Director. The meeting was held to ask Walters to persuade Pat Gray to keep the FBI's investigation away from the source of the cash found in the possession of the Watergate burglars. Walters was told that President Nixon believed an ongoing FBI investigation about the source of the cash could expose CIA activity in Mexico. Shortly after the meeting adjourned Walters told Pat Gray to taper off the FBI probe in Mexico. The FBI slowed its investigation about the source of the cash until Walters later gave Gray written assurance that nothing had been found to suggest the FBI's investigation would jeopardize any CIA activity.[176]

The FBI then resumed its investigation and the details of the money laundering scheme eventually came to light. Some Texas supporters of President Nixon's re-election campaign who wanted to remain anonymous obtained four cashier's checks totaling $89,000 from a Mexican bank. The four cashier's checks were issued to a Mexican lawyer who endorsed them in blank. Those endorsed checks were delivered to CREEP. Several days later a Minnesota businessman who also wanted to remain anonymous gave a $25,000 campaign contribution in cash to Nixon's campaign finance chairman for the Midwest. That cash was used to buy a cashier's check from a bank in Boca Raton, Florida that was also delivered to CREEP. Gordon Liddy, acting on behalf of CREEP, sent those five cashier's checks to Bernard Barker who deposited them for collection in his account at the Republic National Bank of Miami. Barker then withdrew the proceeds of those checks, totaling $114,000, in a series of installments in cash. He delivered $112,000 of the cash to Gordon Liddy for storage in CREEP's safes.[177]

Pat Gray continued to keep John Dean informed about the progress of the FBI's Watergate investigation. Gray gave Dean copies of FBI witness interviews, reports and other internal FBI documents on dozens of occasions. Regular conversations between Pat Gray and John Dean kept the White House informed about what the FBI was learning during the course of its investigation. As a result, John Dean in the White House and the in-house lawyers at CREEP were able to coach witnesses in preparation for their FBI interviews or grand jury testimony with knowledge about what other witnesses had told the FBI. Gray also allowed Dean to sit in on FBI interviews of more than a dozen witnesses, including Dwight Chapin, Charles Colson, John Ehrlichman, Gordon Strachan and David Young. At Dean's request, Gray put a hold on distributing FBI leads to the Watergate prosecutor. Gray also delayed FBI interviews of some White House staff members, including an FBI interview of Kathleen Chenow who had been the secretary for the Plumbers.[178]

The initial criminal prosecution of participants in the Watergate conspiracy was directed by Henry Petersen, the Assistant Attorney General in charge of the Criminal Division at the Department of Justice. After graduating from law school at the Catholic University of America, Petersen joined the Department of Justice and stayed there throughout his career. In his role as Assistant Attorney General in charge of the Criminal Division, Henry Petersen gave instructions to the lead prosecutor in the Watergate break-in case, Earl Silbert, who was the Chief Assistant U. S. Attorney for the District of Columbia.[179] At John Dean's request Petersen made it clear to Silbert that he was investigating a break-in and should not go wandering off into other areas. As the initial Watergate criminal investigation continued, Petersen gave status reports to John Dean. From those reports Dean learned in advance who was going to be contacted and interviewed by the FBI. Petersen also gave information to Dean about the grand jury proceedings in the Watergate break-in case, even though grand jury proceedings are supposed to be kept secret. Dean persuaded Petersen to excuse Colson, Krogh, Young, Chapin and Strachan from appearing personally in front of the grand jury. They were allowed instead to give their testimony to prosecutors at the Department of Justice. Transcripts of their testimony were then read to the grand jury. This unusual procedure protected those Watergate participants from being asked questions by members of the grand jury.[180]

The grand jury investigating the Watergate break-in handed down criminal indictments against the five burglars, Gordon Liddy and Howard Hunt on September 15, 1972. Gordon Liddy had already been dismissed by CREEP on June 28. John Mitchell had resigned as Director of CREEP on July 1 and returned to his law firm, though he continued to be involved in the cover-up.

Mitchell's successor was Clark MacGregor, a former Congressman who would lead CREEP and President Nixon's re-election campaign through the November election. The criminal case against the seven defendants involved in the Watergate break-in would not go to trial until after the election.[181]

After the indictments were handed down and before the Watergate break-in case went to trial, John Dean attended a meeting with Henry Petersen and Earl Silbert at the Department of Justice. Howard Hunt had requested certain documents from the prosecutors in order to prepare his defense to the criminal charges against him. Hunt was entitled to see those documents under the rules governing criminal cases. Silbert asked Dean about two Hermes notebooks which Hunt claimed were missing from the documents the prosecutors had turned over to him. Hunt claimed those two notebooks, which contained information about the GEMSTONE project, were vital to his defense. Dean said he did not remember seeing Hermes notebooks and seemed unfamiliar with that descriptive term. He took Henry Petersen aside and told Petersen that some of Howard Hunt's documents containing politically embarrassing information had been turned over to Pat Gray. Sometime later, John Dean was in his office one weekend and decided to look for the two Hermes notebooks. He found them in one of his office safes. Dean did not contact Earl Silbert or Henry Petersen to let them know he had found Howard Hunt's Hermes notebooks. Instead, he put both notebooks through his office shredder.[182]

In addition to destroying incriminating evidence and putting pressure on the FBI and the prosecutors to confine their investigations to the Watergate break-in, participants in the cover-up were also involved in payments of "hush money." The hush money was paid in cash to the Watergate break-in participants for their lawyers' fees and for their silence. The payment of hush money was authorized by John Mitchell, John Ehrlichman and Bob Haldeman within a few days after the participants in the Watergate break-in were arrested. Mitchell, Ehrlichman and Haldeman also authorized John Dean to ask Herbert Kalmbach to raise the money needed to make the payments. Kalmbach met with Dean on June 29 and agreed to accept the assignment. He was told by Dean that Anthony Ulasewicz would be an appropriate person to distribute the cash. Ulasewicz was a former New York City police officer who had been hired by John Ehrlichman as an investigator and who was paid for his services with campaign funds.[183]

Kalmbach raised about $220,000 for the hush money payments. Most of the money consisted of campaign funds controlled by CREEP. The rest of the cash was donated by an outside contributor. By the middle of September $187,500 in cash had been distributed in various surreptitious ways by Anthony Ulasewicz. He gave $25,000 to Howard Hunt's criminal defense lawyer, William Bittman, $8,000 to Gordon Liddy and $154,500 to Howard Hunt's wife for redistribution among the Watergate break-in participants. On September 21 Herbert Kalmbach met with John Dean and Fred LaRue in Dean's office at the White House to let them know that he and Anthony Ulasewicz were not willing to continue raising and distributing the hush money. Kalmbach arranged to have the rest of the money he had raised turned over to Fred LaRue. Kalmbach then burned the records of his cash receipts and disbursements in an ashtray. The task of raising and distributing cash for hush money payments was assumed by LaRue. Between the September 21 meeting and the day of the election, Fred LaRue paid out an additional $20,000 in cash to the Watergate break-in participants.[184]

On November 7, 1972 President Nixon was elected to serve a second term. He won re-election in a landslide victory. Nixon received 60.8 percent of the popular vote and 520 electoral votes. McGovern was soundly defeated, winning only 18 electoral votes. He did not even win the electoral votes of his home state, South Dakota.[185] The cover-up was successful, at least in the short term. The truth about Watergate would not be uncovered until after the election.

President Nixon began his second term on January 20, 1973. The criminal trial of the seven defendants in the Watergate break-in case had started earlier in the month. After several days of trial, Howard Hunt and the four men from Miami changed their pleas to guilty. Gordon Liddy and James McCord stood trial and were found guilty of all charges on January 30. Less than a month after Liddy and McCord were convicted, President Nixon told White House Counsel John Dean to start reporting directly to him.[186]

Sentencing of the seven defendants in the Watergate break-in case was scheduled for March 23. As the sentencing date approached, Howard Hunt sent John Dean a secret demand for more money. By that time, at John Dean's direction, Fred LaRue had already given Howard Hunt's lawyer, William Bittman, $210,000 of additional cash from campaign funds for distribution among the Watergate break-in defendants and their lawyers.[187]

Dean discussed Hunt's demand with John Ehrlichman and, at Ehrlichman's direction, with John Mitchell. On March 21 Dean had a secret meeting in the Oval Office to inform President Nixon about the situation. Shortly after that meeting, Dean told Fred LaRue that Hunt was demanding an immediate payment of $75,000. LaRue called John Mitchell who told him to make the payment. LaRue took $75,000 in cash out of CREEP funds he had been storing in his filing cabinet, put the cash in an envelope, and left the envelope in William Bittman's home mailbox.[188] The total payments of cash to the Watergate break-in defendants would add up to nearly half a million dollars.[189]

President Nixon continued to involve himself more directly in efforts to monitor and confine the scope of the prosecutors' investigation. Nixon had a number of secret meetings and phone conversations about the Watergate investigation with Henry Petersen, the Assistant Attorney General who was overseeing the investigation for the Department of Justice. Petersen told Nixon what prospective witnesses were telling the prosecutors and how witnesses were testifying before the grand jury. In a phone conversation on April 18, Petersen told Nixon that the prosecutors had learned about the Plumbers' burglary of Dr. Fielding's office. Nixon told Petersen to stay out of that area because it involved a national security matter. Petersen passed Nixon's instruction on to Earl Silbert, the Assistant U. S. Attorney who was conducting the Watergate investigation.[190]

In a nationally televised speech on April 30, 1973 President Nixon announced the resignations of John Ehrlichman, Bob Haldeman and Richard Kleindeist and the firing of John Dean.[191] After resigning as Attorney General, Kleindeist pled guilty to a misdemeanor charge of giving false testimony during his Senate confirmation hearing. The false testimony related to efforts by the White House to interfere with a Department of Justice antitrust investigation of the International Telephone and Telegraph Company. He received a one-month suspended jail sentence.[192]

Nixon nominated Secretary of Defense Elliot Richardson to succeed Richard Kleindeist as Attorney General. Elliot Richardson was a lawyer. After serving as a platoon leader in World War II at Normandy, he attended Harvard Law School where he was editor and president of the Harvard Law Review. Following his graduation from law school Richardson clerked for U. S. Supreme Court Justice Felix Frankfurter. He then returned to his home state of Massachusetts where he served as U. S. Attorney for Massachusetts and was later elected Attorney General of Massachusetts.[193]

On May 9, 1973 the Senate Judiciary Committee opened its confirmation hearings on Elliot Richardson's nomination as Attorney General. The Senate had already passed a resolution calling for the appointment of a Special Prosecutor to investigate Watergate. Richardson assured the Committee that he would appoint a Special Prosecutor who would be independent and adequately staffed. The following week Richardson named Archibald Cox as the Special Prosecutor. Cox was a Harvard Law School Professor who had served as Solicitor General of the United States under Presidents Kennedy and Johnson. On May 23, 1973 the Senate Judiciary Committee approved the nomination of Elliot Richardson as Attorney General and the appointment of Archibald Cox as Special Prosecutor.[194] The Office of Special Prosecutor soon began its investigation of the Watergate conspiracy to determine whether any crimes had been committed. The Senate Watergate Committee chaired by Senator Ervin had already started to hold its public hearings.

Over the next several weeks the truth about Watergate began to come to light. A key element of the Watergate conspiracy was the creation of a secret cash fund controlled by CREEP that could be used to pay for clandestine activities. The total amount of cash in the secret fund was more than $1.7 million. The sources of the money in the secret fund were unspent contributions left over from the 1968 presidential campaign and the results of aggressive fundraising activities that took place before a new campaign finance law went into effect on April 7, 1972. Aggressive fundraising before the April 7 deadline raised secret campaign contributions that were often made in cash. Corporations made illegal campaign contributions totaling around $780,000. Some campaign contributions were made in anticipation of political favors or ambassadorships.[195] Herbert Kalmbach, President Nixon's personal lawyer and a member of his inner circle of advisers, would later plead guilty to a criminal charge of promising an ambassadorship in exchange for a $100,000 contribution to Nixon's re-election campaign.[196]

The secret cash fund was used to pay Donald Segretti and his staff for the dirty tricks operation. Gordon Liddy received $199,000 in cash from the fund and he used some of that cash to pay for the Watergate break-in. Nearly all the hush money that was paid to the Watergate break-in defendants came from the secret fund. We will probably never know how all the money in the fund was spent. The original records of the cash receipts and disbursements for the secret fund were destroyed six days after the Watergate break-in at the suggestion of President Nixon's personal lawyer, Herbert Kalmbach.[197]

On July 16, 1973 a presidential aide testifying before the Senate Watergate Committee disclosed the existence of a voice-activated tape recording system that was installed by the Secret Service a little over two years earlier in President Nixon's offices in the White House and in the Executive Office Building. Over five thousand hours of conversations had been secretly recorded on the White House tapes.[198]

Soon after that testimony was given, Special Prosecutor Archibald Cox subpoenaed some of the White House tapes. President Nixon wanted to avoid producing the actual tapes. He offered to comply with the subpoena by having the tapes transcribed and by producing edited transcripts. When Archibald Cox refused to withdraw the subpoena for the actual tapes, Nixon ordered Attorney General Elliot Richardson to fire him. Richardson apparently believed that firing Cox would interfere with the independence of the Special Prosecutor, contrary to the commitment Richardson had made to the Senate Judiciary Committee in his confirmation hearing. He refused to fire Cox and resigned as Attorney General. Nixon then ordered the Deputy Attorney General, William Ruckelshaus, to fire Cox. Ruckelshaus also refused and said he was submitting a letter of resignation. Before his letter of resignation reached the White House, Nixon fired Ruckelshaus and designated Solicitor General Robert Bork as Acting Attorney General. Bork followed Nixon's order and fired Cox. The White House then announced that President Nixon had fired Archibald Cox, abolished the Office of Special Prosecutor, and returned the Watergate investigation to the Department of Justice.[199] In response to widespread negative public reaction to that announcement, President Nixon agreed several days later to have a new Special Prosecutor appointed. Leon Jaworski became the new Special Prosecutor who continued the investigation Archibald Cox had started.[200] Jaworski pursued enforcement of the subpoena for the actual White House tapes all the way to the United States Supreme Court.

On July 24, 1974 the Supreme Court rejected Nixon's arguments against enforcement of the subpoena and ordered production of the actual tapes.[201] Nixon produced the subpoenaed tapes the following week. The tape recording of a meeting Nixon had with Bob Haldeman on June 23, 1972 revealed that President Nixon personally approved the plan to have the Deputy Director of the CIA contact Pat Gray, the Acting Director of the FBI, for the purpose of trying to derail the FBI's investigation about the source of the cash found in the possession of the Watergate burglars.[202] When that tape became public towards the end of July, the House Judiciary Committee was in the midst of approving Articles of Impeachment against President Nixon. The production and public disclosure of the contents of the June 23 tape became the final nail in President Nixon's political coffin.

On August 9, 1974 President Nixon resigned in disgrace and Vice-President Gerald Ford became our thirty-eighth President. A month later, President Ford granted Richard Nixon a full pardon for all offenses against the United States which he committed or may have committed during his term of office. As a result of the pardon Richard Nixon, who had been named as an unindicted co-conspirator by the grand jury investigating the Watergate cover-up, no longer faced a risk of criminal prosecution.[203]

A number of the other lawyers involved in the Watergate conspiracy did face criminal prosecution as well as incarceration. John Mitchell became the first former Attorney General of the United States to serve a prison sentence. The jury in the Watergate cover-up case found Mitchell guilty of obstruction of justice, conspiracy to obstruct justice, and perjury.[204] The same jury found John Ehrlichman guilty of obstruction of justice, conspiracy to obstruct justice and perjury. Ehrlichman was also convicted in the case arising from the burglary of Dr. Fielding's office and was sent to prison.[205] Gordon Liddy was convicted of conspiracy, burglary and illegal wiretapping in the Watergate break-in case and conspiracy to violate Dr. Fielding's Fourth Amendment rights in the case arising from the burglary of his office. Liddy served the longest prison sentence of any of the participants in the Watergate conspiracy.[206] Charles Colson, John Dean, Herbert Kalmbach, Bud Krogh and Donald Segretti pled guilty to various charges and were sent to prison.[207] Robert Mardian was convicted in the Watergate cover-up case of conspiracy to obstruct justice. He appealed his conviction and was granted a new trial by the Court of Appeals on the grounds that the trial judge should have declared a mistrial when his lead defense attorney became incapacitated by illness during the trial. After the Court of Appeals granted Mardian a new trial the Special Prosecutor dismissed the case against him.[208] Kenneth Parkinson, an in-house lawyer at CREEP, went to trial as a defendant in the Watergate cover-up case and was acquitted.[209] Gordon Strachan was also indicted in the Watergate cover-up case, but the Special Prosecutor decided to try his case separately for strategic reasons. Before Strachan's case went to trial, the Special Prosecutor dropped the charges against him.[210] David Young was given immunity from prosecution in exchange for his cooperation with the government in the case against John Ehrlichman involving the burglary of Dr. Fielding's office.[211]

Many of the lawyers who participated in the Watergate conspiracy were blinded by personal ambition and by a desire to win a landslide victory in the 1972 presidential election at all costs. They zealously pursued the objectives of their clients or superiors without exercising the independent professional judgment that is expected from members of the legal profession. They ignored the morality of what they were doing and what they were being asked to do. They disregarded the fundamental principles of honesty, integrity and public service that are essential to instilling public respect for the legal profession and public confidence in the rule of law. Although they were sworn to uphold the law, they acted as though they were above the law.

The extensive publicity about Watergate over the course of two years made it difficult for the American public to perceive lawyers as ethical professionals committed to serving the cause of justice and protecting the rights guaranteed to all of us by the Constitution. Instead, Watergate reinforced a number of negative beliefs about lawyers – including the belief that lawyers use their knowledge of the law to outsmart and manipulate the system in order to achieve the selfish goals of their clients or their own selfish goals, without regard for the effects of their activities on other people or on the system itself.

In one sense Watergate was unique because the ethical misconduct and criminal behavior of so many lawyers who actively participated in the conspiracy received widespread publicity for an extended period of time. However, it would be a mistake to dismiss Watergate as an aberration and discount the activities and conduct of the lawyers involved in the conspiracy as extreme examples of lawyers behaving badly. In chapter eight we will see how the concept of zealous representation and a win-at-all costs mentality continue to influence the behavior of lawyers and lead some to compromise their personal integrity and disregard the ethical rules governing lawyers. We will first take a look in the next two chapters at ways the private practice of law has become less of a professional endeavor and more of a highly competitive commercial enterprise.[212]

Six

The Private Practice of Law Becomes a Commercial Enterprise

The private practice of law started becoming more of a commercial enterprise in 1977 when the Supreme Court decided that lawyers have a constitutional right under the First Amendment to advertise their services. In *Bates v. State Bar of Arizona*[213] some lawyers practicing in the Phoenix metropolitan area placed an advertisement in the daily newspaper describing their legal clinic and listing the fees they charged for certain routine legal services. They conceded their ad violated a state disciplinary rule against lawyer advertising, but argued that application of the disciplinary rule to the newspaper ad violated their constitutional right under the First Amendment to engage in commercial speech. A majority of the Supreme Court agreed. Justice Harry Blackmun, who wrote the Court's opinion, described the role of commercial speech in a free market:

> [C]ommercial speech serves to inform the public of the availability, nature and prices of products and services, and thus performs an indispensable role in the allocation of resources in a free enterprise system.[214]

Justice Blackmun rejected the State Bar of Arizona's argument that the "hustle of the marketplace will adversely affect the profession's service orientation, and irreparably damage the delicate balance between the lawyer's need to earn and his obligation selflessly to serve."[215] He pointed out that bans on lawyer advertising originated historically as a "rule of etiquette" which "has become an anachronism."[216]

Justice Lewis Powell wrote one of the dissenting opinions. He made the prescient observation that the Court's decision "will effect profound changes in the practice of law, viewed for centuries as a learned profession."[217]

Arizona's ban on lawyer advertising was typical of restrictions existing across the country. Lawyers were expected to obtain new business from referrals and from recommendations based on their community service activities and their reputation. The Supreme Court's decision in *Bates v. State Bar of Arizona* opened the floodgates to lawyer advertising. We now see lawyers' ads on television, in newspapers, on billboards, in airports, on the sides of buses and on the outside back covers of telephone books. People injured in an automobile accident often receive solicitation letters in the mail from lawyers who monitor motor vehicle accident reports. Lawyers have even been known to arrange for semi-trailers containing x-ray machines and other diagnostic equipment to be parked outside large work sites in order to screen workers for occupational disease as they end their shifts.[218] Practices such as these reinforce a negative perception of lawyers as ambulance chasers on the hustle to drum up new business.

While advertising by lawyers can help make people aware of available legal services and increase competition, aggressive lawyer advertising can also have negative effects. Lawyers who try to distinguish themselves in advertisements or in their website content by claiming they will "fight for your rights," or by suggesting they are as tough and aggressive as a well known character in action movies, may lead their clients into contentious litigation that does not serve the clients' best interests. Lawyer ads inviting people who have received a particular surgical implant to call a toll-free telephone number and find out whether they are eligible for a large settlement may cause people who received that implant needless anxiety and concern. Ads that create unrealistic expectations about the results of a claim or lawsuit will create dissatisfaction among clients when the expected results are not obtained. An unhappy client is not only upset with his or her lawyer. Dissatisfied clients are likely to have negative feelings and opinions about the legal profession as a whole.

In addition to the effects of lawyer advertising, the emergence of large law firms has changed the economics of private law practice dramatically. In 1965 the largest law firm in the United States had 125 lawyers. By 2012 at least 350 law firms in the United States had more than 100 lawyers.[219] Of those 350 law firms, roughly 150 firms had at least 250 lawyers and 24 firms had more than 1,000 lawyers.[220] The law firms with at least 250 lawyers are sometimes collectively referred to as "Big Law." The influence of Big Law within the legal profession has made the private practice of law more of a commercial enterprise, particularly in larger law firms, with the generation of revenue from legal fees as a primary goal.

According to the results of a study published in 2014, profits per partner in the 200 largest law firms averaged roughly half a million dollars for the previous year.[221] In a number of the most profitable firms the average profits per partner exceeds two million dollars a year.[222] Those per partner averages are based on all the partners in the firms, including both income partners and equity partners. Income partners are generally paid a salary and bonus, though they do not own an interest in the firm. Equity partners are the firm's owners, and their compensation is usually much higher than the compensation paid to income partners. For the equity partners in the most profitable law firms, average profits per partner have ranged from $2 million to $4.2 million a year.[223] All of these figures are averages. Some partners make less than the average, while others make considerably more.

To support these profit levels for the partners and pay the significant overhead costs required to operate a large law firm, the lawyers in the firm need to bill clients a considerable amount of money for legal services. The partners also need to have large numbers of newer associate attorneys in the firm who can bill clients and generate profits. Billings to clients are generally based on the number of hours of legal work performed by a lawyer multiplied by the lawyer's hourly rate. The firm sets a standard hourly rate and a billable hour goal for each lawyer at the beginning of the year. To cover increases in salaries and overhead costs from year to year, lawyers are under pressure from within the firm to increase their hourly rates periodically. It is not uncommon to see rates in the range of $750 to $1,000 an hour, or more, for experienced partners in Big Law firms practicing in the largest metropolitan areas. Common billable hour goals for associates in the larger firms are in the range of 2,000 to 2,400 billable hours a year.[224] In some firms associates who exceed their goals will be considered for a bonus at the end of the year, giving them an incentive to generate even more billable hours.

Billable hour goals at the larger firms require associates to put in very long hours at work. Let's consider a hypothetical associate who devoted 2,100 billable hours to client work last year. The associate was also required to attend law firm meetings and perform administrative tasks that could not be billed to clients. In many states, lawyers need to attend continuing legal education programs in order to maintain their license to practice law. If the associate hopes to become a partner in the firm some day, he or she needs to devote time to bar association activities, writing articles, public speaking and networking in order to develop a reputation that will attract clients to the firm. So the associate who billed 2,100 hours probably worked at least 2,700 hours last year. Assuming four weeks off work during the year for vacations, holidays and a day or two home sick with the flu, this associate worked during the rest of the year at least 56 hours a week on average. That average is consistent with the results of a study conducted by the American Bar Foundation and the National Association for Law Placement.[225] The average of 56 hours a week does not include any time for lunch or time for breaks during the day. It also does not include commuting time. If we add a couple of hours a day for the associate to commute to and from the office, we can see that little time was left over for the associate to have much of a life outside of work.

In order to compete for sophisticated and lucrative corporate legal work, Big Law firms want to recruit top law school graduates from the leading law schools. To attract top graduates willing to work the long hours the firm will require, Big Law firms offer starting salaries that would seem astronomical to most people. It is not uncommon for a brand new lawyer who joins a Big Law firm in New York as an associate to be paid a starting salary of $160,000 a year with the possibility of additional compensation in the form of bonuses.[226] This salary is paid to a beginning lawyer with no clients and with no experience practicing law. Other major metropolitan areas follow New York's lead. Starting salaries for first-year associates who join Big Law firms in many other large metropolitan areas are somewhat less than they are in New York, but still well over $100,000 a year. Not surprisingly, the experienced lawyers in a firm expect to be paid more than a first-year associate. When entry level salaries are raised to recruit top law school graduates, salaries for the more experienced lawyers in the firm need to be raised as well. The result is an inflated salary structure that can only be supported by high levels of billings to clients. Judge Harry Edwards, a senior federal appellate court judge who had been a law professor at the University of Michigan and at Harvard, succinctly described the relationship between high salaries and overhead costs and the substantial number of billable hours many law firms need to generate:

> [M]any, many law firms have transformed themselves into "money machines," where partners and associates finance their huge salaries and luxurious surroundings by billing a tremendous number of hours.[227]

The salaries offered by Big Law firms also have a ripple effect on somewhat smaller law firms that want to compete for major corporate legal work. Some corporate legal departments that hire outside law firms choose a Big Law firm as the safe choice, at least for "bet the company" litigation and other major legal matters. Big Law firms are institutions with known reputations. If a major legal matter turns out poorly for the corporation, the general counsel in charge of the legal department is unlikely to be criticized by the CEO or the Board of Directors for having hired a Big Law firm. Other corporate legal departments are more interested in finding less expensive alternatives to Big Law firms and they are willing to consider somewhat smaller law firms for major projects.[228] To compete for those projects, the smaller firms need to have highly qualified lawyers available to do the work. At least to some extent, those firms compete with Big Law firms to hire the top graduates from leading law schools. They typically offer somewhat less onerous billable hour requirements as a trade off for lower starting salaries and lower average profits per partner. However, for a top law school graduate to be interested in joining a smaller firm the salary gap cannot be too great. Increases in Big Law firm starting salaries put pressure on the somewhat smaller law firms to raise their starting salaries as well.[229] As starting salaries go up, billings to clients for legal work must go up in order to generate more money to pay the higher salaries. Even if an associate in one of those smaller firms is "only" expected to devote 1,900 billable hours a year to client work, he or she will still need to work roughly 52 hours a week on average, assuming the associate is off work four weeks during the year for vacations, holidays and a couple of sick days. That average does not include time for lunch, time for breaks, or time for commuting to and from work.

Law firm pressure to generate billable hours can put lawyers at odds with the interests of their clients. A lawyer's "leave no stone unturned" approach may not be the most efficient way to solve the client's legal problem. Law firm partners may be inclined to over-staff projects, assigning four or five lawyers to work on a legal matter when one or two lawyers would suffice. Lawyers may over-work files in order to log billable hours, particularly when an economic downturn has led to a reduction in the amount of legal work that is available. Some lawyers have been known to drag out the resolution of litigation so they can keep on billing their client. All of these practices make legal services far more expensive than they need to be, reflecting poorly on the reputation of lawyers and the legal profession as a whole.

In one client's fee dispute lawsuit with a large law firm, embarrassing internal law firm emails came to light. In an email to two of his colleagues, a lawyer wrote that he heard the firm was already $200,000 over its estimate for handling the client's legal matter. One of the recipients of that email replied by writing that another lawyer in the firm had "random people working full time on random research projects in standard [name omitted] 'churn that bill, baby!' mode. That bill shall know no limits." In another email one of the lawyers asked a colleague, "Didn't you use 3 associates to prepare for a first day hearing where you filed 3 documents?" The colleague replied, "And it took all of them 4 days to write those motions . . . . Perhaps if we paid more money we'd have more skilled associates."[230] The fee dispute lawsuit was eventually settled out of court.

The pressure to generate client billings also tends to make lawyers less willing and able to perform *pro bono* legal services for people who cannot afford to pay a lawyer. People of modest means who do not qualify for legal aid, and many people in the middle class, simply do not have the money to pay legal fees. When a large percentage of the population does not have meaningful access to the legal services they need, the legitimacy of the legal system is undermined and the reputation of the legal profession suffers.[231]

Lawyers also suffer. Particularly in larger firms, partners as well as associates need to devote many hours to their law practice, day in and day out. A significant number of lawyers seem to live to work. They do not have the luxury of working to live. Long hours with no end in sight can take a stressful toll.

Intense and relentless competition is also a source of stress. In most large firms, associates compete with other associates for the relatively few equity partner positions that will be available. Lawyers compete with lawyers in other firms for legal work, trying to wrestle clients away from other firms and trying to keep the clients they already have.[232] In some firms, lawyers find themselves competing with their law firm colleagues for "client origination" credits that will affect their compensation. The lawyer who receives credit for bringing a client to the law firm may receive a larger bonus this year and a larger percentage share of the firm's profits next year. Startling examples of the cutthroat competition that can occur within a firm are described in an article by Noam Scheiber published in the *New Republic*.[233] In one example, partners in the Chicago office of a large firm tried to poach clients from the firm's New York office by claiming they would be less expensive than their New York partners. In the same firm, some younger lawyers who brought clients to the firm discovered later on that more senior lawyers in the firm claimed and received all of the credit. Such behavior hardly creates an environment of collaboration and mutual trust among professional colleagues.

Another source of stress for lawyers is profound uncertainty about the future of their law practice and the stability of their law firm. Clients can decide to change lawyers for any number of reasons. Some of those reasons are completely beyond the control of the lawyers currently representing a client. For example, a management change in a corporate legal department may put a new manager in charge of the legal work being handled by a law firm. The new manager may have his or her favorite law firm or may simply want to try out somebody new. Changes in the economy may also have an adverse effect on a lawyer's practice. During an economic downturn many companies may be reluctant to engage in merger and acquisition activity until the economy becomes more stable. Lawyers who specialize in mergers and acquisitions may suddenly have a shortage of legal work. The stability of a lawyer's firm may be jeopardized if one of the partners with a significant client base decides to move to a different firm in order to advance his or her career or simply to make more money. The perception that lawyers make more money in larger law firms has led some firms to merge with other firms. The number of mergers involving law firms in the United States set a record in 2013.[234] A law firm merger creates a change in culture, and some lawyers who had a secure position in their firm before the merger may find themselves and their practice area out of step with the combined firm after the merger.

Lawyers practicing in larger firms are acutely aware that large firms have collectively laid off hundreds of lawyers in recent years.[235] One law firm saw its annual profits per partner drop by about six percent from 2006 to 2007, to roughly $2.73 million per partner. In 2008 that firm laid off 131 lawyers, reducing the number of lawyers in the firm by nearly twenty percent.[236] A year later another firm laid off 190 associates, representing twenty percent of the firm's associates.[237] Still another law firm laid off 60 associates in 2013, representing about seven percent of the firm's associates, and reduced annual compensation for roughly ten percent of the firm's partners. Those cuts were made when the firm was financially strong, with no debt and with compensation for the partners averaging $2.2 million a year. The firm did not lay off partners presumably because the partnership agreement only allowed partners to be fired for cause.[238] Another large firm did lay off both equity partners and income partners.[239] Law firm partners are not immune from a layoff if the firm's focus drifts away from their practice area or if they are unable to continue generating substantial billable hours and more business for the firm.[240] The lawyers who are laid off need to find another place to practice law. That can be a difficult challenge for an associate or a fairly new partner, as well as for a more experienced partner without a significant client base.

Lawyers also need to find a new place to practice when their law firm goes out of business. A number of large law firms have decided to close their doors after experiencing a loss of business and reduced partnership profits. One of Chicago's oldest firms, with 301 lawyers, was dissolved after a business slowdown and reduced partnership profits led some of the more productive partners to leave for other firms.[241] A Philadelphia firm with 287 lawyers that had been in business for 106 years suffered the same fate.[242] A New York firm with roughly 700 lawyers dissolved after it became overextended with many satellite offices in different parts of the world.[243] A firm in Boston that had over 400 lawyers in 2002 dissolved three years later after a number of lawyers defected to join other firms.[244] Sometimes a scandal involving a handful of lawyers in a firm can cause the firm to break apart. A 600 lawyer firm headquartered in Dallas went out of business after a few lawyers hired to set up a tax shelter practice in the firm's Chicago satellite office were prosecuted for helping clients commit tax fraud.[245]

Some law firm partners discover that the dissolution of their firm may jeopardize their personal financial security even if they are able to find positions in other law firms. Firms that dissolve with obligations to creditors may need to file for bankruptcy protection. The bankruptcy trustee may be able to sue former partners to recover money for the bankruptcy estate that can be used to pay creditors of the firm. For example, after a 450 lawyer firm headquartered in San Francisco dissolved and filed for bankruptcy, the trustee sued 223 former partners of the law firm seeking to recover up to $275 million in compensation they allegedly received while the firm was insolvent. More than 200 of those partners agreed to cash settlements they paid from their personal assets.[246] The bankruptcy trustee may also sue partners for unpaid capital contributions they agreed to make to buy their partnership interest in the law firm, even though the firm no longer exists.[247] If a partner borrowed money from a bank to make his or her capital contribution to the firm, the partner will be personally liable to the bank to repay the loan even though the partnership interest has become worthless.[248] Partners will also remain personally liable on any guarantees of the law firm's obligations they may have given to landlords, banks and other financial institutions. When a law firm in financial distress goes out of business, the partners may find themselves digging out of a financial hole for quite some time.

Seven

C ivil litigation in the United States has become a highly lucrative industry for lawyers in private practice. Data reported by the Administrative
Office of the United States Courts and by the National Center for State Courts
suggest that roughly 9.5 million civil lawsuits are filed in federal and state
courts each year.[249] That estimate does not include civil cases filed in courts
of limited jurisdiction, such as small claims court, or cases filed in specialty
courts such as bankruptcy court. It also does not include domestic relations
or family law cases, criminal cases, juvenile court cases or traffic cases. If we
assume that the offices of court clerks are open and able to receive case filings
nine hours a day, excluding weekends and government holidays, the 9.5 million new civil lawsuits filed each year in the United States are being filed at an
average rate of slightly more than one new lawsuit per second.

Many lawsuits are legitimate. A person who is injured or damaged by the
misconduct of another person or a company may not obtain fair compensation without filing suit. A company may need to file a lawsuit in order to
protect its patents or trademarks from infringement by another company. A
lawsuit may be the only effective way short of a criminal prosecution to hold
an organization accountable for gross misconduct. Filing suit can be the best
way to challenge illegal or unconstitutional action by administrative agencies.

These are only a few of the many situations in which it may be necessary to file a civil lawsuit.

Yet one may wonder why so many millions of civil lawsuits are filed in the United States each year. Perhaps we are living in a litigious society that has become preoccupied with the vindication of individual rights. Maybe some people consider themselves to be victims in life and want to have someone else officially blamed for their misfortune. Others may want to file suit as a way of getting even for a perceived wrong. And some lawyers actively solicit clients for litigation by advertising and by using more creative methods to recruit clients. For those lawyers new lawsuits represent a business venture, an investment of time and money intended to produce a profit. Some of those lawyers have even been known to refer to their clients collectively as "inventory."

Very few people file suit on their own behalf. Most civil lawsuits are filed by lawyers in private practice who have their own financial incentives for encouraging clients to sue. A lawyer may be in competition with other lawyers for the chance to represent a client. By confidently expressing a willingness to file suit the lawyer can show the potential client that he or she will be an effective advocate who is not afraid of going to court on a client's behalf. Many plaintiffs who bring a lawsuit are represented by lawyers who charge a contingent fee that will be based on a percentage of the amount of money the lawyer recovers for the client. Contingent fee lawyers often believe that filing suit before engaging in settlement negotiations will put the adverse party on the defensive and produce a larger settlement. Some contingent fee lawyers are willing to take almost any case that has the potential to produce a settlement and generate a fee. In commercial cases lawyers typically represent plaintiffs on the basis of an hourly fee arrangement. Those lawyers have a financial incentive to encourage clients to file suit since a lawsuit is likely to generate a significant number of billable hours. Lawyers who defend civil lawsuits are usually paid by the hour. They have a financial stake in the litigation process since defending a lawsuit provides many opportunities to generate legal fees.

More than ninety percent of all civil lawsuits are resolved by a settlement before they come to trial. Yet the path to a settlement can be very expensive.

Lawyers generally engage in pretrial discovery to learn as much as they can about their adversary's case and to prepare their own case for settlement or trial. Sometimes lawyers conduct extensive pretrial discovery in an effort to wear down their adversary as a prelude to settlement negotiations. And some clients want their lawyers to engage in aggressive practices during pretrial discovery simply because they want to make life difficult and expensive for the adverse party.

The court rules give lawyers a number of tools for conducting pretrial discovery in civil lawsuits. Using these tools can be expensive for clients and financially rewarding for lawyers being paid by the hour. In most civil cases, depositions are taken of the parties and the key witnesses and transcripts of the deposition testimony are prepared. Lawyers and paralegals then read the transcripts and prepare summaries of the deposition testimony. Lawyers often submit written interrogatories and requests for admissions that must be answered in writing by the party to whom they are directed. The lawyers for the parties usually submit document requests to each other, requiring the lawyers and their clients to review business and personal records, emails and other electronically stored information for written and electronic documents that might be relevant to the claims or defenses in the lawsuit. Once potentially relevant documents are collected, they need to be reviewed by lawyers and paralegals to identify privileged material that will be held back from the documents that are turned over to the opposing party. In cases involving technical, scientific or medical issues, expert witnesses are retained to review information and prepare reports expressing opinions within the scope of their expertise. When a lawsuit is filed on behalf of a plaintiff claiming damages for personal injuries, he or she will likely be examined by one or more doctors or other medical experts.

The cost of this pretrial discovery ranges from many thousands of dollars in a routine case to millions of dollars in complex litigation. Pretrial motions and mandatory conferences with the judge add even more expense to the cost of litigating a case that is resolved before trial. Occasionally, the court will decide the outcome of a case before trial by granting a motion to dismiss the complaint or a motion for summary judgment. Most other cases are settled.

Cases go to trial if they are not resolved by a motion to dismiss the complaint, by a motion for summary judgment or by a settlement. After the trial is over the outcome of the case may be appealed. The legal fees and costs associated with taking a case to trial, and pursuing an appeal, can be substantial.

Most people and small businesses cannot afford to pay litigation fees and costs from their own funds. A party with a claim that is unlikely to produce a significant contingent fee will have difficulty finding a lawyer willing to take the case. A defendant in a lawsuit who does not have adequate liability insurance or substantial assets may not be able to pay a lawyer enough money to prepare an effective defense and may even be driven into bankruptcy.

When insurers and self-insured companies are paying for litigation fees and costs, they will eventually pass those expenses on to consumers in the form of higher insurance premiums and higher prices for goods and services. The costs of unnecessary activities that are motivated by a desire to avoid the risk of litigation, such as the practice of defensive medicine, are also borne by consumers.[250] Taxpayers fund the judicial system that needs to handle all the lawsuits that are filed. In a very real sense we are all subsidizing the litigation industry as it exists today. Perhaps that is one of the reasons the litigation explosion in the United States has such a negative impact on the reputation of the legal profession.[251]

Publicity about questionable lawsuits also tarnishes the reputation of the profession. In the rest of this chapter we'll take a look at examples of lawsuits that appear to be frivolous, or at least a poor use of the legal system. None of the cases appear to have been motivated by a genuine desire to seek justice. All of these lawsuits were filed by lawyers.

Sometimes a defendant is sued in a case simply because it has deep pockets. A pedestrian was struck by a car on a rural highway in Park City, Utah while walking after dark along a route she had obtained on her Blackberry from Google Maps. She sued Google as well as the driver of the car that struck her, claiming that Google was negligent in the directions it provided on Google Maps. The Court dismissed the negligence claims against Google. As the

Court pointed out, "it is clear that Google was not required to anticipate that a user of the Google Maps service would cross the road without looking for cars."[252]

Some lawsuits seem to be motivated by a desire to have someone else blamed for a personal tragedy. At two o'clock early one December morning, the driver of a 1991 Honda Civic accidentally backed her car down a boat ramp into Galveston Bay. Her passenger, who was not wearing a seatbelt, was able to get out of the car by crawling through the passenger side window. The driver was unable to get out of the car. She drowned. After sunrise several hours later, a dive team found the car. All the windows were rolled up and all the doors were closed. The driver's body was found in the back seat. An autopsy revealed that her blood alcohol level at the time was .17, nearly twice the legal limit for driving a car. It was probably even higher several hours earlier when the accident occurred. The driver's parents sued Honda, claiming the passive restraint system that operated automatically when the driver's door closed was defectively designed. It is fairly easy to challenge the design of a product with the benefit of hindsight. The jury awarded $65 million to the parents and the estate of the driver. Honda appealed. The Court of Appeals of Texas reversed the award and rendered judgment in favor of Honda.[253] The Court decided there was no evidence that a safer alternative design for the passive restraint system was available and would have significantly reduced the risk of the driver's death.

A defendant can be sued for not meeting a person's unrealistic expectations. Nearly five years after starting work for a financial institution in New Jersey, a marketing manager was diagnosed with general anxiety disorder and depression that was aggravated by New Jersey rush hour traffic. She wanted the financial institution to allow her to retain her managerial position while changing her schedule to avoid the rush hour commute. She asked for permission to come to work late, after morning rush hour, and to leave early, before afternoon rush hour. Essentially, she wanted to retain her full-time managerial position while working in the office

part-time. Her employer did not agree to that request and she was ultimately fired. She later filed suit for compensatory and punitive damages
and for attorneys' fees.[254] Even if the lawsuit was eventually settled out of
court, the employer probably spent many thousands of dollars in legal fees
to defend the case.

Defendants can be named in lawsuits and required to defend themselves even
when there is no evidence to support the claims against them. The patient of
a gastroenterologist needed a liver biopsy to diagnose problems he was having with his liver. After the biopsy was performed the patient was admitted
to the hospital for observation. The gastroenterologist then left on vacation
and an on-call physician assumed responsibility for the patient's care. When
the patient's condition worsened the on-call physician ordered a series of tests
that revealed perforations of the patient's gall bladder and colon. The patient
received treatment for those complications and ultimately recovered. He filed
a medical malpractice lawsuit against the hospital, the gastroenterologist, the
physician who performed the liver biopsy and the on-call physician. The
patient's medical expert witness in the lawsuit refused to express any opinions
critical of the care provided by the on-call physician, whose interventions may
have saved the patient's life.

The lawyer for the on-call physician then asked the patient's lawyer to
dismiss his client from the case. The patient's lawyer refused to dismiss the
on-call physician unless he made a settlement offer. The on-call physician declined to make a settlement offer because there was no evidence he had done
anything wrong.

A while later, another lawyer was brought into the case to assist the
patient's initial lawyer. He agreed to dismiss the on-call physician shortly
before the case went to trial against the other defendants. After the trial was
over, the trial judge imposed sanctions on the patient's initial lawyer who
was required to reimburse the on-call physician for the time he devoted to
preparing his defense of the case. The patient's lawyer appealed the award of
sanctions. The Ohio Court of Appeals affirmed the sanctions award. The
Court decided the lawyer had engaged in frivolous behavior by refusing to

dismiss the on-call physician without an offer of money as soon as it became clear that there was no expert testimony to support a malpractice claim against him.[255]

Some people seem to think it is easier to file a lawsuit than to take personal responsibility for their own behavior. They may also receive a financial windfall in the process. A twenty-four year old law student began hearing voices and started hitting himself in the face. He was involuntarily committed to a mental hospital for psychiatric observation and treatment. After a brief stay in the hospital he returned to his law school classes. About a year and a half later he disrupted a law school class to announce that he had telepathic powers. At the urging of a law school dean he sought counseling at the university's student health clinic and began out-patient treatment with a clinic psychiatrist. Over the next ten weeks he had six counseling sessions with the psychiatrist who also prescribed medication for him. The psychiatrist, who was about to retire, offered to make a referral to another psychiatrist who could continue therapy sessions with the student and refill his prescription.

After the psychiatrist retired, the student stopped taking his medication and did not seek further psychiatric treatment. Eight months later the student went downtown and randomly fired an M-1 rifle at unarmed people, killing two of them. Police officers shot him in the legs to make him stop. He was charged with two counts of first degree murder and found not guilty by reason of insanity. He then filed a malpractice lawsuit against the psychiatrist, claiming the psychiatrist's negligence caused him to be shot in the legs, endure a murder trial and face confinement in a mental institution for an indefinite period of time. The jury awarded the student $500,000. An appellate court reversed the award and rendered judgment in favor of the psychiatrist.[256] Though the psychiatrist ultimately won the case on appeal, tens of thousands of dollars were most likely spent for his defense.

Lawsuits can be filed for inexplicable reasons. In November of 2003 a small photography business was hired by a couple to photograph their wedding and wedding reception the following month. The couple agreed to pay the photographers $4,100 for their services. After the wedding, the groom complained that the photographers failed to capture the final fifteen minutes of the reception, including the last dance and the bouquet toss. Six years later, in 2009, the groom sued the photographers for $48,000 in compensatory damages and additional amounts for punitive damages and attorneys' fees. The compensatory damages sought in the case were based on the estimated cost of recreating the wedding so it could be filmed again. In filing the complaint the Big Law firm lawyer representing the groom was not deterred by the fact that the couple had separated and were getting a divorce. The bride had returned to her native Latvia and reportedly could not be found. By the time the court dismissed most, but not all, of the claims in the lawsuit the owner of the photography business and its founder, an immigrant then in his 80s, had spent roughly $50,000 of their own money defending the case.[257] Because not all of the claims were dismissed, the owner and the founder of the photography business had to continue spending even more of their own money defending themselves.

Some lawsuits are motivated by greed. The Huffington Post launched its for-profit website in 2009. Much of the website content was written by bloggers who understood and agreed they would not be paid for writing content posted on the website. They made their submissions with no expectation of monetary compensation. Instead, they received widespread public exposure for themselves and their work. Within two years the website became quite popular, receiving more than 26 million unique visitors a month. In 2011 the Huffington Post was sold to AOL for around $315 million. Some of the bloggers filed a class action lawsuit against the Huffington Post and AOL seeking damages of more than $105 million, or roughly one-third of the selling price. They claimed their unpaid submissions to the blog added value to the Huffington Post, entitling them to share in the proceeds of the sale. The court dismissed the lawsuit, noting it was "an effort to change the rules of the game after the game has been played, and equity and good conscience require no such result."[258]

Lawyers who file class action lawsuits know they can be very expensive to defend. A company sued in a class action case may decide it will be more economical and less distracting to the company's business to settle the class action rather than mount an aggressive defense. A number of class action suits are filed with the expectation that a settlement will produce a fee for the lawyers, even if the members of the class only receive coupons or nominal payments.

A class action lawsuit was filed against the franchisor of Blimpie restaurants in Illinois.[259] The suit was based on a claim that the advertising for Super Stacked™ Subs was misleading. The class action complaint alleges that Super Stacked™ Subs do not contain double portions of meat as advertised. The complaint cites the nutritional information on Blimpie's website revealing that Super Stacked™ Subs do not contain twice as much protein as submarine sandwiches with a single portion of meat. Yet Blimpie does not, and could not, claim that Super Stacked™ Subs contain twice as much protein as the regular sandwiches. The bread and cheese on the regular sandwiches contain protein. Super Stacked™ Subs only add a double portion of meat.[260] And it is hard to see how a Blimpie's customer could possibly be misled. Sandwiches are made to order. A customer could easily see whether the person making the sandwich was putting on one portion of meat or two portions of meat. The customer could also complain if the amount of meat on the sandwich appeared to be less than the amount that was ordered.

One of Blimpie's competitors, SUBWAY®, discovered it is not immune from class action litigation. It turns out that SUBWAY® "Footlong" submarine sandwiches are not always twelve inches long. Nine separate class action lawsuits were filed in federal courts across the country against the franchisor of SUBWAY® restaurants. The Judicial Panel on Multidistrict Litigation consolidated the federal class actions into a single proceeding known as *In Re: Subway Footlong Sandwich Marketing and Sales Practices Litigation*.[261] The plaintiffs then filed a consolidated class action complaint asserting claims of false and deceptive advertising and marketing practices "intended to trick unsuspecting consumers . . . into believing that they are receiving more food for their money than they are actually receiving."[262] It apparently does not matter to the plaintiffs' lawyers that baked goods, such as submarine sandwich rolls, are unlikely to be uniform in length when they come out of the oven. It also does not seem to matter to the lawyers that people who buy a SUBWAY® "Footlong" submarine sandwich can see exactly what they are getting. Perhaps anyone who really cared about the precise length of their submarine sandwich could measure the sandwich with a pocket tape measure or a twelve-inch length of string before paying the cashier.

Courts rarely allow plaintiffs seeking damages for personal injuries to be joined together in a class action, even when their claims arise from the same event or exposure or from use of the same product. The facts unique to each person's claim are thought to predominate over the facts that are common to all claims, making class action treatment inappropriate. In these situations the lawyers representing the plaintiffs file separate lawsuits, sometimes naming several claimants as plaintiffs in each lawsuit. Lawyers will often advertise and engage in other activities to recruit plaintiffs for the litigation. They understand that a defendant may not be willing or able to spend the considerable amount of money necessary to carefully examine and litigate the merits of each claim. By filing lawsuits on behalf of as many plaintiffs as they can find, the lawyers believe they will create leverage so they can pressure a defendant to pay money to settle claims even if the claims have dubious merit.[263]

A consolidated federal court proceeding that was litigated in 2004 and 2005 illustrates the methods some lawyers use to generate claims and create evidence in support of those claims. Thousands of plaintiffs filed lawsuits claiming they were suffering from silicosis, which is a scarring of the lungs caused by inhaling silica dust. The lawsuits pending in various federal courts were consolidated by the Judicial Panel on Multidistrict Litigation for the purpose of certain pretrial proceedings and transferred to Judge Janis Graham Jack in the Southern District of Texas.[264] Judge Jack required each of the plaintiffs to submit a Fact Sheet disclosing, among other things, the plaintiff's diagnosis with supporting medical information and the names of the plaintiff's treating physicians. When the Fact Sheets were submitted and analyzed, an interesting pattern came to light. Hardly any of the plaintiffs had been diagnosed with silicosis by a treating physician. The diagnosis of silicosis for more than 9,000 plaintiffs was made by 12 doctors affiliated with a handful of plaintiffs' law firms and mobile x-ray screening companies.[265] The screening companies were businesses that offered free chest x-rays to see whether evidence supporting a claim for compensation could be found. As Judge Jack, who had been a registered nurse before becoming a federal District Court Judge,[266] pointed out:

> A review of all of the submitted Fact Sheets is telling. In the approximately 9,083 Fact Sheets submitted in this MDL as of the date of the . . . hearings, approximately 8,000 treating doctors are named. But when it comes to the doctors who diagnosed these Plaintiffs with silicosis, 12 names appear. Twelve doctors diagnosed all 9,083 plaintiffs. This small cadre of non-treating physicians, financially beholden to lawyers and screening companies rather than to patients, managed to notice a disease missed by approximately 8,000 other physicians — most of whom had the significant advantage of speaking to, examining and treating the Plaintiffs.[267]

The litigation screening company that generated the diagnosis of silicosis for more than half the plaintiffs in the consolidated proceeding was hired by a law firm that only paid the screening company for plaintiffs with a positive diagnosis who hired the law firm to represent them.[268] That screening company hired a radiologist in private practice who made 3,617 "diagnoses" of silicosis in 48 days that were submitted in support of plaintiffs' claims. All of his reports used the same wording to describe the diagnosis.[269] Another doctor who submitted reports in support of some of the plaintiffs' silicosis claims "performed 1,239 diagnostic evaluations in 72 hours."[270] After conducting hearings to assess the reliability of the medical reports, Judge Jack found that "on a number of different levels, the claims in this MDL defy all medical knowledge and logic."[271] She concluded that the diagnoses of silicosis submitted in support of nearly all of the plaintiffs' claims "were driven by neither health nor justice: they were manufactured for money."[272]

Eight

ZEALOUS REPRESENTATION

I n 1969 the American Bar Association, or ABA, adopted and published its Model Code of Professional Responsibility which created an affirmative duty for lawyers to represent their clients zealously. The proclaimed duty of zealous representation has had a profound impact on the legal profession and the behavior of lawyers ever since.

The stated mission of the ABA, founded in 1878, is to serve as the legal profession's "national representative."[273] Currently about one-third of the lawyers in the United States are members of the ABA. Among its many functions, the ABA has developed model statements of ethical principles and model ethical rules to promote uniform national standards for the professional conduct of lawyers. The ABA does not have the authority to license, regulate or discipline members of the legal profession. That authority is exercised by the individual states and the District of Columbia. The ABA's influence as a national voice for the legal profession has led nearly all of the states and the District of Columbia to adopt, with minor modifications, the statements of ethical principles and model ethical rules developed by the ABA.

The 1908 Canons of Professional Ethics represented the ABA's first effort to create uniform standards for the ethical behavior of lawyers.[274] The Canons were a set of normative principles intended to guide the behavior of lawyers in order to maintain public confidence in the integrity of our system for the administration of justice. As stated in the Preamble:

> In America, where the stability of Courts and of all departments of government rests upon the approval of the people, it is peculiarly essential that the system for establishing and dispensing Justice be developed to a high point of efficiency and so maintained that the public shall have absolute confidence in the integrity and impartiality of its administration. The future of the Republic, to a great extent, depends upon our maintenance of Justice pure and unsullied. It cannot be so maintained unless the conduct and the motives of the members of our profession are such as to merit the approval of all just men.

> No code or set of rules can be framed, which will particularize all the duties of the lawyer in the varying phases of litigation or in all the relations of professional life. The following canons of ethics are adopted by the American Bar Association as a general guide, yet the enumeration of particular duties should not be construed as a denial of the existence of others equally imperative, though not specifically mentioned.[275]

The formulation of the Canons as a set of normative principles, rather than a collection of specific rules, is illustrated by Canon 15. That Canon, entitled "How Far a Lawyer May Go in Supporting a Client's Cause," states:

> Nothing operates more certainly to create or to foster popular prejudice against lawyers as a class, and to deprive the profession of that full measure of public esteem and confidence which belongs to the proper discharge of its duties than does the false claim, often set up by the unscrupulous in defense of questionable transactions, that it is the duty of the lawyer to do whatever may enable him to succeed in winning his client's cause.

It is improper for a lawyer to assert in argument his personal belief in his client's innocence or in the justice of his cause.

The lawyer owes entire devotion to the interest of his client, warm zeal in the maintenance and defense of his rights and the exertion of his utmost learning and ability, to the end that nothing be taken or withheld from him, save by the rules of law, legally applied. No fear of judicial disfavor or public unpopularity should restrain him from the full discharge of his duty. In the judicial forum the client is entitled to the benefit of any and every remedy and defense that is authorized by the law of the land, and he may expect his lawyer to assert every such remedy or defense. But it is steadfastly to be borne in the mind that the great trust of the lawyer is to be performed within and not without the bounds of the law. The office of attorney does not permit, much less does it demand of him for any client, violation of law or any manner of fraud or chicane. He must obey his own conscience and not that of his client.[276]

While the language seems archaic and the term "warm zeal" is not defined, Canon 15 makes some very important points: Public esteem for the legal profession is diminished by the "false claim" that it is a lawyer's duty to do whatever may enable the lawyer to succeed in winning the client's cause. A lawyer is not allowed, and cannot be required, to violate the law or engage in "any manner of fraud or chicane." A lawyer must be guided by the lawyer's own conscience and not by the conscience of the client, since a lawyer should be morally accountable for his or her conduct during the course of representing a client.[277] Another Canon makes the point that "it should never be forgotten that the profession is a branch of the administration of justice and not a mere money-getting trade."[278]

Unlike the 1908 Canons of Professional Ethics, the ABA's 1969 Model Code of Professional Responsibility consisted of new Canons with statements of Ethical Considerations and specific Disciplinary Rules. The new Canons were "statements of axiomatic norms, expressing in general terms the standards of professional conduct expected of lawyers in their relationships with the public, with the legal system, and with the legal profession."[279] The ABA described the Ethical Considerations as "aspirational in character [representing] the objectives toward which every member of the profession should strive. They constitute a body of principles upon which the lawyer can rely for guidance in many specific situations."[280] The Disciplinary Rules were mandatory. They stated "the minimum level of conduct below which no lawyer can fall without being subject to disciplinary action."[281] With these definitions in mind, let's take a close look at Canon 7 of the 1969 Model Code of Professional Responsibility.

Canon 7 states the "axiomatic norm" and standard of "professional conduct expected of lawyers" that a lawyer should represent a client zealously within the bounds of the law.[282] The Ethical Considerations for Canon 7 underscore the point that the "duty of a lawyer, both to his client and to the legal system, is to represent his client zealously within the bounds of the law."[283] The Ethical Considerations acknowledge that "[t]he bounds of the law in a given case are often difficult to ascertain."[284] "While serving as an advocate, a lawyer should resolve in favor of his client doubts as to the bounds of the law."[285] Even when a lawyer is not serving as an advocate, Ethical Consideration 7-6 indicates that reasonable doubts about a client's state of mind or intention should generally be resolved in favor of the client:

> Whether the proposed action of a lawyer is within the bounds of the law may be a perplexing question when his client is contemplating a course of conduct having legal consequences that vary according to the client's intent, motive, or desires at the time of the action. Often a lawyer is asked to assist his client in developing evidence relevant to the state of mind of the client at a particular time. He may properly assist his client in the development and preservation of evidence of existing motive, intent, or desire; obviously, he may not do anything furthering the creation or preservation of false evidence. In many cases a lawyer may not be certain as to the state of mind of his client,

and in those situations he should resolve reasonable doubts in favor of his client.[286]

Zealous representation was made a mandatory requirement for ethical lawyering by Disciplinary Rule 7-101. That Disciplinary Rule, entitled "Representing a Client Zealously," states that "A lawyer shall not intentionally: (1) Fail to seek the lawful objectives of his client through reasonably available means permitted by law and the Disciplinary Rules, ..."[287] As the Model Code was adopted by the states and was taught to increasing numbers of law students, the concept of zealous representation took root as a guiding principle for the legal profession's understanding of a lawyer's proper role.

The 1969 Model Code of Professional Responsibility was replaced fourteen years later by the Model Rules of Professional Conduct. The Model Rules, adopted by the ABA in 1983, have since been amended from time to time and remain in effect today. They represent yet another approach to writing a set of uniform ethical standards for lawyers. The ABA's Model Rules of Professional Conduct is a collection of authoritative rules with formal comments that are intended to serve as guides for interpreting the rules.[288] While the Model Rules do not clearly state that it is a lawyer's duty to represent clients zealously within the bounds of the law, they retain the concept of zealous representation. According to the Preamble, the basic principles underlying the Model Rules "include the lawyer's obligation zealously to protect and pursue a client's legitimate interests, within the bounds of the law, while maintaining a professional, courteous and civil attitude towards all persons involved in the legal system."[289] "As advocate, a lawyer zealously asserts the client's position under the rules of the adversary system."[290] The Comment to Rule 1.3, addressing diligence in the client-lawyer relationship, is even more specific. It states that a "lawyer must also act with commitment and dedication to the interests of the client and with zeal in advocacy on the client's behalf."[291]

Since 1969, when the ABA's Model Code was published, the normative principle of zealous representation has worked its way into the core of the legal profession's psyche.[292] Zealous representation is not a defined term in the Model Code of Professional Responsibility or in the Model Rules of Professional Conduct. In the absence of a definition within the rules, words are given their ordinary meaning.[293] According to a dictionary definition, "zealous" means "marked by fervent partisanship for a person, a cause, or an ideal."[294] Robert Gordon, a Professor at Stanford Law School, has pointed out that fervent partisanship in representing clients invites lawyers "to creatively stretch the law, facts, and procedural maneuvers to benefit clients, even at some cost to the effective functioning of the legal framework as a whole."[295] In a similar vein Paula Schaefer, a law professor at the University of Tennessee with previous experience practicing at a Big Law firm, observed that "[z]ealous advocacy is understood to require the attorney to be a partisan of the client, even to the detriment of others."[296] Professor Schaefer also pointed out that a "popular conception of zealous advocacy is that it obligates an attorney to suspend personal morality in favor of zealously pursuing the client's agenda."[297]

In chapter five we saw how the zealous pursuit of a client's agenda led the lawyers of Watergate to disregard their ethical responsibilities as lawyers, to manipulate and abuse the legal system and, in a number of cases, to engage in criminal conduct. We will now take a look at several more recent examples of what can happen when lawyers allow zealous representation – fervent partisanship on behalf of a client – to become the primary guide for their professional behavior. The examples involve lawyers representing clients in civil lawsuits, prosecuting attorneys in criminal cases, and lawyers advising clients in business transactions.

On January 18, 1986 a two year old child suffered seizures resulting in severe and permanent brain damage caused by Somophyllin Oral Liquid, a theophylline-based medication that had been prescribed for her asthma. A lawsuit was filed on her behalf against the physician who prescribed the medication and Fisons Corporation, the drug company that manufactured Somophyllin. One of the critical issues in the case was whether Fisons knew that theophylline-based medications were potentially dangerous when given to children with viral infections. During the course of pretrial discovery in the case Fisons was asked to provide certain information and to produce specific categories of documents. The lawyers for Fisons responded by objecting "to all discovery requests regarding Fisons products other than Somophyllin Oral Liquid as overly broad, unduly burdensome, harassing, and not reasonably calculated to lead to the discovery of admissible evidence."[298] In response to a request for copies of any letters Fisons sent to physicians "concerning theophylline toxicity in children," the lawyers for Fisons replied: "Such letters, if any, regarding Somophyllin Oral Liquid will be produced."[299] Based on the responses and objections signed by its lawyers, Fisons did not produce two "smoking gun" documents that were in its possession. The first document was a June 30, 1981 letter that Fisons sent to a small number of physicians more than four years before the plaintiff was injured and more than two years before she was born. That letter discussed an article confirming reports "of life threatening theophylline toxicity when pediatric asthmatics . . . contract viral infections."[300] The second document was an inter-departmental Fisons memo dated July 10, 1985, six months before the plaintiff was injured, describing "an epidemic of theophylline toxicity" and "a dramatic increase in reports of serious toxicity to theophylline."[301] Fisons kept those two documents in files relating to Intal, which was a different product manufactured by Fisons that competed with Somophyllin. Intal was a cromolyn sodium product that did not contain theophylline.

Fisons' lawyers argued that the smoking gun documents were not documents "regarding Somophyllin Oral Liquid." Instead, they were documents "regarding" Intal because they were intended to support the marketing of Intal as an alternative to Somophyllin.[302] The Washington State Supreme Court rejected that argument and described how Fisons avoided producing the documents "by giving evasive or misleading responses to interrogatories and requests for production."[303] The lawyers for Fisons claimed they were just doing their job and vigorously representing their client.[304] They were apparently not concerned about the morality of concealing information regarding severe and permanent complications associated with the use of a pharmaceutical product by children.[305] The Court soundly rejected the lawyers' argument that "[d]iscovery is an adversarial process and good lawyering required the responses made in this case."[306]

In a product liability case against Suzuki Motor Company and its American subsidiary, the U. S. Court of Appeals for the Eleventh Circuit pointed out that the Rules of Civil Procedure governing the pretrial discovery process "were intended to promote the search for truth that is the heart of our judicial system."[307] The plaintiff in the case had suffered serious head and spinal cord injuries when his 1988-½ Suzuki Samurai collided with another car and rolled over. The Court sharply criticized the defendants and their lawyers for engaging in "an unrelenting campaign to obfuscate the truth."[308] From the beginning of the discovery process, they "stubbornly withheld discoverable information by improperly objecting to interrogatories and by providing only partial responses to the interrogatories they answered."[309]

For example, the defendants and their lawyers objected to terms used in the plaintiff's interrogatories such as "tests, research or other investigation," "risk of rollover," "risk of personal injury," "change, alteration or modification" and "engineer" on the grounds that those terms were ambiguous and were not defined.[310] When the plaintiff asked for information about other vehicles similar to the Samurai for several model years, the defendants and their lawyers only provided information about the Samurai for the 1988-½ model year.[311] The defendants and their lawyers also engaged in a "deliberate cover up of damaging evidence regarding General Motors' refusal to market the Samurai in the United States."[312] They falsely claimed that "they were 'unaware of any decision by General Motors not to market the Samurai' and 'there was no decision not to market a vehicle of the same design as the Samurai.'"[313] Documents the plaintiff's lawyer eventually obtained from General Motors showed that "tests led General Motors to decline to market Suzuki's sport utility vehicle in the United States because of 'perceived rollover tendencies.'"[314] The trial judge concluded that "Suzuki deliberately withheld this information from the plaintiff and that Suzuki counsel participated in the cover up."[315] The Court of Appeals found it "appalling that attorneys, like defense counsel in this case, routinely twist the discovery rules into some of 'the most powerful weapons in the arsenal of those who abuse the adversary system for the sole benefit of their clients.'"[316] The Court also criticized the ABA's Model Rules of Professional Conduct:

All attorneys, as 'officers of the court,' owe duties of complete candor and primary loyalty to the court before which they practice. An attorney's duty to a client can never outweigh his or her responsibility to see that our system of justice functions smoothly. This concept is as old as common law jurisprudence itself.

. . . . . .

Unfortunately, the American Bar Association's current Model Rules of Professional Conduct underscore the duty to advocate zealously while neglecting the corresponding duty to advocate within the bounds of the law. . . . Too many attorneys, like defense counsel in this case, have allowed the objectives of the client to override their ancient duties as officers of the court. In short, they have sold out to the client.[317]

Some zealous advocates try to get away with misrepresenting the law applicable to a case. A Department of Justice lawyer was reprimanded by the federal Court of International Trade for submitting a brief which omitted critical language from what she cited as precedential authority and for attempting to conceal a Supreme Court opinion adverse to her position. The case involved a claim against the United States for the refund of certain customs duties that had been paid on imported products. The claimant filed a motion for summary judgment seeking a favorable dispositive ruling before trial. Under the Court's scheduling order, the government's response to the summary judgment motion was due on May 5. Lawyers, particularly when they are handling a case in a federal court, understand that deadlines in scheduling orders need to be taken seriously. Near the end of the day on May 4, the Department of Justice lawyer filed a motion for a thirty-day extension of time. The Court denied the motion for an extension of time and ordered the government to file its response "forthwith." The government's response was filed twelve days later. The Court refused to consider the government's response as untimely and granted the claimant's motion for summary judgment. The Department of Justice lawyer then filed a motion for reconsideration, arguing that the government had filed its response to the summary judgment motion in compliance with the Court's order that it do so "forthwith."[318]

In support of her argument that "forthwith" means "within a reasonable time under the circumstances of the case; promptly and with reasonable dispatch," the lawyer cited a definition in *Black's Law Dictionary* and quoted from several judicial opinions. Her misquotations from two of the opinions she cited led to the reprimand. She quoted the following sentence from one of the judicial opinions: "'Forthwith' means immediately, without delay, or as soon as the object may be accomplished by reasonable exertion." She omitted from that quotation the very next sentence of the judicial opinion, which reads: "The Supreme Court has said of the word that 'in matters of practice and pleading it is usually construed, and sometimes defined by rule of court, as within twenty-four hours.' *Dickman v. Northern Trust Co.,* 1900 176 U. S. 181, 193." The lawyer's other misquotation was from a dissenting opinion by Supreme Court Justice Clarence Thomas, which she quoted as stating that "[a]lthough we have never undertaken to define 'forthwith' . . . , it is clear that the term 'connotes action which is immediate, without delay, prompt, and with reasonable dispatch.'" What Justice Thomas actually wrote in his dissenting opinion was: "Although we have never undertaken to define 'forthwith' as it is used in the SSA, it is clear that the term 'connotes action which is immediate, without delay, prompt, and with reasonable dispatch.'" In the very next sentence of his opinion Justice Thomas cited the Supreme Court's opinion in *Dickman v. Northern Trust Co.* By omitting the phrase, "as it is used in the SSA [the Suits in Admiralty Act]," the Department of Justice lawyer made Justice Thomas' language seem to be more generally applicable than it actually was. She again omitted the reference to the *Dickman v. Northern Trust Co.* case which would have indicated that "in matters of pleading and procedure" the word "forthwith" usually means within twenty-four hours, and not twelve days.[319] In essence, the Department of Justice lawyer tried to mislead the Court by omitting critical language from precedents she quoted. As the U. S. Court of Appeals for the Federal Circuit pointed out in its opinion affirming her reprimand:

The effect of [her] editing of this material and ignoring the Supreme Court decision that dealt with the issue – a decision that seriously weakened her argument – was to give the Court of International Trade a misleading impression of the state of the law on the point. She eliminated material that indicated that her delay in filing the [government's response] had not met the court's requirement that she file "forthwith," and presented the remaining material in a way that over-stated the basis for her claim that a "forthwith" filing requirement meant she could take whatever time would be reasonable in the circumstances.[320]

In our adversarial system of justice, judges do not conduct their own investigation of the facts in a case and they do not routinely perform their own legal research. They necessarily rely on the candor of the lawyers for the parties to fairly and accurately present the facts of the case and the applicable law to the court. Misrepresenting the law in an argument to a court is, in addition to being unethical, fundamentally inconsistent with the way our system of justice is designed to work.

Sometimes zealous representation seems to have no limits. *Fharmacy Records v. Nassar*[321] was a copyright infringement case brought by the plaintiffs who claimed they had primary rights to a rhythm line, or beat, that was duplicated by the defendants and incorporated into a successful rap tune. The basic issue in the case was who created the beat first. Pretrial discovery in the case was contentious. The defendants' computer forensics expert expressed the opinion that a zip disk purportedly containing the original file for the beat had been intentionally wiped clean and that information on Fharmacy's studio computer had been intentionally backdated. The defendants ultimately filed a motion asking the Court to dismiss the case, contending that "the plaintiffs and their attorney have engaged in intentional misconduct and have committed a fraud upon the Court by manipulating, fabricating, and destroying evidence."[322] The Court agreed, and dismissed the case after recounting a list of discovery abuses and observing that "the conduct at issue is not merely contestable, but in contravention of basic notions of fairness and professional responsibility."[323] The Court noted:

It must be emphasized that this is not a case involving mere games-manship or garden variety discovery abuses. The actions of the plain-tiffs and their attorney in this case are so egregious that they have forfeited their right to proceed in court. The plaintiffs clearly have no respect for the civil justice system, and it would be unfair to require the defendants to defend this case any further.[324]

The plaintiffs and their lawyer challenged the Court's dismissal of the case by filing a motion for reconsideration and a motion to disqualify the judge. The motion to disqualify was based on the following argument: The plaintiffs' lawyer had been involved several years earlier in a case against the Girl Scouts; lawyers in the firm representing the Girl Scouts bore animos-ity towards the plaintiffs' lawyer after he won the case; the judge practiced law at the law firm that represented the Girl Scouts; although the judge did not join the law firm until a few years after the Girl Scouts case was over, he nevertheless adopted the law firm's personal bias against the plaintiffs' lawyer; and, a reasonable person would believe that the judge and the lawyers in the firm who had worked on the Girl Scouts case would network and discuss that case with one another since they were all alumni of the University of Notre Dame.[325] The Court described those allegations of judicial bias as "feckless and irresponsible" and denied the motion to disqualify:

The plaintiffs point to no concrete evidence from which person-al bias could be inferred; instead they rely upon an agglomeration of disconnected facts to spin a yarn that challenges the most active imagination.[326]

The Court then denied the motion for reconsideration, having "documented the disturbing conduct of the plaintiffs and their attorneys in the manipula-tion and destruction of evidence in the case, which resulted in a finding that dismissal was an appropriate sanction."[327] The U. S. Court of Appeals for the Sixth Circuit affirmed the dismissal of the case as an appropriate sanction for the plaintiffs' discovery abuses.[328] The trial judge then awarded the defendants more than $517,000 in attorneys' fees against the plaintiffs and their lawyer.[329] That award was also upheld on appeal.[330]

Some lawyers seem to believe that zealous representation of their client gives them a license to misrepresent, distort and hide evidence in order to win the client's case. DuPont was named as a defendant in a number of lawsuits brought by owners of commercial nurseries who had used Benlate 50 DF, a fungicide product that was manufactured by DuPont. The plaintiffs in the lawsuits claimed that Benlate damaged their nursery plants because it was contaminated with highly toxic herbicides, known as sulfonylureas, that were also manufactured by DuPont. Perhaps the most critical issue in the lawsuits was whether the soils in the plaintiffs' nurseries were contaminated with sulfonylureas. To test the plaintiffs' soils DuPont hired one of the few analytical laboratories in the country that was able to analyze soil for the presence of sulfonylureas at low levels. DuPont was required by the rules governing pretrial discovery and by various court orders to disclose the results of those tests to the plaintiffs. However, DuPont and its lawyers took extraordinary steps to conceal the test results from the plaintiffs and falsely denied that Benlate was contaminated.[331] The federal District Court Judge who was presiding over one group of cases described the conduct of DuPont and its lawyers in these words:

> This Court had never experienced the kind of deliberate refusal to comply with discovery orders that was evidently taking place . . . .
> It became apparent to the Court that DuPont was using its in-house legal staff, local Wilmington, Delaware, counsel, national coordinating counsel, and others to carry out a deliberate effort to restrict legitimate discovery in these and similar cases.[332]

As one example of the lawyers' behavior in that group of cases, a DuPont employee who was the contamination prevention coordinator for the facility where DuPont manufactured the active ingredient in Benlate was scheduled to give a deposition. The evening before his deposition he met with one of the lawyers in the Big Law firm that was representing DuPont. He gave the lawyer some documents from the manufacturing facility that had not been produced to the plaintiffs earlier. The documents related to the contamination of Benlate with sulfonylureas. Rather than producing the documents and proceeding with the deposition, the lawyer falsely represented that the witness was unavailable and that his deposition would need to be rescheduled.[333]

DuPont, with the knowledge and active participation of at least some of its lawyers, also carried out a scheme to manipulate and misrepresent the results of the analytical tests of the plaintiffs' soils. The analytical laboratory's scientists who tested the plaintiffs' soils initially found sulfonylureas in several of the soil samples. The analytical laboratory promptly reported those findings to DuPont's lawyers. The laboratory was then ordered by DuPont to go back and "confirm (defirm)" the positive findings.[334] The Court found that: "Testing procedures were changed. The minimum detection limit was raised. Tests were repeatedly redone and massaged. Soil samples that were found to be positive were 'homogenized' with other parts of the soil sample."[335] Laboratory test summaries were then prepared showing no sulfonylureas in the soil samples taken from the plaintiffs' properties. The Court noted that the summaries "were not summaries of all of the findings produced by the [analytical laboratory's] tests, but were selected charts and tables showing only parts of the findings which DuPont believed to be adequate to lead an expert witness to testify that there was no evidence of Benlate contamination of the *Bush Ranch* Plaintiffs' property."[336] DuPont and its lawyers did not have the analytical chemists who actually tested the plaintiffs' soils testify at trial. Instead, they hired another expert who was given the summaries, and not the raw test data, on which to base his expert opinions and trial testimony. Not surprisingly, the expert testified that the analytical laboratory charts he reviewed showed that no sulfonylureas were present in the soils on the plaintiffs' properties.[337] The Court characterized the expert witness as "a mouthpiece through which DuPont furthered its fraudulent scheme."[338] With respect to the conduct of DuPont's lawyers, the Court had this to say:

Although it was the lawyers for the Dupont corporation whose acts of concealment and misrepresentation were the immediate cause of damage, the circumstances may justify imposition of sanctions on the corporation.[339]

The Court then imposed sanctions on DuPont potentially totaling more than $100 million.[340] The U. S. Court of Appeals for the Eleventh Circuit, while reversing the sanctions on procedural grounds, suggested "DuPont and its counsel may very well have engaged in criminal acts" and "we assume that the appropriate United States Attorney will shortly begin an investigation of this matter (if he or she has not already done so)."[341] The sanctions issue was later settled, with DuPont agreeing to pay $11 million and its Big Law firm agreeing to pay $250,000.[342]

Unlike the lawyers for the parties in a civil lawsuit, the prosecutor in a criminal case has a special role as a minister of justice in addition to his or her role as an advocate.[343] In a case decided in 1935 the Supreme Court pointed out that prosecutors have the responsibility to treat defendants fairly and to see that justice is done. The Court in that case reversed a conviction and granted the defendant a new trial based on persistent misconduct by the prosecutor in his cross-examination of witnesses and his argument to the jury. The prosecutor's misconduct included misstating the facts in his cross-examination of witnesses, persistently cross-examining witnesses about testimony the witnesses had not given, insinuating the existence of prejudicial facts that were not in evidence, and bullying and arguing with witnesses.[344] The Court found that the prosecutor "overstepped the bounds of that propriety and fairness which should characterize the conduct of such an officer in the prosecution of a criminal offense."[345] The Court described the special role of a prosecutor in our system of criminal justice in these words:

The United States Attorney is the representative not of an ordinary party to a controversy but of a sovereignty whose obligation to govern impartially is as compelling as its obligation to govern at all; and whose interest, therefore, in a criminal prosecution is not that it shall win a case, but that justice shall be done. As such, he is in a peculiar and very definite sense the servant of the law, the twofold aim of which is that guilt shall not escape or innocence suffer. He may prosecute with earnestness and vigor – indeed, he should do so. But, while he may strike hard blows, he is not at liberty to strike foul ones. It is as much his duty to refrain from improper methods calculated to produce a wrongful conviction as it is to use every legitimate means to bring about a just one.[346]

A prosecutor has awesome power. When a prosecutor abuses that power he or she undermines public confidence in the integrity of our criminal justice system and public respect for the rule of law. In the words of Chief Justice Earl Warren:

When society acts to deprive one of its members of his life, liberty or property, it takes its most awesome steps. No general respect for, nor adherence to, the law as a whole can well be expected without judicial recognition of the paramount need for prompt, eminently fair and sober criminal law procedures. The methods we employ in the enforcement of our criminal law have aptly been called the measures by which the quality of our civilization may be judged.[347]

The Supreme Court has developed specific rules to protect the due process rights of defendants in criminal cases. One of those rules, established in the case of *Brady v. Maryland*[348] and known as the *Brady* rule, requires the prosecutor, upon request, to disclose evidence to the defense that might be exculpatory. That rule is needed to protect the due process rights of defendants because the pretrial discovery tools that are commonly used in civil litigation are not available to the defendant in a criminal case. The defendant does not have the right to take depositions of the prosecution's witnesses or to require the prosecutor to produce all the documents and other evidence in the prosecutor's possession that might be relevant to the case. Unfortunately, zealous representation of the government in pursuit of a conviction leads some prosecutors to disregard the *Brady* rule or to engage in other conduct that is inconsistent with their obligations as ministers of justice. Let's take a look at four examples.

Sherman White was convicted of aggravated robbery, murder and assault with intent to commit murder. He was sentenced to three terms of life imprisonment without parole and began serving that sentence in 1972. White was involved, along with five other men, in the robbery of a tavern. The bartender and two patrons were shot and killed, and other patrons at the tavern were injured. White himself did not assault or shoot anyone. He testified at his trial that he was coerced to participate in the robbery and merely stood by the door. A surviving patron of the tavern testified that White was an active participant who demanded his wallet during the robbery. The testimony of that eyewitness clearly undermined White's defense of coercion. After White was convicted and sentenced, new evidence came to light that raised serious doubts about the credibility of the eyewitness' testimony. According to a police department memorandum written during the investigation of the robbery, the eyewitness had identified one of the other participants in the robbery as the man who took his wallet. Based on another police department memorandum, that other participant apparently admitted taking the eyewitness' wallet. The prosecutor withheld those memoranda and other exculpatory evidence from White's defense lawyer. The U. S. Court of Appeals for the Eighth Circuit granted White's petition for a writ of *habeas corpus* in 1999 and held that he was constitutionally entitled to either be released from custody or be granted a new trial:

> The crime was committed, and the trial held, in 1972. Sherman White has been in prison for 27 years after a trial in which the State withheld material evidence that would have helped him.[349]

The Court also noted that White had a credible coercion defense based on his testimony at the trial.[350]

When Justin Wolfe was a young marijuana dealer in Northern Virginia his main drug supplier was shot and killed by Owen Barber. Wolfe was convicted by a state court jury of capital murder for hire and was sentenced to death. To obtain the conviction the prosecutors had to convince the jury beyond a reasonable doubt that Wolfe hired Barber to kill the victim. There was no physical evidence connecting Wolfe to the murder. The prosecutors' theory of the case was that Wolfe had a motive for killing the victim because Wolfe owed the victim money, the victim was upset with Wolfe for not paying his debt, and Wolfe believed he would make more money from his drug deals if the victim were out of the way.[351]

At Wolfe's criminal trial the prosecutors' case was based on Barber's testimony that he had been hired by Wolfe to commit the murder. Barber also testified at the trial that he had no relationship to the victim, enabling the prosecutors to argue that Barber had no motive for the killing apart from his arrangement with Wolfe. The prosecutors presented testimony from four other witnesses to corroborate certain aspects of Barber's testimony. However, as the prosecutors later acknowledged, they would not have been able to prosecute Wolfe on the murder for hire charge without Barber's testimony against him.[352]

Wolfe's state court appeals from his conviction and death sentence were not successful. He then filed a petition in federal court for a writ of *habeas corpus*. After conducting an evidentiary hearing the U. S. District Court granted the writ and vacated Wolfe's conviction and sentence.[353] The Court's decision was based on numerous violations of the *Brady* rule by the prosecutors and on the prosecutors' presentation of Barber's trial testimony which they should have known to be false.

The prosecutors improperly withheld significant information that would have enabled Wolfe's lawyer to impeach the testimony of the prosecution's witnesses and to develop alternative theories to explain the murder. The prosecutors withheld evidence that Barber told his roommate he had acted alone in committing the murder.[354] They failed to disclose the investigating detective's report outlining his initial interview with Owen Barber. During that initial interview, before Barber said anything to implicate Wolfe the detective told Barber that he believed Barber killed the victim for Justin Wolfe and suggested that cooperation could mean the difference between execution or life in prison.[355] The prosecutors failed to disclose that they "choreographed and coordinated witness testimony through a series of joint meetings."[356] They "withheld evidence of Barber's personal dealings with the victim, including a claim that Barber owed [the victim] money, a claim that [the victim] had a hit out on Barber and a claim that Barber and [the victim] had recently associated with each other socially."[357] That information, if disclosed, would have completely undermined the prosecutors' theory of the case that Barber had no relationship to the victim and no personal motive for killing him. The prosecutors also failed to disclose the existence of tape recordings of meetings with key witnesses who suggested other people who may have had a motive for the murder. The prosecutors failed to disclose investigation reports containing information about conflicts within the victim's drug operation and about a rumor on the street that the victim was a police informant. The information in those reports suggested other possible motives for killing the victim that did not involve Wolfe. The prosecutors withheld evidence of prior inconsistent statements made by one of their corroborating witnesses, and did not disclose their off the record agreement not to prosecute another corroborating witness who had loaned Barber the car Barber used to commit the murder. They also failed to disclose the existence of statements given by three eyewitnesses who each saw a second car leaving the scene of the murder shortly after the shots were fired.[358]

In addition to withholding significant information that should have been disclosed to Wolfe under the *Brady* rule, the prosecution "violated Wolfe's due process rights by presenting Barber's trial testimony despite having information in its possession indicating that the testimony was false."[359] As the Court noted:

> The [prosecution] was in possession of information indicating that Barber knew [the victim] and that Barber stated that he acted alone, yet it allowed Barber's testimony that he did not know [the victim] and that Wolfe hired him to commit the murder to go uncorrected.

As the Court has repeatedly indicated, Barber's testimony was critical to Wolfe's criminal trial because it was the only testimony establishing the murder for hire element of the charge.[360]

The prosecutors tried to justify their violations of the *Brady* rule by arguing that when information is disclosed it can be used by at least some defendants and their lawyers "to fabricate a defense around what is provided."[361] The Court rejected that argument:

> Essentially, in an effort to ensure that no defense would be "fabricated," [the prosecutors'] actions served to deprive Wolfe of any substantive defense in a case where his life would rest on the jury's verdict. The Court finds these actions not only unconstitutional in regards to due process, but abhorrent to the judicial process.[362]

The Court quoted language from a Supreme Court opinion to make the point that the adversarial system of prosecution should not "descend to a gladiatorial level unmitigated by any prosecutorial obligation for the sake of the truth."[363] The Court then went on to express the opinion that the prosecutors had acted unethically, "in contravention of the 1999 Virginia Code of Professional Responsibility."[364]

The District Court's judgment vacating Wolfe's conviction and sentence was affirmed by the U. S. Court of Appeals for the Fourth Circuit.[365] In its opinion, the Court of Appeals rebuked the prosecutors' office for repeated violations of the *Brady* rule in death penalty cases,[366] and summarily dismissed some of the prosecutors' appellate arguments as "weak – though strident – contentions."[367] As the Court of Appeals noted:

> Wolfe had to labor for years from death row to obtain evidence that had been tenaciously concealed by the Commonwealth, and that the prosecution obviously should have disclosed prior to Wolfe's capital murder trial.[368]

When prosecutors are seeking the death penalty in a case, strident arguments attempting to justify their tenacious concealment of critical evidence from the defendant are really out of place.

This next example does not involve a capital crime or a violation of the *Brady* rule. It is a white collar criminal tax fraud case brought by prosecutors who zealously sought convictions in utter disregard of the constitutional rights of the defendants.

KPMG, one of the country's largest accounting firms, learned that the firm and several of its partners and employees were subjects of a federal criminal investigation of fraudulent tax shelters. The firm believed that it needed to avoid being indicted in order to be able to remain in business. Representatives of the firm had meetings with the federal prosecutors in New York attempting to persuade them to refrain from indicting KPMG. At the same time, consistent with its policy and past practice, KPMG started paying the legal fees for its current and former employees who were subjects of the investigation.[369]

Prosecutors have considerable discretion in deciding whether to seek a criminal indictment. During the KPMG investigation federal prosecutors were bound to follow a policy statement issued by Deputy Attorney General Larry Thompson that was known as the Thompson Memorandum. That policy statement identified a number of factors for prosecutors to consider in deciding whether to seek an indictment against a business organization such as KPMG. Among the factors to be considered were the organization's cooperation in the investigation and whether the organization appeared to be protecting its culpable agents and employees. According to the Thompson Memorandum, an organization's payment of attorneys' fees for culpable agents and employees, when such payments were not required by state law, could be considered by the prosecutor in evaluating the organization's cooperation.[370]

At their meetings with the lawyers for KPMG, the prosecutors made comments that were interpreted as expressing their displeasure about the firm's payment of legal fees for its employees. KPMG got the message. Desperate to avoid its own indictment, the firm capped the legal fees it would pay for an employee during the investigation. It took the unprecedented step of making its payment of legal fees conditioned on the employee's cooperation with the government. Whenever prosecutors notified KPMG's law firm that an employee was not cooperating, the law firm advised the lawyer for the employee that payment of the employee's legal fees would end unless the government indicated within ten business days that the employee agreed to cooperate. KPMG also agreed to stop paying legal fees for an employee who was indicted.[371] Even that was not enough. One of the prosecutors persuaded KPMG to send a supplemental memo to employees to explain that employees did not have to be assisted by a lawyer and could "deal directly with government representatives without counsel."[372] After making all these concessions, KPMG was able to persuade the Department of Justice to enter into a deferred prosecution agreement. Under the terms of that agreement, KPMG avoided being indicted by admitting to engaging in a fraud that generated at least $11 billion in phony tax losses, by paying $456 million in fines and penalties, by agreeing to make specific changes to its business operations, and by continuing to cooperate with the government.[373] On the same day the agreement was signed several KPMG employees were indicted. More employees were indicted two months later. As soon as an employee was indicted, KPMG stopped paying legal fees for the employee's defense pursuant to its agreement with the government.[374]

The KPMG employees asked the Court to dismiss the indictment against them on the grounds that the prosecutors violated their constitutional rights by persuading KPMG to limit and eventually end its payment of their legal fees. The Court noted that the government "let its zeal get in the way of its judgment,"[375] violating the employees' right to fundamental fairness under the Due Process Clause of the Fifth Amendment and their Sixth Amendment right to the effective assistance of legal counsel of their choice.[376] The Court stressed the unfairness of the prosecutors' efforts to restrict the employees' access to legal counsel, particularly in a complicated case that was going to cost millions of dollars[377] for an employee to defend:

Justice is not done when the government uses the threat of indictment – a matter of life and death to many companies and therefore a matter that threatens the jobs and security of blameless employees – to coerce companies into depriving their present and even former employees of the means of defending themselves against criminal charges in a court of law. If those whom the government suspects are culpable in fact are guilty, they should pay the price. But the determination of guilt or innocence must be made fairly – not in a proceeding in which the government has obtained an unfair advantage long before the trial even has begun.[378]

The Court also noted that the government "was economical with the truth"[379] in its early responses to the employees' motion to dismiss the indictment, and had this pointed comment for the prosecutors:

Every court is entitled to complete candor from every attorney, and most of all from those who represent the United States. These actions by the USAO [the United States Attorney's Office] are disappointing. There should be no recurrence.[380]

The Court dismissed the indictment against the thirteen current or former employees who were affected by the government's coercion of KPMG to limit and then cut off its payment of their legal fees.[381] The dismissal was affirmed by the U. S. Court of Appeals for the Second Circuit.[382]

In the aftermath of Hurricane Katrina six unarmed civilians were shot by members of the New Orleans Police Department in an incident on Danziger Bridge. Two of the victims died and three of the other four were seriously injured. Murder and attempted murder charges were brought in state court against seven police officers. A state court judge dismissed those charges based on misconduct by the state prosecutor.[383] In 2008 the U. S. Department of Justice took over the case and began an investigation. Two years later, several members of the New Orleans Police Department were indicted by a federal grand jury. The criminal case against five of the indicted defendants went to trial in the U. S. District Court for the Eastern District of Louisiana in the summer of 2011. The trial lasted several weeks. All five of the defendants were convicted by the jury. They were each sentenced to prison, for terms ranging from 6 years to 65 years.[384]

After the defendants were convicted and sentenced, evidence of misconduct by at least one of the federal prosecutors in the U. S. Attorney's Office for the Eastern District of Louisiana was brought to the Court's attention. The federal District Court Judge presiding over the case began an investigation. Two federal prosecutors from Georgia were brought in to assist. Over the next several months the judge prodded the investigation along and the truth started coming out. Finally, by 2013 the judge had seen enough. In a lengthy opinion filed on September 17, 2013 the Court granted the defendants' motion for a new trial. The ruling was based on a deliberate pattern of prosecutorial misconduct which deprived the defendants of their fundamental right to a fair trial and which undermined confidence in the integrity of the proceedings.[385] The prosecutors' misconduct involved repeated violations of specific rules governing pretrial publicity. The rules are intended to ensure that defendants in criminal cases receive a fair trial.[386]

Rule 3.8 of the Louisiana Rules of Professional Conduct required the prosecutors to "refrain from making extrajudicial comments that have a substantial likelihood of heightening public condemnation of the accused . . .".[387] As federal prosecutors, they were also bound to follow the guidelines in the United States Attorneys Manual governing media relations:

> At no time shall any component or personnel of the Department of Justice furnish any statement or information that he or she knows or reasonably should know will have a substantial likelihood of materially prejudicing an adjudicative proceeding.[388]

More specifically, the Manual prohibited the prosecutors from making observations about a defendant's character, statements about the identity or credibility of prospective witnesses, statements about evidence or argument in the case, and expressions of opinion about a defendant's guilt.[389] The prosecutors were also bound to follow federal regulations governing the release of information by Department of Justice personnel in criminal cases:

> At no time shall personnel of the Department of Justice furnish any statement or information for the purpose of influencing the outcome of a defendant's trial, nor shall personnel of the Department furnish any statement or information, which could reasonably be expected to be disseminated by means of public communication, if such a statement or information may reasonably be expected to influence the outcome of a pending or future trial.[390]

In addition to those rules, the U. S. District Court for the Eastern District of Louisiana had adopted Local Criminal Rules, applicable to both prosecutors and defense lawyers in criminal cases, which prohibited the release of information or opinion for dissemination by any means of public communication "if there is a reasonable likelihood that such dissemination will interfere with a fair trial or otherwise prejudice the due administration of justice." The Local Rules expressly prohibited the release of statements concerning "[a]ny opinion as to the accused's guilt or innocence or as to the merits of the case or the evidence in the case."[391]

Two high-ranking federal prosecutors in the U. S. Attorney's Office for the Eastern District of Louisiana, and a senior federal prosecutor in the Civil Rights Division of the Department of Justice in Washington, D. C., were determined to see the defendants convicted. They decided to surreptitiously circumvent the rules prohibiting prosecutors from making public comments about the case. The three federal prosecutors posted anonymous blogs at nola.com, the website for the New Orleans *Times-Picayune*. Many residents of New Orleans and the surrounding areas obtained news and other information from that website, especially after the *Times-Picayune* cut back on the number of days each week it published newspapers in print. None of the three prosecutors identified themselves as lawyers or as prosecutors involved in the case. They concealed their identities.

One of the New Orleans federal prosecutors, Sal Perricone, had been a detective in the New Orleans Police Department and a Special Agent in the FBI before becoming Senior Litigation Counsel in the U. S. Attorney's Office.[392] He used names for his blog posts such as "Henry L. Mencken1951," "dramatis personae," "legacyusa" and "campstblue."[393] During the federal investigation leading up to the indictments in the case, Perricone posted vitriolic comments about the New Orleans Police Department, describing the Department as "corrupt," "totally disfunctional" [sic], with a command structure "only concerned with their own aggrandizement and enrichment."[394] In another post he called for the resignation of "the top brass of the police department" and wrote that "[n]one of them have the people's interest at heart. NONE."[395] In several posts he described Warren Riley, the Superintendant of the Department who would be a defense witness at the trial, as "racist," "inept" and "delusional."[396] In a post six months before the trial of this case, Perricone commented about the ongoing trial of another case involving post-Katrina activities of the police, characterizing the New Orleans Police Department as "a collection of self-centered, self-interested, self-promoting, insular, arrogant, overweening, prevaricating, libidinous fools."[397] In another post, he previewed and debunked the defense he expected from the defendants in this case.[398] Five weeks before the trial started, he posted a comment blaming former Mayors of New Orleans "for allowing criminals on the police force today."[399] Ten minutes before the Court was called to order on the first day of trial, Perricone posted a comment about the defendants that "NONE of these guys should had have [sic] ever been given a badge."[400] During the trial, on the morning after one of the defendants had testified, Perricone posted this comment about that defendant's testimony:

> Where is Madison's [one of the shooting victim's] gun? Come on, officer, tell us. You shot because you wanted to be part of something, you thought, was bigger than you. You let your ego control your emotions. You wanted to be viewed as a big man among the other officers.

That's the creed of the NOPD and I hope the jury ignores your lame explanation and renders justice for Mr. Madison. To do less, is to sanction any cop who decides it is in his best interest to put a load of buckshot in the back of a disabled american [sic] in broad daylight.[401]

Then while the jury was deliberating Perricone continued to post comments online including statements such as "GUILTY AS CHARGED," "With all the shots fired on the bridge that day, how many hit an ARMED subject?" and "I don't think the jury will leave the dead and wounded on the bridge."[402]

The other New Orleans federal prosecutor, Jan Mann, supervised the work of the New Orleans members of the prosecution team in the case and used "eweman" for her blog posts.[403] She posted inappropriate comments on the nola.com website from November 2011 to March 2012, after the defendants were convicted and while they were waiting to be sentenced.[404]

The third federal prosecutor, Karla Dobinski, was a trial attorney in the Civil Rights Division of the Department of Justice. The Court seemed particularly troubled by her participation in the blogging activity because she was the "taint team" leader assigned to the prosecution team. Her role in the federal criminal case was to protect the constitutional rights of defendants who had been compelled to give incriminating statements during the state's criminal investigation. Particularly in cases involving allegations of police misconduct, statements may be compelled during an investigation despite objections based on the Fifth Amendment privilege against self-incrimination in exchange for a grant of immunity by the state prosecutor. A state prosecutor's grant of immunity is not binding on the federal government. In a subsequent federal prosecution, the "taint team" is responsible for purging information that might disclose the existence or content of immunized statements from the materials turned over to the federal prosecution team. Through that process, the constitutional rights of the defendants are protected and the federal prosecution is not tainted by incriminating information that was disclosed over Fifth Amendment objections.[405] Karla Dobinski, the "taint team" leader working on the case, used the assumed name "Dipsos" for her blog posts.[406] During the final week of trial, she posted six comments encouraging two other bloggers, in particular, to keep posting comments. Those two other bloggers "repeatedly posted pro-prosecution statements strongly condemning the defendants, their witnesses, and their entire defense. Expressing her appreciation for their posts, she proclaimed: 'You are performing a valuable public service!'"[407] The Court made clear its frustration with Dobinski's behavior:

> Less than 65 days before the start of this trial, Dobinski took the stand to explain in detail all of her extensive efforts to protect defendant Bowen's constitutional rights; yet before the jury even got the case for decision, she *personally* fanned the flames of those burning to see him convicted. Such gravely poor judgment surely calls into question the careful and meticulous effort she claims she exerted in protecting Bowen's rights.[408]

After discussing in considerable detail the evidence of misconduct by the three federal prosecutors, the Court made these observations in its opinion and order granting the defendants a new trial:

> The Court is, of course, also very cognizant that, on September 4, 2005, two men died, while three others were seriously injured, under tragic circumstances at the hands of some of the defendants herein, and that the state court criminal justice system was corrupted to the prejudice of at least one victim, Lance Madison. Mr. Madison's riveting testimony – both at trial and at sentencing – is surely not soon forgotten. Indeed, it echoes in this case, making the abuses set forth herein all the more astonishing. This case started as one featuring allegations of brazen abuse of authority, violation of the law, and corruption of the criminal justice system; unfortunately, though the focus has shifted from the accused to the accusers, it has continued to be about those very issues. After much reflection, the Court cannot journey as far as it has in this case only to ironically accept grotesque prosecutorial misconduct in the end.[409]

Prosecutors are "officers of the court bound to special rules of professional conduct."[410] The Court quoted from a 2012 opinion by the U. S. Court of Appeals for the Ninth Circuit to make the point that the "Department of Justice has an obligation to its lawyers and to the public to prevent prosecutorial misconduct. Prosecutors, as servants of the law, are subject to constraints and responsibilities that do not apply to other lawyers; they must serve truth and justice first."[411] The three federal prosecutors who posted anonymous blogs in their zealous desire to see the defendants convicted circumvented the rules governing pretrial publicity and abandoned their responsibility to maintain the integrity and fairness of the criminal justice process.

In trials and other adversarial proceedings, a lawyer's zealous representation of a client can be challenged by a lawyer representing the opposing party and, in some cases, by the judge presiding over the case. A competent lawyer will call the court's attention to misrepresentations that are made by the lawyer's opponent about the facts of the case or the applicable law. However, when a lawyer is representing a client in a business transaction there may not be an opposing lawyer in a position to challenge the lawyer and point out flaws in the lawyer's advice.

The attitude of fervent partisanship that is inherent in the concept of zealous representation can lead some lawyers to pursue their clients' objectives so aggressively that they bend the law beyond the breaking point. We'll take a look at three examples. The first example involves criminal violations of the federal securities laws by a lawyer who helped his client conceal its dire financial condition from investors. The second involves criminal violations of the federal income tax laws by a lawyer who wrote legal opinions in support of fraudulent tax shelters. The third is a civil enforcement action for violations of the federal securities laws by the in-house general counsel of a publicly traded company who helped the company, which was her client as well as her employer, overstate its reported financial performance by backdating sizeable grants of stock options to key executives.

Refco Inc. and its corporate affiliates provided brokerage and related services to customers investing in the international currency and commodity futures markets. The firm had a reputation for fostering a culture of bending the rules and for playing just over the edge.[412] Refco made loans to its customers so they could trade on margin and leverage their capital into larger trades. The trades generated substantial commissions and profits for Refco. In the late 1990s several global financial crises caused a number of Refco's customers to suffer massive trading losses. Loans to those customers became uncollectible receivables that should have been written off or at least disclosed in Refco's financial statements. The uncollectible receivables totaled hundreds of millions of dollars. Disclosure of those receivables would have had dire financial consequences for Refco.[413]

Joseph Collins, a partner in a Big Law firm, was Refco's principal outside lawyer. Refco was Collins' largest client, reportedly paying the law firm around $5 million a year in legal fees. Collins and his firm were alleged to have helped Refco's management carry out a scheme to conceal the uncollectible receivables from investors and from the public. The uncollectible receivables were transferred from the books of Refco Inc. to the books of an affiliated corporation that was controlled and partially owned by the CEO of Refco Inc. The transfer was accomplished by treating the transferred amount as a loan by Refco Inc. to the affiliated corporation, even though the affiliate had no liquid assets or operational functions and had no ability to repay the loan. Then, to avoid having to disclose the loan as a related party transaction on Refco's periodic financial statements, "round-trip" loans were arranged with the cooperation of some of Refco's solvent customers. Those round-trip loans straddled the end of each financial reporting period, so that Refco's books would show loans to the participating customers instead of the loan to Refco's affiliate. A few days after the end of the financial reporting period, the transactions would be unwound and the "loans" would be "repaid." Apart from some short term interest paid to the participating customers, no money changed hands in these paper transactions. The round-trip loans essentially enabled Refco to lend money to itself, on paper, with the assistance of the customers who were willing to participate in the plan in exchange for the interest payments they received on the short-term "loans."[414]

Collins and his law firm allegedly helped Refco carry out this scheme by explaining the transactions to customers who were thinking about participating, by negotiating the terms of the round-trip loans, by drafting the documents for the transactions, and by marking the participating customers' promissory notes as paid in full when the transactions were unwound. While the scheme was continuing to conceal the uncollectible receivables from investors and from the public, Collins and his law firm participated in drafting documents submitted to the Securities and Exchange Commission in connection with a public offering of Refco bonds and an initial public offering of Refco stock. When the initial public offering began trading on the New York Stock Exchange, the CEO of Refco Inc., who owned 38 percent of the firm, reportedly netted $1 billion.[415]

Two months later, a new controller at Refco discovered the scheme to hide the uncollectible receivables and Refco publicly disclosed that its financial statements could no longer be considered reliable. Within a week the value of Refco Inc. stock dropped from $29 a share to 65 cents a share. Refco filed for bankruptcy the following week.[416] The purchasers of Refco Inc. stock then filed a class action lawsuit for securities fraud seeking to recover the losses they sustained as a result of the scheme to conceal the uncollectible receivables and Refco's true financial condition. Their claims against Collins and his law firm for aiding and abetting Refco's fraudulent conduct were dismissed because the federal securities laws do not provide a basis for a private suit against those who aid and abet a fraud perpetrated by others.[417] Although he escaped civil liability to the Refco investors, Collins settled a formal complaint filed by the Securities and Exchange Commission that alleged he aided and abetted a financial fraud.[418] Collins was also convicted by a jury of conspiracy, criminal securities fraud, false filings with the Securities and Exchange Commission and wire fraud, and was sentenced to prison.[419] The U. S. Attorney for the Southern District of New York, whose office prosecuted Collins, described him as "a lawyer deeply and corruptly enmeshed in coordinating and concealing the massive accounting fraud that ultimately led to Refco's collapse."[420] Attempting to justify his behavior and avoid a conviction, Collins testified in his criminal trial that "I have a duty to represent my client zealously."[421]

A tax shelter investment can reduce a taxpayer's income tax obligation by providing the taxpayer with a loss that can be used as an offset against other income. A legitimate tax shelter investment will have economic substance as well as a business purpose other than merely avoiding the payment of income tax. For example, a wealthy individual who expects to receive $5 million in gross income this year may decide to buy a start-up company that is expected to have losses of $1 million a year for the next few years until it becomes established and starts generating profits. By purchasing the start-up company, the taxpayer can reduce gross income this year from $5 million to $4 million and save hundreds of thousands of dollars in income tax. The taxpayer can also anticipate making money from the start-up company in future years once it becomes profitable.

In contrast to legitimate tax shelter investments that produce a loss in the short term, abusive tax shelters have no business or investment purpose. Their sole purpose is to help purchasers of the tax shelter avoid paying income tax. An abusive tax shelter may involve an extraordinarily complex series of transactions that generate tax "losses" on paper even though the purchaser of the tax shelter is not actually losing money. If the Internal Revenue Service audits a taxpayer's return and decides that a loss claimed by the taxpayer is attributable to an abusive tax shelter, the IRS can disallow the claimed loss, refigure the taxpayer's income tax obligation, and assess interest as well as substantial penalties.

In the 1990s tax shelters became popular tools for helping wealthy individuals and corporations substantially reduce their income tax liabilities. Purchasers of tax shelters often obtained independent "opinion letters" attesting to the legality, economic substance and business purpose of their tax shelter investment. These opinion letters were thought to minimize the risk of penalties if the IRS audited a return and disallowed the losses associated with the tax shelter. Without the risk of substantial penalties, a taxpayer could take the chance of being audited and, at worst, simply end up paying the tax that had been avoided, plus interest.[422]

Many of these opinion letters were written by lawyers at prominent law firms. The lawyers often felt pressure from long-standing clients to write an opinion letter supporting a tax shelter investment the client wanted to make. Lawyers succumbed to this pressure even if it meant lending their names to tax shelter investments of questionable legality. They wanted to accommodate their clients and preserve their client relationships. And the legal fees for writing an opinion letter could be substantial.[423] According to one news report, a Big Law firm was paid a $1 million fee for writing a twelve page opinion letter for Enron supporting a tax shelter investment that was going to save Enron $78 million in taxes.[424]

In 2002 a Subcommittee of the U. S. Senate began an investigation into the development, marketing and implementation of abusive tax shelters by accounting firms, lawyers, financial advisors and banks. The Subcommittee focused on generic abusive tax shelter products that were developed for sale to multiple clients. After conducting an extensive investigation and holding two days of hearings, the Subcommittee issued a Report on April 13, 2005.[425] In its Report the Subcommittee noted that abusive tax shelters were causing the U. S. Treasury to lose billions of dollars a year in unpaid income taxes.[426] The Report describes abusive tax shelter products that were developed and marketed by three major accounting firms, including KPMG. A few months after the Subcommittee's Report was published, indictments were issued against several individuals associated with KPMG. Later on, the Department of Justice entered into a deferred prosecution agreement with KPMG. Earlier in this chapter we considered the dismissal of the indictments against several KPMG employees on the grounds that their constitutional rights under the Fifth and Sixth Amendments were violated when the government pressured KPMG to limit and then cut off its payment of their legal fees. We will now examine the activities and eventual criminal conviction of Raymond Ruble, a lawyer who played key roles for KPMG in the development and marketing of the firm's generic tax shelter products.

In the late 1990s KPMG made a strategic business decision to develop tax shelter products that could be marketed to multiple clients. At least some of the KPMG partners wanted the firm to become an industry leader in the field.[427] Raymond Ruble, a partner in a prominent Wall Street law firm, provided legal advice and technical assistance to help KPMG develop at least one of its generic tax shelters, known as BLIPS.[428] Once KPMG's tax shelters were developed, the accounting firm asked Ruble to provide opinion letters to KPMG clients attesting to the legality and the investment purpose of the tax shelter. KPMG was already providing its own opinion letters, but believed that offering clients a second opinion letter from a Wall Street law firm would help with marketing. As KPMG told its clients who were worried about IRS penalties:

> The opinion letters that we issue should get you out of any penalties. However, the [Internal Revenue] Service could try to argue that KPMG is the promoter of the strategy and therefore the opinions are biased and try to assert penalties. We believe there is a very low risk of this result. If you desire additional assurance, there is at least one outside law firm in NYC that will issue a co-opinion.[429]

With respect to three of KPMG's generic tax shelters, that outside law firm in New York City was Raymond Ruble's firm.

Ruble was hardly providing KPMG clients with an independent second opinion about the validity and business purpose of its tax shelters. He used language in his opinion letters that he borrowed from the templates for KPMG's opinion letters. Ruble and KPMG compared drafts of their respective opinion letters to make sure they were compatible.[430] KPMG did not really want a lawyer's independent second opinion about the validity of its tax shelters. KPMG only wanted to be able to tell its clients that a Wall Street law firm would give an opinion supporting the tax shelter. Ruble was glad to oblige. Ruble's law firm estimated that it received more than $23 million in legal fees for opinion letters and other work on the KPMG tax shelter products.[431]

Raymond Ruble was indicted by a federal grand jury on charges related to his participation in the KPMG tax shelter scheme. After a ten week jury trial he was convicted of multiple counts of tax evasion relating to BLIPS clients who had received legal opinion letters from him.[432] The U. S. Attorney's Office that prosecuted the case issued a press release quoting comments made by the federal District Court Judge during the sentencing hearing four months later:

> In discussing the specific offense conduct of the defendants, Judge KAPLAN stated that, 'while BLIPS and the other shelters they were involved in all were dressed up as investment opportunities, that is not what they were all about. They were designed to create tax losses so that the super-rich people could avoid paying income taxes.' Judge KAPLAN said, '. . . there does come a time when a scheme is so raw, so brazen, and so outrageous that it crosses the line that separates bad or incompetent or unsuccessful tax planning from crime.' Judge KAPLAN also stated, 'these defendants were not prosecuted and they were not convicted for making mistakes in judgment on debatable questions in good faith,' adding 'these defendants knew that they were on the wrong side of the line.'[433]

Ruble was sentenced to serve 78 months in prison followed by two years of supervised release.

In 2007 the U. S. Securities and Exchange Commission filed suit against Nancy Heinen, a lawyer who had been General Counsel of Apple Computer, Inc. The SEC alleged that while she was Apple's General Counsel Heinen caused stock option grants made during 2001 to be backdated in order to conceal millions of dollars in executive compensation. In the first backdated grant, 4.8 million stock options were awarded to six senior executives of the company. As one of the company's senior executives, Heinen received 400,000 of those stock options. In the second backdated grant, 7.5 million stock options were awarded to Apple's CEO, Steve Jobs.[434]

Many publicly traded companies, including Apple, grant stock options to senior executives as part of their compensation. Once an executive's stock options have vested, the executive can exercise the options and receive the difference between the market price of the stock when the options are exercised and the exercise price specified in the grant. If a company's stock price has increased in the market above the specified exercise price, the additional compensation received by the executive can be substantial.

The SEC has established specific accounting and disclosure rules that publicly traded companies need to follow when they grant stock options. Under the accounting rules, a company is not required to report an expense in its financial statements for stock options that are granted with an exercise price at the current market price for the stock. Stock options granted at the current market price may or may not increase in value in the future. Unless and until the market price of the company's stock increases, the options are essentially worthless. However, if stock options are granted with an exercise price that is below the current market price for the stock when the options are granted, the accounting rules require the difference between the exercise price and the current market price, multiplied by the number of options in the grant, to be reported as a compensation expense in the company's financial statements. For example, if a company grants 100,000 stock options at an exercise price of $10.00 per share when the current market price for the stock is $12.00 per share, the company is required to report $200,000 of compensation expense attributable to the stock option grant.

In 2001 Apple could have paid additional compensation to its senior executives and CEO by giving them substantial bonuses and reporting the bonus amounts as additional compensation in its financial statements. However, declaring and paying bonuses would have increased Apple's reported operating expenses and reduced its reported net income. To pay the executives additional compensation without having to report bonuses, the SEC alleged that Heinen carried out a plan to backdate the stock option grants to earlier dates when the stock price was lower than it was when the decisions to grant the options were made. An additional reason for backdating the grants was that Apple was representing in its financial statements and in other documents filed with the SEC that its stock options were granted at an exercise price equal to the fair market value of the stock on the date of the grant.

The SEC alleged that Heinen selected the dates to which the stock option grants would be backdated and then directed her legal department staff to document Board of Directors approval of the grants by preparing a backdated consent resolution and by preparing fictitious minutes of a special meeting of the Board of Directors that never occurred. The SEC also alleged that Heinen caused official corporate minutes to be altered to conceal the backdating.[435] As a result of the backdating scheme, Apple failed to report $39.2 million of compensation expense, thereby understating its net loss for fiscal year 2001 and overstating its net income for fiscal year 2002 by material amounts.[436]

Heinen resigned as Apple's General Counsel in May of 2006. Seven months later, on December 29, 2006, Apple filed restated financial statements that recognized $39.2 million in additional pre-tax compensation expense associated with the two backdated stock option grants.[437] During the SEC's investigation of the backdating scheme, Heinen declined to answer questions based on her rights under the Fifth Amendment privilege against self-incrimination.[438] She later agreed to a settlement of the SEC's suit against her. Under the terms of the settlement, Heinen agreed to pay $2.2 million, agreed to be barred from serving as an officer or director of any public company for five years, and agreed to a three-year suspension from appearing or practicing as an attorney before the SEC.[439]

The examples in this chapter illustrate a number of different ways that an overriding commitment to zealous representation can lead lawyers to engage in behavior that diminishes public respect for the legal profession. The elevation of zealous representation to become the defining principle for a lawyer's role also has a corrosive effect within the legal profession itself. And the fervent partisanship that is the essence of zealous representation often promotes needless conflict and does not serve clients well.

Too many lawyers seem to regard their commitment to zealous representation as an excuse for rude, contentious and uncivil behavior.[440] They may think that contentious behavior, in its various forms, will make them more effective as advocates or as negotiators by intimidating the lawyers and the parties on the other side of a case. They allow themselves to be carried away by a competitive impulse that leads them to approach nearly every issue that comes up in a deposition or a court hearing or a negotiation as a fight that must be won. Their nasty comments to opposing counsel are not tempered by any notion of professional restraint.[441] An article in the *Chicago Tribune*[442] reported this exchange between lawyers, found in the transcript of a deposition taken in 1993, after one of the lawyers, "Mr. V," asked the other lawyer, "Mr. A," for a copy of a document he was using to question the witness:

Mr. V: Please don't throw it at me.

Mr. A: Take it.

Mr. V: Don't throw it at me.

Mr. A: Don't be a child, Mr. V. You look like a slob the way you're dressed, but you don't have to act like a slob.
. . . . .

Mr. V: Stop yelling at me. Let's get on with it.

Mr. A: Have you not? You deny I have given you a copy of every document?

Mr. V: You just refused to give it to me.

Mr. A: Do you deny it?

Mr. V: Eventually you threw it at me.

Mr. A: Oh, Mr. V, you're about as childish as you can get. You look like a slob, you act like a slob.

Mr. V: Keep it up.

While this is an extreme example of uncivil behavior, it illustrates the type of nasty and unproductive sparring between lawyers that occurs far too often. Countless articles have been written about the decline in civility within the legal profession as a cause of widespread dissatisfaction among lawyers.

Zealous representation can also be counterproductive for clients. When a lawyer is representing a client in dealings with officials in a regulatory agency, fervent partisanship on behalf of the client will probably not be received well by the regulatory officials. A lawyer who is narrowly focused on the zealous pursuit of a client's stated agenda may fail to apply the independent professional judgment that could enable the lawyer to discourage the client from pursuing an agenda that ultimately leads to massive liabilities.[443] Sometimes a confrontational approach taken in the spirit of zealously representing a client can actually be an obstacle to achieving the client's objectives. Consider this example related to me by a professional colleague practicing law in a major metropolitan area: The owner of a well-known and established restaurant was approached by a developer who wanted to build a skyscraper. The developer already had architectural plans for the skyscraper and needed to buy the property where the restaurant was located. He was willing to have the restaurant rebuilt at a prime location on the main floor of the skyscraper. After some negotiations, the restaurant owner and the developer signed a contract which allowed the developer to buy the restaurant property and allowed the restaurant owner to rebuild the restaurant inside the skyscraper. After signing the contract the restaurant owner had second thoughts and went to see his lawyer. The lawyer wrote a belligerent and confrontational letter to the developer demanding a release from the contract. The developer's lawyer sent a blunt letter in response, basically saying, "Your client signed a contract, and if he's backing out we'll see you in court." After a number of sleepless nights the restaurant owner called the developer and requested a meeting without their lawyers.

The developer agreed, and when they met the restaurant owner explained that the restaurant had been a successful family business for several decades and the restaurant property was owned free and clear. He went on to say that he was in his early sixties and really did not want to incur new debt to rebuild the restaurant. As a result of that meeting the developer had the architectural plans changed so the skyscraper could be built around the restaurant. The restaurant owner was able to keep the restaurant property, avoid incurring debt and reclaim his peace of mind – once he got his zealous lawyer out of the way.

Nine

Legal Ethics

Lawyers take pride in being members of a self-policing profession. Their professional conduct is said to be governed by comprehensive ethical rules that have been adopted by each of the states and the District of Columbia. A lawyer may be disciplined for violating the ethical rules of a state where he or she is admitted to practice. An ethical violation can be reported to a state's Board of Professional Responsibility, or an organization with a similar name, that will investigate the reported violation. The organization may have the authority to admonish the lawyer or to issue a formal reprimand. For more serious ethical violations that may warrant suspension from the practice of law for a period of time or the ultimate sanction of disbarment, the organization will make a disciplinary recommendation to the licensing agency for lawyers which is usually the State Supreme Court.

Yet the existence of ethical rules and a process for their enforcement does not necessarily mean that lawyers are guided in their practice by high ethical standards.[444] In 1995 former Chief Justice Warren Burger made this observation about the profession's approach to legal ethics:

[T]he organized Bar's failure to set and maintain high ethical standards for the legal profession has caused much of the decline in professionalism among lawyers and the corresponding decline in the public esteem of lawyers.[445]

The ethical rules adopted by nearly all of the states are currently based on the ABA's Model Rules of Professional Conduct. The fundamental problem with the Model Rules is that clear statements of aspirational ethical principles are missing. The Model Rules do not attempt to guide the professional behavior of lawyers with stated normative principles or ethical ideals akin to the norm of zealous representation.[446] The Model Rules are simply a set of rules supplemented by comments that are intended to provide guidance for interpreting and applying the rules. A set of rules cannot anticipate and address every conceivable ethical issue that might arise in the practice of law. The language of a rule can be interpreted narrowly to justify behavior that is inconsistent with the intent of the rule.[447] And literal compliance with the Model Rules does not guarantee ethical behavior. Ethical rules do not create ethical lawyers any more than the rules of the road create careful drivers.

A lawyer who is found guilty in our criminal justice system of a crime involving dishonesty or moral turpitude will ordinarily be suspended from the practice of law or disbarred. In the absence of a criminal conviction, relatively few violations of the ethical rules result in disciplinary action against the offending lawyer unless the ethical violation involves mishandling client funds in a lawyer's trust account.

The disciplinary process begins when a formal complaint is filed about a lawyer's ethical violation. Lawyers are generally reluctant to file ethical complaints about other lawyers, except in egregious situations. Clients are usually unfamiliar with the ethical rules and may not be aware that an ethical violation has occurred. They may also be reluctant to file a complaint, preferring to avoid having to disclose the situation that led them to hire a lawyer. If an ethical complaint is filed against a lawyer, it will be investigated and acted on by the Board of Professional Responsibility or a similar organization consisting of lawyers. Unless an ethical violation is part of a continuing pattern of professional misconduct, the lawyers considering and acting on the complaint will be unlikely to take or recommend formal disciplinary action against the lawyer who is the subject of the complaint.

Senior U. S. Court of Appeals Judge Harry Edwards has pointed out that "some lawyers cross the line of ethical behavior in overly zealous representation of their clients."[448] In the previous chapter we saw a number of examples of lawyers who crossed the line of ethical behavior as that line is defined by the ABA's Model Rules of Professional Conduct. From a review of the pertinent Model Rules we will see that the professional misconduct of those lawyers cannot be attributed to a lack of ethical rules.

Model Rule 3.4 prohibits lawyers from altering, destroying or concealing evidence, falsifying evidence, or failing to make a reasonably diligent effort to comply with proper pretrial discovery requests.[449] Model Rule 3.3, entitled "Candor Toward the Tribunal,"[450] prohibits a lawyer from knowingly making a false statement of law or fact to a court or failing to disclose controlling legal authority that is adverse to the lawyer's position. That rule also prohibits a lawyer from knowingly offering evidence the lawyer knows to be false. Model Rule 3.1 prohibits a lawyer from asserting a claim or defense in a case "unless there is a basis in law and fact for doing so that is not frivolous."[451] Model Rule 3.8 addresses the special responsibilities of a prosecutor in a criminal case. Under that rule, a prosecutor is required to "make timely disclosure to the defense of all evidence or information known to the prosecutor that tends to negate the guilt of the accused or mitigates the offense, . . ."[452] The rule also requires a prosecutor to "refrain from making extrajudicial comments that have a substantial likelihood of heightening public condemnation of the accused . . . ."[453] Trial publicity is governed by Model Rule 3.6 which prohibits the lawyers in a firm or government agency that is investigating or litigating a matter from making "an extrajudicial statement that the lawyer knows or reasonably should know will be disseminated by means of a public communication and will have a substantial likelihood of materially prejudicing an adjudicative proceeding in the matter."[454] A lawyer's violation or attempted violation of any of these rules is defined by Model Rule 8.4 as professional

misconduct. That rule also includes in the definition of professional misconduct "conduct involving dishonesty, fraud, deceit or misrepresentation" and
"conduct that is prejudicial to the administration of justice."[455]

Those ethical rules did not prevent the types of professional misconduct
illustrated in the previous chapter by lawyers who apparently believed they
were properly guided by a desire to zealously represent their clients. In the
rest of this chapter we will consider two other types of unethical practices by
some lawyers – charging clients excessive legal fees, and representing clients
with conflicting interests. Both of these practices can be attributed to the
commercialization of the private practice of law.

Excessive Legal Fees

Lawyers are ethically prohibited from charging a client an unreasonable fee. Rule
1.5 of the ABA's Model Rules of Professional Conduct and the Comment to that
rule identify a number of factors to consider in deciding whether a fee is reasonable. Those factors include the time, labor and skill required of the lawyer, the
lawyer's experience and reputation, the novelty and difficulty of the legal matter,
the results the lawyer obtains, and fees customarily charged for similar services.[456]

Partners in some of the largest law firms charge fees based on hourly billing
rates as high as $750 to $1,200 an hour. Is that reasonable? Consider that much
of a partner's time working on a legal matter is spent attending meetings with the
client, reading documents and legal memoranda, and directing the activities of
other lawyers and paralegals working on the matter. Time spent by junior associates during their first year or two of practice at a large firm is often billed to clients
at $200 an hour or more. Junior associates are still learning how to practice law
and they have not yet developed the efficiencies that come with experience.

It is not uncommon for lawyers to raise their hourly rates from time to
time. Like doctors, business people and other professionals, lawyers need to
be able to cover their costs of doing business, keep up with inflation, and
perhaps make a bit more money than they did the year before. Lawyers who
only raise their hourly rates for new legal work give their existing clients and

prospective new clients a fair choice. Clients who are not willing to pay the higher hourly rate can choose to hire a different lawyer to handle the new legal matter from beginning to end. However, many of the larger law firms expect periodic increases in their hourly rates every year or two for existing legal work. That expectation sets the stage for a negotiation between the client and the law firm that often becomes adversarial in nature. The law firm knows that it will be very expensive for the client to change lawyers in the middle of a lawsuit or a complex business transaction. The client hopes the law firm wants to keep the client's legal work badly enough that the firm will be reasonable in its negotiations for an increased hourly rate.

Clients can also find themselves being expected to pay higher hourly rates for a lawyer's services in an ongoing lawsuit or business transaction if the lawyer moves to a different law firm that is accustomed to charging clients high hourly rates. The lawyer will be under considerable pressure at his or her new law firm to start charging a higher hourly rate that is consistent with the firm's rate structure. From the perspective of a client who was very happy with the lawyer at the former law firm, the only thing that really changed about the lawyer is the lawyer's office address.

The number of hours a lawyer bills to clients is the other component of legal fees based on hourly billings. As client resistance to paying higher and higher hourly rates continues to grow, lawyers find themselves under increasing pressure to bill more hours in order to generate the legal fees their firms expect them to produce. In the 1980s it was fairly common for law firms to expect lawyers to bill 1,750 to 1,800 hours a year. In 2002 the ABA published a report proposing an expectation that lawyers bill 1,900 hours a year. According to a more recent report, the *average* billable hour requirement at the largest Big Law firms is slightly more than 2,200 hours a year.[457]

High billable hour expectations can put lawyers at odds with the interests of their clients in a number of ways. Consider this hypothetical example of a lawyer who has been hired to represent a client in a lawsuit on the basis of an hourly fee: The lawyer recommends the "traditional litigation approach" of engaging in pretrial discovery for a while, filing pretrial motions with the court in an effort to narrow the issues for trial, and then participating in settlement

negotiations shortly before trial. The lawyer may genuinely believe it is important to fully develop the facts and legal arguments in the case in order to make
sure the client's legal rights are vindicated to the greatest possible degree. The
lawyer is also well aware that the traditional litigation approach will generate a
substantial number of billable hours and tens of thousands of dollars, or more,
in legal fees. However, what the client may really want is to resolve the lawsuit
as quickly as possible and to avoid spending a lot of money on legal fees. The
client would be perfectly happy to forego the pretrial discovery process and
participate in mediation early in the case to achieve a resolution of the dispute
that is reasonably acceptable. Yet the lawyer has not recommended an early
mediation as an alternative approach to resolving the lawsuit, and may even
talk the client out of foregoing the pretrial discovery process. In this example,
is it reasonable for the lawyer to charge a fee based on the number of hours
the lawyer devoted to the traditional litigation approach in the case, when the
client would have preferred a quicker and far less expensive alternative?

Some lawyers actively put their need to generate billable hours ahead of
the interests of their clients. They may postpone settlement discussions that
could resolve a lawsuit in order to have a chance to spend more time engaging
in pretrial discovery. They may even encourage other lawyers to sue their client. For example, a lawyer representing one of the defendants in the personal
injury litigation arising from exposure to silica dust in the workplace called a
lawyer representing plaintiffs to suggest that his client be named as a defendant.[458] Another lawyer practicing in Massachusetts at a large law firm was
disciplined for performing unnecessary work and for billing a client for tasks
that were performed and billed by other lawyers in the firm. He "knowingly
spent more time than necessary on this billed work in order to increase his
billable hours at the firm."[459]

Pressure to generate billable hours also rewards inefficiency. A junior associate who is still learning how to practice law may draft and re-draft and
revise and edit a fairly simple document in order to avoid making a mistake
and displeasing the supervising partner. Eight hours might be spent preparing
a document that a more experienced lawyer could have prepared in an hour
and a half. The associate who did the work will probably record all eight hours

of billable time on his or her time sheets. Many firms will bill the client for all eight hours at the associate's hourly rate. Law firms may also overstaff cases in order to increase billable hours, by assigning three associates to work on a project when one associate would be enough. Inefficiency can also result from a lawyer's fatigue near the end of the day. To meet high billable hour expectations a lawyer will need to work long hours day after day during the week, with some time spent working most weekends. At the end of a long day, an hour of the lawyer's time may not have the same value for a client as an hour earlier in the day when the lawyer's mind was fresh. Yet the hour at the end of the day will be billed to the client at the lawyer's hourly rate, with no discount for the fatigue factor.

Some lawyers cheat. They pad their time sheets by recording more time than the amount of time they actually spent. Four hours is billed for preparing a document that only took the lawyer two and a half hours to prepare. A research project that took six hours is billed as though it took seven and a half. Some lawyers double bill their clients, charging two clients for the same block of time. For example, a lawyer representing Client A in a lawsuit may need to take a four-hour airplane flight to attend a deposition that is being taken in another city. The lawyer bills Client A for the four hours spent on the airplane traveling to the deposition. That is understandable, since the airplane flight is keeping the lawyer away from the office where he or she could be performing other billable work. One might think that the lawyer would spend time during the flight preparing for the deposition. After all, Client A is being billed for the four hours. Instead, the lawyer spends three of those hours on the airplane working on a document for Client B and bills Client B for three hours of time. Four hours on the airplane becomes seven hours of billable time. Until the ABA adopted a formal ethical opinion in 1993 condemning the practice, many lawyers considered that form of double billing to be acceptable.[460] And despite the ABA's formal ethical opinion, double billing still occurs.

Chief Justice William Rehnquist served as a member of the lawyer disciplinary board when he practiced law in Arizona. As he noted, "if one is expected to bill more than two thousand hours per year, there are bound to be temptations to exaggerate the hours actually put in."[461] Clients usually have no way of knowing how much time their lawyers actually spend working on their legal matter. Lisa Lerman, a law professor at The Catholic University of America who has focused on legal ethics, pointed out that "[a] remarkable amount of padding and double billing can be hidden."[462] Clients who do not hire lawyers on a regular basis also have no way of knowing whether their legal matter was overstaffed or whether all the work their lawyers performed was necessary. Professor Lerman succinctly described the effects of dishonest billing practices on the relationship between lawyers and their clients, on the reputation of the legal profession, and on the economy:

> If lawyers are deceiving their clients to increase their own earnings, this raises fundamental questions about the integrity of the profession. The expectation that lawyers should be scrupulously truthful in billing their clients is not naïve or unreasonable, but is absolutely basic to the establishment and maintenance of a relationship of trust and confidence between lawyer and client. . . . The harm caused by billing fraud is very serious. Clients are being harmed by being charged too much for legal services, any by being charged for services they do not need. Clients and lawyers are harmed by the dishonesty of lawyers who lose track of the difference between truthfulness and rationalizing. . . . .

> Obviously, there is also harm to the legal profession. Dishonest billing feeds public concerns about lawyers' lack of candor and greed, and demonstrates that the financial self-interest increasingly tends to dominate other professional values. Also, there may be substantial harm to the economy from the wasted services that are provided to our federal government and to our corporations. The legal bills of large institutions are ultimately paid by taxpayers, shareholders, consumers, and employees.[463]

Despite the harm to clients and to the reputation of the legal profession that results from dishonest hourly billing practices, lawyers who engage in those practices are seldom caught and rarely disciplined.

Excessive numbers of billable hours charged to clients and high hourly rates do not provide the only path to an unreasonable fee. Contingent fee arrangements can also produce unreasonable legal fees.

Contingent fees have traditionally been based on one-third of the amount of money recovered for a client, after out of pocket expenses are deducted. For example, a lawyer may recover $230,000 for a client who was injured in a motor vehicle accident. If the lawyer incurred $20,000 for expert witness fees, court reporter fees, deposition transcript fees and other out of pocket expenses while working on the case, the lawyer's fee would be one-third of $210,000, or $70,000, under the traditional contingent fee arrangement. The net recovery for the client would be the remaining $140,000 of the total amount recovered. Over the years the traditional contingent fee arrangement has been modified as a number of contingent fee lawyers charge clients forty percent, or even fifty percent, of the amount of money recovered. Some even charge a fee based on a percentage of the total recovery, and then deduct the out of pocket expenses from the client's share. All these modifications to the traditional contingent fee arrangement produce a larger fee for the lawyer and a smaller net recovery for the client.

Even the traditional contingent fee arrangement can produce a legal fee that is excessive. After the September 11, 2001 terrorist attacks on the World Trade Center, more than 10,000 people filed suit against the City of New York and its private contractors claiming they had sustained injuries due to their participation in rescue, recovery and cleanup operations at the World Trade Center site. Many of the people filing suit had sustained serious injuries as a result of their heroic efforts. The cases were filed in the U. S. District Court for the Southern District of New York where they were consolidated and assigned to Judge Alvin Hellerstein. The consolidated cases were litigated for several years. The litigation was complex and expensive. The lawyers representing the plaintiffs borrowed millions of dollars to pay the out of pocket costs needed to prosecute the cases. They took considerable financial risk as the legal principles governing the cases made the outcome far from certain. After intense negotiations, the parties agreed on a settlement process that would produce a total settlement amount in the range of $575 million to $632.5 million. The lawyers representing the plaintiffs would be reimbursed for their out of pocket costs and would then receive their agreed one-third of the remaining settlement proceeds.[464] Judge Hellerstein rejected the settlement after concluding that it "was unfair to the plaintiffs, giving them too little and giving the lawyers too much."[465] The settlement would have generated legal fees for the plaintiffs' lawyers between $189 million and $216 million, which Judge Hellerstein believed to be excessive.[466] The parties resumed their negotiations. The lawyers representing the plaintiffs agreed to reduce their contingent fee percentage from one-third to twenty-five percent, and the City of New York and its contractors agreed to increase the total amount they would pay into the settlement fund. Judge Hellerstein approved the revised settlement that increased the amount of money being paid to the plaintiffs by $125 million and reduced the fees paid to their lawyers by roughly $50 million. The plaintiffs' lawyers still received well over $150 million in legal fees and were also reimbursed for their out of pocket expenses.[467]

Conflicts of Interest

Ethical conflicts of interest are addressed by the ABA's Model Rules of Professional Conduct. It is unethical for a lawyer or law firm to undertake a client representation that is directly adverse to a current client, unless both clients give their informed written consent.[468] The basis for that rule is that "[l]oyalty and independent judgment are essential elements in the lawyer's relationship to a client."[469] Former clients of a lawyer or law firm are also protected, though to a somewhat lesser degree. It is unethical for a lawyer or law firm to represent a client with interests adverse to the interests of a former client, in a matter that is the same as or "substantially related" to the representation of the former client, unless the former client gives informed written consent to the representation of the new client.[470] That rule is primarily intended to protect the confidentiality of information the former client shared with the lawyer or law firm. Despite these rules, some lawyers put their personal and financial interests, and the financial interests of their law firms, ahead of the interests of their current and former clients. Let's take a look at examples of several different ways some lawyers and law firms ignore or try to circumvent the ethical rules governing conflicts of interest.

The first example involves a law firm that wanted to defend a client in a lawsuit that was brought by a former client of the firm. Residential Funding Company, LLC ("RFC") purchased residential mortgage loans from a corporate predecessor of HSBC Finance Corporation ("HSBC") and included those loans in mortgate-backed securities trusts which RFC sold to investors. When litigation resulted from the sale of those trusts, RFC hired a large law firm to defend it in suits brought by investors as well as in suits brought by the Federal Housing Finance Authority and the Federal Home Loan Bank of Chicago. The law firm had regular communications about the lawsuits with other lawyers representing RFC and interviewed several RFC witnesses about the company's business practices. The law firm also gave advice to RFC about potential claims by institutional investors.

  After the individual lawsuits against RFC were resolved by a comprehensive settlement, RFC filed suit against HSBC claiming that the residential mortgage loans it had purchased from HSBC's corporate predecessor were defective. One of the partners in the law firm that defended RFC in the individual lawsuits had represented HSBC for nearly twenty years in other matters. HSBC wanted to hire that partner to defend the lawsuit brought by RFC. After expressing some reservations about conflict of interest issues, the law firm eventually agreed to represent HSBC in the lawsuit.[471] RFC objected, and asked the Court to disqualify the law firm from representing HSBC because the firm "was representing HSBC against its former client RFC on a substantially related matter in which HSBC's interests were materially adverse to RFC's and RFC had not given informed consent, confirmed in writing."[472] HSBC opposed the disqualification motion by making the unsupported argument that the defense of investor claims against RFC and the pursuit of affirmative claims by RFC against the seller of the mortgage loans were matters "not related on their face." HSBC also argued that, in any event, RFC had waived its right to seek disqualification of the law firm. HSBC's waiver argument was based on RFC's failure to respond within forty-eight hours to an ambiguous voicemail message the law firm partner left for RFC's principal outside lawyer. The Court rejected both arguments and disqualified the law firm from representing HSBC, noting that the partner who left the voicemail message "was more concerned about moving forward with his representation of HSBC than he was about obtaining RFC's consent."[473]

A different law firm was disqualified from representing the plaintiff in a Superfund cost recovery case with respect to claims against some of the defendants. Roosevelt Irrigation District, as plaintiff, filed suit against dozens of defendants seeking to recover the costs it incurred as a result of the contamination of its municipal groundwater wells. The Irrigation District claimed its wells were contaminated with hazardous substances migrating from three Superfund sites for which the defendants were responsible. The judge presiding over the case ruled that the law firm representing the Irrigation District had ethical conflicts which precluded the firm from prosecuting the claims asserted against five of the defendants – Honeywell, Corning, Univar, Salt River Power District and Dolphin.[474] The reasons for disqualification were somewhat different for each of those defendants.

A lawyer who had represented Honeywell and Corning on issues relating to their involvement in two of the Superfund sites joined the law firm representing the Irrigation District about a month before the lawsuit was filed. Shortly before changing law firms, the lawyer represented Honeywell in discussions with a lawyer at the Irrigation District's firm and analyzed the Irrigation District's draft complaint in his capacity as Honeywell's lawyer. In the Court's words, by changing law firms he "switched sides" in the case.[475]

Univar, Salt River Power District and Dolphin had been members of joint defense groups that were formed to try to negotiate joint cleanup agreements for two of the Superfund sites with the state environmental agency. Both of the joint defense groups included members that were represented by lawyers in the firm currently representing the Irrigation District. The members of the joint defense groups signed joint defense agreements. The lawyers representing the members of the joint defense groups met regularly to share technical information and have frank discussions about the potential liability of their clients and about their strategies for addressing the contamination of the Superfund sites. The Court decided that the exchange of relevant confidential information pursuant to the joint defense agreements created implied attorney-client relationships and duties of confidentiality between the members of the joint defense groups and the lawyers representing each of the members. The Court noted the public's expectation "that attorneys and law firms will not divulge confidential information once obtained from former clients."[476] Since a member of each joint defense group was represented at the time by lawyers in the law firm now representing the Irrigation District, that law firm could not prosecute claims on behalf of the Irrigation District against other members of the joint defense groups.

Some interesting conflict of interest issues arose in another environmental case which involved the investigation and clean up of contamination at the former Mare Island Naval Shipyard in Vallejo, California. After the Navy closed the Shipyard, part of the land was conveyed to Lennar Mare Island, LLC ("LMI") which assumed certain obligations for investigating and cleaning up the contamination. LMI hired CH2M Hill Constructors, Inc. ("CCI") to do the work. Pursuant to the contract between LMI and CCI, environmental insurance policies were purchased from Steadfast Insurance Company. The parties became involved in a dispute about insurance coverage under the Steadfast policies. LMI sued Steadfast claiming that its refusal to pay claims was costing LMI millions of dollars. Steadfast responded to the suit by asserting claims against both LMI and CCI, seeking a declaratory judgment about the scope of coverage provided by the environmental insurance policies it issued. After Steadfast hired a Big Law firm to represent it in the lawsuit, CCI filed a motion asking the Court to disqualify the law firm from representing Steadfast. CCI's motion was based on the fact that the law firm was currently representing CCI's parent corporation, CH2M

HILL Companies, Ltd. ("CH2M"). The law firm had also represented CCI directly on a prior occasion.[477]

In opposing the motion for disqualification, Steadfast argued that the law firm's current client was the parent corporation, CH2M, and not the CCI subsidiary which was a former client of the firm. Under the ethical rules governing conflicts of interest, as Steadfast pointed out, if CCI was a former client of the law firm disqualification would be required only if the firm's prior representation of CCI was "substantially related" to the current lawsuit. The Court rejected Steadfast's argument, concluding that "CCI and CH2M are a unified client" of the law firm which "has advised CH2M on strategic decisions in matters that impact the entire corporate family."[478] CH2M considered the law firm to be its "top strategic law firm" which billed CH2M around $1 million for work performed for CH2M and its subsidiaries in 2014. According to its general counsel, CH2M was "wholly dependent" on the law firm "for nearly all of the most important corporate and regulatory issues currently facing the company."[479] The law firm had actually given legal advice to the CH2M board member who had responsibility for the Mare Island project.[480]

Steadfast then argued that CH2M and its subsidiaries had waived any conflict of interest by virtue of an advance waiver provision in the original 2005 retention agreement between CH2M and the law firm. A number of Big Law firms include advance waiver provisions in their retention agreements, essentially asking clients to waive conflicts of interest that might arise in the future, in order to give the law firm maximum flexibility to represent other clients. The advance waiver provision in the law firm's retention agreement with CH2M was fairly typical:

[We are] a large law firm with multiple offices around the world. Because of the firm's size and geographic scope, as well as the breadth and diversity of our practice, other present or future clients of the firm inevitably will have contacts with you. Accordingly, to prevent any future misunderstanding and to preserve the firm's ability to represent you and our other clients, we confirm the following understanding about certain conflicts of interest issues:

a) Unless we have your specific agreement that we may do so, we will not represent another client in a matter which is substantially related to a matter in which we represent you and in which the other client is adverse to you. We understand the term "matter" to refer to transactions, negotiations, proceedings or other representations involving specific parties.

b) In the absence of a conflict as described in subparagraph (a) above, you acknowledge that we will be free to represent any other client either generally or in any matter in which you may have an interest.

c) The effect of subparagraph (b) above is that we may represent another client on any issue or matter in which you might have an interest, including, but not limited to: . . . (iii) Litigation matters brought by or against you as long as such matters are not the same as or substantially related to matters in which we are, or have been, representing you.[481]

It is interesting to note that the law firm partner who worked most often with CH2M believed the advance conflict waiver provision in the retention agreement gave the firm permission to represent Steadfast in the lawsuit.[482] The Court disagreed, and found the advance waiver provision was too broad, general, indefinite and stale to cover the current lawsuit.[483] The Court also offered these comments about the untenable position in which the law firm had placed its client, CH2M:

[The law firm] realized it faced a conflict but determined it would take on representation of Steadfast, then told CH2M of its decision asserting it was covered by the broad advance waiver from nine years ago; it then inferred CH2M's acceptance from its silence. In this way, [the law firm] effectively forced CH2M's general counsel into 'an impossible position of having to brief the directors on litigation [the law firm] intended to prosecute against [CH2M] in meetings where [he] would need [the law firm] to advise the board on strategic matters.'

[Citation to general counsel's reply declaration omitted.] He concluded [the law firm] 'could not represent [CH2M] in its most serious matters involving the executive team and its Board of Directors, while attacking the integrity of the company in another matter representing a client adverse to the company.'[484]

The law firm was disqualified from representing Steadfast in the lawsuit. It undoubtedly cost the law firm's client, CH2M, many thousands of dollars in legal fees to achieve that result.

The ethical rules governing conflicts of interest with current clients are quite restrictive. A lawyer cannot agree to represent a client whose interests are directly adverse to those of a current client unless both clients give their informed written consent. Particularly in litigation, clients are unlikely to give their consent because they do not want to see their lawyer or law firm representing a party adverse to them in a lawsuit. Some lawyers try to get around the ethical rules governing conflicts with current clients by ending their professional relationship with a current client in order to undertake the representation of a new client.

A case decided by the Supreme Court of Florida provides an example.[485] Flight attendants who claimed they were suffering from diseases caused by exposure to second-hand smoke in airplane cabins filed a class action suit against several tobacco companies. The class action suit was resolved by a settlement agreement. Under the terms of the settlement, the tobacco companies agreed to fund a foundation that would sponsor scientific research for the early detection and cure of diseases associated with cigarette smoking. Flight attendants who were members of the class action retained their right to file individual suits for compensatory damages, but agreed to forego any claims for punitive damages. The research foundation was formed and several of the flight attendants became members of the foundation's board. Two of the lawyers who were representing flight attendants in their individual suits for compensatory damages became concerned that the foundation was not functioning effectively. They filed suit against the foundation on behalf of a handful of the flight attendants, accusing the foundation's board of misusing funds and seeking an accounting, an injunction and other relief. When some flight attendants objected to the lawyers' suit against the foundation on conflict of interest grounds, the lawyers withdrew from their individual cases. One of the lawyers withdrew from a flight attendant's individual case after representing her for a decade; that flight attendant was also a member of the foundation's board.[486]

Two flight attendants who were members of the foundation's board filed a motion to disqualify the lawyers who were representing other flight attendants in their suit against the foundation. The Florida Supreme Court upheld the trial court's decision disqualifying the lawyers. The Court noted that lawyers have an ethical duty to decline a representation that is directly adverse to the interests of a current client. A lawyer cannot avoid that duty "by taking on representation in which a conflict of interest already exists and then convert a current client into a former client by withdrawing from the client's case."[487] The Court quoted from an earlier opinion to make the point that "a lawyer or law firm 'may not simply [choose] to drop one client 'like a hot potato' in order to treat it as though it were a former client for the purpose of resolving a conflict of interest dispute.'"[488]

A fairly bizarre conflict of interest involving a lawyer named Joseph Parise came to light in *Huston v. Imperial Credit Commercial Mortgage Investment Corp.*,[489] a lawsuit filed as a class action under the federal securities laws on behalf of purchasers of the common stock of the defendant ("ICCMIC"). An initial public offering ("IPO") of approximately 34,500,000 shares of ICCMIC's common stock was held in October 1997. Parise was the managing director and senior vice president of ICCMIC. He participated in drafting the IPO documents and also attended strategy sessions discussing the IPO. He made a number of road show presentations for the IPO. He responded to questions from the Securities and Exchange Commission about the IPO documents. According to the CEO of ICCMIC, Parise gave legal as well as business advice about the IPO and the IPO documentation. The Court found that Parise was acting as a lawyer representing ICCMIC in connection with the IPO.[490]

On Parise's recommendation his brother-in-law, John Huston, bought 1,500 shares of ICCMIC common stock in the IPO. Parise left ICCMIC in June of 1998. In early 2000 he entered into a memorandum of understanding and fee-splitting agreement with a law firm. The memorandum of understanding described a joint representation arrangement between Parise and the law firm for prospective litigation. The fee-splitting agreement described Parise's anticipated level of involvement in a securities lawsuit and contemplated that his share of the legal fees would range from $180,000 to $7.2 million depending on the amount of money recovered in the case.[491] Parise referred John Huston, his brother-in-law, to the law firm.[492] In March of 2001 the law firm filed a class action complaint in the lawsuit naming John Huston as plaintiff and class representative. The complaint asserts that the prospectus for the IPO "contains materially false and misleading statements and omits from disclosure material facts and risks."[493] Parise, who had participated in drafting the documents for the IPO, also drafted the complaint.[494] Needless to say, both Parise and the law firm were disqualified from continuing to represent the plaintiff in the class action suit.

Another lawyer allowed his personal as well as his financial interests to lead him to engage in activity contrary to the interests of a client of his law firm. John McAleese was a partner in a Big Law firm that represented Apple Inc. on various matters including patent prosecutions related to the touch-based user interface of Apple's iPhone and similar devices. McAleese was not an intellectual property lawyer and never worked on Apple matters. His wife, Jennifer McAleese, was a co-founder and 35 percent owner of FlatWorld Interactives, LLC. The other co-founder of FlatWorld was Slavoljub Milekic who owned the remaining 65 percent of FlatWorld. Milekic had filed a patent which FlatWorld believed was being infringed by Apple in the "swiping mechanism" used in its iPhone and iPad products.

Since early 2007 when FlatWorld was founded, John McAleese received numerous emails from his wife Jennifer on his law firm computer about potential patent litigation. He emailed a partner in his law firm asking for the name of a company that might be interested in purchasing patents and enforcing the patents against infringers. He used his office computer to edit letters Jennifer had drafted claiming that FlatWorld's patent was being used by Apple. He helped FlatWorld look for a purchaser of its patent. He also helped FlatWorld retain a law firm to sue Apple. On April 19, 2012 FlatWorld sued Apple for patent infringement, claiming that touch-based and gesture-based technology used in Apple products, including the iPhone and iPad, infringes on FlatWorld's patent.[495] Apple first learned about John McAleese's involvement with Flatworld on February 25, 2013 when an Apple director with oversight of legal matters saw McAleese's name on a log of privileged documents. The director sent an email the same day to one of the partner's in McAleese's law firm expressing the director's concern. The partner forwarded that email to John McAleese. After receiving the email, McAleese called Jennifer about Apple's concerns and also called one of the lawyers representing FlatWorld in the patent infringement case to discuss the matter, in violation of Apple's attorney-client privilege with its law firm.[496]

The Court in the patent infringement case concluded that John McAleese had acted in a legal capacity on FlatWorld's behalf, contrary to the interests of his law firm's client, Apple.[497] The Court explained how McAleese breached the duty of undivided loyalty to his law firm's client:

'Attorneys have a duty to maintain undivided loyalty to their clients to avoid undermining public confidence in the legal profession and the judicial process.' [Citation omitted.] John McAleese breached that duty. Since 2007, John McAleese had acted as FlatWorld's attorney in a manner contrary to the interests of [the law firm's] (and thus McAleese's) client, Apple.

. . . An attorney cannot be adverse to one of his firm's clients even if the attorney never worked on that client's matters. 'For attorneys in the same firm to represent adverse parties is patently improper.' [Citation omitted.][498]

Three months after his involvement with FlatWorld came to light, John McAleese was no longer a member of Apple's law firm.[499] What happened to him? He soon became a partner in another Big Law firm.

A direct conflict of interest led a client to file suit against a different Big Law firm. Axcess International, Inc. hired the law firm in 1998 to prepare and file patent applications and prosecute its patents for radio frequency identification technology. Without seeking or obtaining the consent of Axcess, the law firm also started representing Savi Technologies, Inc., a competitor of Axcess, and helped Savi obtain patents for its competing radio frequency identification technology. In 2010 Axcess sued the law firm in Texas state court asserting claims of professional negligence and breach of fiduciary duty. The trial court judge dismissed the breach of fiduciary duty claim. The case went to trial on the professional negligence claim. The jury found the law firm negligent and awarded damages of $40.53 million, which was about eight percent of the law firm's annual revenue. The jury also found that Axcess knew or reasonably should have known about the law firm's wrongful conduct by May 2007, roughly three years before Axcess filed suit. Because the statute of limitations for a professional negligence claim in Texas is two years, Axcess' claim was time-barred. The statute of limitations in Texas for a breach of fiduciary duty claim is four years, but that claim had been dismissed by the trial court judge before trial. Both sides appealed the result.[500] The appeal was still pending when this book was published.

The Supreme Court has noted that a lawyer who is "burdened by an actual conflict of interest . . . breaches the duty of loyalty, perhaps the most basic of counsel's duties."[501] Loyalty is a lawyer's most basic duty because it creates the level of trust that provides the foundation for an effective lawyer-client relationship.[502] A lawyer needs to be fully informed about a client's situation in order to be able to give the client the benefit of the lawyer's best professional judgment. A client needs to trust a lawyer well enough to disclose the most sensitive details about its business operations and strategies or the most intimate details of his or her personal situation.

Clients need to know that their lawyer will represent them wholeheartedly and will not compromise their representation out of concerns about other clients of the lawyer or the lawyer's firm. Clients want to have confidence that their lawyer or law firm will not drop them like a hot potato in order to represent a more lucrative client, or sue them on behalf of some other client. Clients do not want to pay significant legal fees and invest time and effort developing a professional relationship with their lawyer only to have to start all over again with a new lawyer. They also do not want to feel stuck being represented by a law firm that is suing them in some other matter on behalf of another client.

In March of 2011 a group of in-house lawyers for some of the Big Law firms, representing thirty-two of the largest law firms in the United States, proposed changes to the ABA's Model Rules of Professional Responsibility that would significantly weaken the ethical rules governing conflicts of interest with current clients.[503] Under the proposal, if a client meets the criteria for being a "sophisticated client" when the client first hires a law firm, the client would essentially be treated like a former client for conflict of interest purposes. A current client of a law firm could be sued by other lawyers in the firm acting on behalf of another client so long as the lawsuit is not "substantially related" to the law firm's representation of the current client. The law firm would not need to obtain the current client's consent. Law firms would also be able to ask a "sophisticated client" to give an open-ended, prospective waiver of future conflicts regardless of the nature of the conflict. The proposal broadly defines a "sophisticated client" as a client that meets any one of six criteria when the client first retains the law firm. A client is deemed to be a "sophisticated client" for conflict of interest purposes if the client: (1) is a publicly traded company; (2) is a repetitive user of legal services; (3) has a balance sheet showing assets in excess of $25 million; (4) has an annual budget for legal services, including expenditures for in-house counsel, in excess of $300,000; (5) operates in at least five jurisdictions; or (6) is a governmental entity that has the power to consent to waivers of conflicts. Under these criteria, most clients who could afford to hire a large law firm would be deemed to be "sophisticated clients." The fact that these changes to the ethical rules governing conflicts of interest were even suggested by some of the largest law firms in the country and put forward as a serious proposal to further their own financial interests suggests that a core value of the legal profession – loyalty to clients – may be in trouble.

Part Three

A PATH TO A BETTER FUTURE

If you do not change direction,
you may end up where you are heading.

LAO TZU[504]

Ten

At the Crossroads

The current state of the legal profession results from the significant developments affecting the profession that we examined in chapters five through nine. In the aftermath of those developments and their convergence over the past several years we have a legal profession in crisis.

Without ethical and moral principles to guide their professional behavior, lawyers are left with a set of ethical rules that can be amended, narrowly interpreted, or rationalized away. Zealous representation has become a normative principle within the legal profession to define a lawyer's proper role. Lawyers acting zealously sometimes lose sight of the ethical rules that should be guiding their behavior and believe a win-at-all-costs approach is what their role requires. They may even surrender their personal integrity and sense of morality to the goals of their clients, and fail to exercise the independent professional judgment that would serve their clients' best interests. Fervent partisanship creates a contentious atmosphere that drives people apart and interferes with their ability to seek common ground. All too often, one person feels the need to win at the expense of somebody else. Incivility among lawyers, while not universal, is widespread. The commercialization of the private practice of law has given money a far too prominent place on the altar of professional values.

At the same time, too many people in our society simply do not have the money to hire a lawyer and do not have meaningful access to our legal system.

The legal profession seems preoccupied with its own self-interest and the self-interest of its members. Time and effort are devoted to calculating, publicizing and comparing average profits per partner at the largest law firms. Yet the society the legal profession serves has little interest in maximizing average profits per law partner. Lawyers tout their ability to win even though winning at any cost may not be what most of their clients want. Companies that sell legal forms to people who cannot afford to pay legal fees are accused of engaging in the unauthorized practice of law. Amendments to the ethical rules are proposed that would make it easier for law firms to represent clients with adverse interests in order to increase law firm revenues.

Our profession is on a path that has led to increasing levels of stress and dissatisfaction among lawyers and a steady decline in public esteem for the legal profession. We can expect the state of the profession to continue to deteriorate if it remains on its current path.

We are at the crossroads. As members of the legal profession we have the opportunity to look beyond ourselves and our own self-interest and choose a better path. We can find that path in the answer to this fundamental question: What higher purpose in our society, beyond ourselves and our own self-interest, does the legal profession serve? The answer to that question will guide us along a path to a destination where lawyers regard themselves as skilled professionals living meaningful lives and where the legal profession is held in high esteem by the society it serves.

We need to ask that question now.

Eleven

A Higher Purpose

We are fortunate in the United States to live in a constitutional democracy that is governed by the rule of law. The Constitution and the Bill of Rights protect us from autocratic rule. They also protect us from mob rule. We remain free to worship or not as we choose, to speak our minds, and to keep government agents out of our personal space unless they have probable cause. The government cannot confiscate our lawful property without paying just compensation. Government officials who abuse their authority or who ignore our constitutional rights can be held accountable in a court of law. People can be convicted and imprisoned for a criminal offense only if their guilt is proven beyond a reasonable doubt. People and organizations causing harm to others can be held accountable in a civil lawsuit. In any court case, whether criminal or civil, the parties are entitled to due process of law in a proceeding that is fundamentally fair.

The legal profession has critical roles in protecting the rights we enjoy in our constitutional democracy. Judges serve as impartial decision-makers in the judicial branch of our government. They are responsible for interpreting the law. Judges also decide whether a particular law, regulation or other governmental action violates the Constitution. They preside over criminal and civil trials and have the responsibility to ensure that the proceedings are fundamentally fair and meet constitutional due process requirements. In performing their judicial function in a case, judges are prohibited from acting with bias or favoritism toward one side or the other.

Judges in our judicial system are not inquisitors. They do not conduct their own investigation about the facts of a case. They are able to maintain their impartiality by relying on the lawyers for the parties to investigate the facts and present their versions of the facts to the court. Judges also rely on the lawyers for the parties to research the law applicable to a case and to present their respective legal arguments. The ability of our judicial system to function well necessarily depends on the quality of our judiciary and on honest and effective advocacy by lawyers.

Lawyers help preserve our constitutional democracy and ensure that we are governed by the rule of law. They may file suit against a government agency that is exceeding its authority or violating constitutional rights. They can also challenge the constitutionality of a statute or regulation. Government prosecutors protect our society from people who break the law. Lawyers defending people accused of crime ensure that the defendant receives a fair trial and is not convicted unless guilt is proven beyond a reasonable doubt. They also protect defendants in criminal cases from searches and interrogations that violate a defendant's constitutional rights. Lawyers in civil cases help people resolve their disputes without resorting to violence. In some civil or criminal cases the lawyers for the parties have the opportunity to persuade the court that the law should evolve and move beyond outdated legal principles. In a very real sense, lawyers make our system of justice work.

Lawyers also help clients comply with the many laws and regulations that seem to permeate modern society. Based on their legal expertise, lawyers draft enforceable contracts, easements and leases. They can help clients negotiate the terms of a business transaction. Lawyers may prepare the documents needed to set up a corporation, a partnership or a limited liability company. They can write the documents a client is required to file with a regulatory agency such as the Securities and Exchange Commission. A lawyer may draft a patent application for an inventor and later help the inventor negotiate a royalty agreement with a purchaser of the patent. Lawyers help clients develop estate plans and draft their wills. In performing these and similar tasks, lawyers rely on their knowledge of the law and the technical skills they have developed as lawyers.

In addition to applying their technical legal skills, lawyers have the opportunity to serve clients as wise counselors and trusted advisors in many of the practical affairs of life. Lawyers counseling clients who are thinking about setting up a business may suggest the best legal structure to use and ways to raise capital to finance the business. They can also offer guidance to help clients deal effectively with investors and employees. A lawyer advising a client who is thinking about buying an existing business may suggest a checklist of issues for the client to investigate before deciding whether buying the business would be a good investment. Lawyers representing businesses in financial distress can help their clients decide whether to raise additional capital, or whether to try to renegotiate the terms of existing loans, or whether reorganization in bankruptcy is the best option for the business. Lawyers counseling individuals who are designing their estate plan or who are contemplating a divorce frequently help guide their clients through the difficult personal decisions and choices that need to be made.

These are only a few examples of the many different situations in which lawyers can give clients practical as well as legal advice. Purely technical legal advice is often inadequate to meet a client's needs. Clients experience a legal problem in the context of their broader personal or business objectives. They may benefit from independent professional guidance about the best course of action to take. The ABA's Model Rules of Professional Conduct recognize that lawyers advising clients are not limited to giving purely legal advice:

> In representing a client, a lawyer shall exercise independent professional judgment and render candid advice. In rendering advice, a lawyer may refer not only to law but to other considerations such as moral, economic, social and political factors, that may be relevant to the client's situation.[505]

As the Comment to Model Rule 2.1 explains:

> Advice couched in narrow legal terms may be of little value to a client, especially where practical considerations, such as cost or effects on other people, are predominant. Purely technical legal advice, therefore, can sometimes be inadequate. It is proper for a lawyer to refer to relevant moral and ethical considerations in giving advice. Although a lawyer is not a moral advisor as such, moral and ethical considerations impinge on most legal questions and may decisively influence how the law will be applied.[506]

Lawyers who take the time to listen to their clients and develop a professional relationship built on mutual trust are able to provide the independent professional judgment and sage advice that will serve their clients well.

Some clients consult a lawyer because they are in trouble. They may be facing a criminal charge and a possible prison sentence. They may be about to go through a divorce. The business they spent thirty years building may be on the verge of collapse. They may still be grieving the death of a spouse or the death of a child. They may have suffered a serious injury that left them permanently disabled. When clients are in trouble, the legal issues they face are only part of their situation. Deeply felt emotions are involved. Dreams may have been shattered. Clients may be afraid of what the future will bring. A lawyer is an independent professional with whom they can share their fears and concerns in confidence. With rare exceptions, what clients tell their lawyer will be protected from disclosure by the attorney-client privilege. While providing skilled legal representation and sound practical advice, a lawyer is in a unique position to help a client in trouble by listening, by caring, and perhaps by offering some hope.

The legal profession has a higher purpose than pursuing its own self-interest and the self-interest of its members. The higher purpose the legal profession serves in our society is to understand and wholeheartedly serve the best interests of clients while upholding the Constitution and preserving the rule of law.

In the next chapter we will consider concrete steps that can be taken to guide lawyers to a path that enables the legal profession to fully express its higher purpose. Along that path, lawyers will find meaning and personal fulfillment in their professional lives as well as the satisfaction of knowing that their profession is held once again in high esteem by the society it serves.

Twelve

G radual incremental change will not be sufficient to enable the legal profession to find a path to a better destination. A fundamental change in direction is needed.

A New Focus for Legal Education

It begins in law school.

Supreme Court Justice Felix Frankfurter emphasized the foundational importance of legal education in these words, written while he was a professor at Harvard Law School:

> In the last analysis, the law is what the lawyers are. And the law and the lawyers are what the law schools make them.[507]

The nature of legal education needs to be changed in three fundamental ways: The walls that have developed between the legal academy and the practice of law should be dismantled. The teaching of legal analysis should not require law students to suppress the emotional and spiritual aspects of human experience; instead, students should be taught that it is acceptable, and even desirable, for them to bring all of their humanity to their professional roles as lawyers. The law school curriculum should be expanded to include courses on interpersonal skills as well as clinical experience to prepare students for their future role as lawyers representing clients.

Law schools excel at teaching students how to think like lawyers. Legal reasoning taught in law school is an essential craft for students to learn. As future lawyers, law students need to learn how to read and analyze appellate court decisions and how to interpret the language of statutes and regulations. They also need to learn how to develop and present arguments based on precedents, whether they arguing for a result based on similarities to a precedent or arguing for the contrary result based on distinctions from a precedent. By developing these skills, students learn how to interpret the law and how to anticipate changes in the law. They also begin to appreciate how the law develops incrementally in our common law system of jurisprudence. When the students become lawyers they will be able to give sound legal advice and make effective legal arguments on behalf of their clients.

However, it should not take three years of law school for students to master the craft of legal analysis. Judge Harry Edwards of the U. S. Court of Appeals for the District of Columbia Circuit has pointed out that the first year of law school and part of the second year should be sufficient for that purpose.[508] The remaining year and a half can be devoted to other courses and clinical programs. Before serving on the Court of Appeals, Judge Edwards was a law professor at the University of Michigan and at Harvard Law School.

The law school curriculum should include a required one-quarter or one-semester class on legal philosophy. The purpose of that class would be to teach law students about the nature of the legal process and the role of lawyers in that process. The students would develop an appreciation of the function of the legal profession in our society and why the profession is a critical institution. They would study examples of how lawyers can help the law evolve, such as the example of Thurgood Marshall who devoted much of his career as a practicing lawyer to chipping away at the "separate but equal" doctrine of *Plessy v. Ferguson* until he found an opportunity to persuade the Supreme Court to reject that doctrine in *Brown v. Board of Education*. The class would also give students the opportunity to consider and discuss the meaning of justice and how judges deal with cases in which strict application of the law would lead to an unjust result.

The law school curriculum should also include a required one-quarter or one-semester class on how to be an ethical professional. Unlike current classes on professional responsibility, which tend to focus on teaching the ABA's Model Rules of Professional Conduct, the proposed class would emphasize ways that lawyers can be ethical people in their professional lives. The class would give students the opportunity to discuss how they can deal with ethical challenges that arise in the practice of law. Students would consider and discuss questions such as these: How do I reconcile a client's proposed course of action with my own moral values? How can I maintain my personal integrity when representing clients? When, and how, do I just say "no" to a client? Is there really a difference between stretching the truth and telling a lie? How can I be an honest person and protect client confidences?

Elective classes should be offered on the interpersonal skills lawyers need in order to practice law effectively. A class on communications would teach students how to recognize and adapt to the different ways people receive and process information. The class could also teach students how to listen deeply and ask open-ended questions so they can really understand a client's broader interests and objectives. A class on basic psychology for lawyers could help students learn how to relate to people who are expressing their feelings and emotions. The class could also teach students how to deal with difficult people without becoming reactive and adversarial. A class on the art of storytelling would teach students interested in a career as a trial lawyer how to present a persuasive case that has emotional as well as intellectual appeal. A class on leadership skills would teach students ways of relating more effectively to clients, colleagues and employees. Classes on negotiation and mediation, currently offered by many law schools, can teach students how to resolve disputes by using alternatives to the adversarial litigation process.

Finally, some form of clinical experience should be mandatory so that law students learn how to relate to clients and help solve a client's problems. Health care professionals spend considerable time in an internship under the supervision and guidance of an experienced professional before they are allowed to treat patients independently. Legal professionals should also be required to have at least some clinical experience before they can obtain a license to practice law.

Zealous Representation and Ethical Renewal

As Chief Justice Earl Warren once said, "In civilized life, law floats in a sea of ethics.[509]

In chapter eight we saw many examples of lawyers whose commitment to zealous representation led them engage in behavior that diminishes the reputation of the legal profession. They also violated a number of the ABA's Model Rules of Professional Conduct in the process. In December of 2003 the Arizona Supreme Court removed the word "zealously" from the ethical rules governing lawyers practicing in Arizona.[510] The ethical rules in Arizona no longer contain any reference to "zealous representation" or "zealous advocacy." The American Bar Association and the rest of the states should follow Arizona's lead. Zealous representation and zealous advocacy – fervent partisanship on behalf of clients – should be excised from the psyche of the legal profession.

An aspirational statement of ethical principles should also be adopted to guide the behavior of lawyers. Specific ethical and disciplinary rules can be written within the framework of the ethical principles. A proposed statement of ethical principles is set forth below:

<u>Ethical Principles for Lawyers</u>

It is the responsibility of each lawyer to understand and wholeheartedly serve the best interests of clients in the context of the legal profession's obligation to uphold the Constitution and preserve the rule of law. A lawyer shall strive in all of his or her professional activities to:

- Act with honesty and integrity
- Treat people with dignity and respect
- Be loyal to clients and serve their best interests
- Exercise independent professional judgment and give clients candid advice
- Represent each client wholeheartedly while taking personal moral responsibility for actions taken on the client's behalf
- Keep clients well informed
- Preserve the confidences of current and former clients
- Safeguard and fully account for client funds and other client property in the lawyer's possession
- Charge each client a reasonable fee based on all the circumstances of the representation, and fully disclose to the client the basis for the fee charged
- Refrain from representing two or more clients with adverse interests, unless the clients give their informed and specific written consent to the representation
- Without first obtaining informed and specific written consent from a former client, decline any representation that would be adverse to the current interests of the former client in a matter substantially related to the representation of the former client
- Act consistent with a lawyer's role as an officer of the court
- Refrain from asserting frivolous claims, defenses or objections
- Devote to pro bono or civic activities at least five percent of the time spent working on client matters

These or substantially similar ethical principles should be adopted by the American Bar Association and by each of the states and the District of Columbia. In the meantime, clients can insist that the lawyers they hire subscribe to these ethical principles. Lawyers can take the initiative and proactively subscribe to these ethical principles in order to gain a competitive advantage in the marketplace. In the process they may also discover that they feel better about practicing law as members of a noble profession.

A few comments about some of these proposed ethical principles may be helpful. The first principle is a commitment to acting with honesty and integrity. Those qualities are the foundation for a lawyer's ability to establish relationships of mutual trust with clients. They also define a lawyer's reputation within the legal community. A lawyer with a reputation for being honest will be more likely to be believed by other lawyers and by judges. Abraham Lincoln had a reputation for being an honest lawyer and he had a very successful law practice. He once suggested that a person who could not be an honest lawyer should find a different occupation.[511] People who act with integrity also inspire trust because their words, their actions and their personal moral values are all aligned. Lawyers who act with integrity will be far more credible than lawyers who do not. In chapter five we saw a notable example of a lawyer acting with integrity. When President Nixon ordered Elliot Richardson to fire the Special Watergate Prosecutor, Archibald Cox, Richardson refused to comply with Nixon's order and resigned his position as Attorney General of the United States. Firing Archibald Cox would have interfered with the independence of the Special Prosecutor, contrary to a commitment Richardson had made in his Senate confirmation hearing. Rather than compromising his integrity and going back on his word, Elliot Richardson just said "no." Lawyers representing clients should follow his example.

Treating people with dignity and respect acknowledges their humanity. Most of us have been in situations where an angry person calmed down after someone took the time to listen respectfully to what the person had to say. People have a deep desire to be treated like human beings. They want to feel that their lives matter, regardless of their role or their social standing or their circumstances in life. As lawyers we have the opportunity to be positive and visible examples of how people ought to treat each other.

The proposed ethical principles place considerable emphasis on loyalty to current and former clients. Loyalty to clients makes it possible to have meaningful professional relationships based on mutual trust. In the absence of trust a lawyer's professional relationship with a client becomes transactional in nature. The client becomes guarded and is not comfortable fully disclosing all the information the lawyer needs to have in order to provide the independent professional judgment that would serve the client's best interests. The lawyer essentially becomes a legal technician and is not able to be the client's trusted advisor.

Loyalty to clients means that a lawyer is guided by a client's best interests. As a starting point we can borrow a basic tenet of the medical profession: First, do no harm. Lawyers should avoid a course of action that is likely to make a client's situation worse. For example, the best interests of clients are not served by lawyers who create controversy where none existed, or who fight over every issue that might come up in litigation, or who charge a fee the client cannot possibly afford to pay. Sometimes a lawyer has the opportunity to persuade a client to avoid self-inflicted harm by discouraging a client from pursuing an agenda that is likely to lead to trouble. Clients should be able to trust their lawyer to recommend a course of action that is best for the client even if it will produce a smaller fee for the lawyer. Being loyal to clients also requires a lawyer to seek a client's specific permission before agreeing to represent another client with adverse or conflicting interests.

A lawyer should represent each client wholeheartedly while taking personal moral responsibility for actions taken on the client's behalf. According to a dictionary definition, "wholehearted" representation is "completely and sincerely devoted, determined or enthusiastic," and "marked by earnest commitment: free from all reserve or hesitation."[512] A lawyer representing a client wholeheartedly is enthusiastic, determined and earnestly committed to the best interests of the client without hesitation. At the same time, lawyers ought to be guided by their own moral compass. They need to remain true to their own values. A lawyer should not try to escape personal moral responsibility for actions taken on a client's behalf by claiming that "I was only representing my client."

Finally, the proposed ethical principles ask lawyers to devote five percent of their billable time to pro bono representation or other civic activities. Eighty hours a year for lawyers billing 1,600 hours, or 120 hours a year for lawyers billing 2,400 hours, seems like a lot of time to expect lawyers to contribute. Yet many people in our society who need legal services cannot afford to pay a lawyer. Volunteer work by lawyers can help civic organizations maintain and improve the quality of life in our communities. Lawyers are members of a privileged profession that is entrusted with the administration of our system of justice. Many lawyers earn a living that is at least comfortable by most standards. Contributing five percent of billable time to pro bono or other civic activities is half a tithe. That does not seem too much to ask.

Curtailing the Litigation Industry

Most people would agree that far too many resources in our society are consumed by the litigation industry. Extraordinary amounts of time and money are devoted to pretrial discovery and other litigation activities. While many lawsuits have merit, many others are marginal at best.

Lawyers ought to resist the temptation to file a marginal case based principally on their desire to earn a quick fee from a nuisance settlement. They should refrain from engaging in pretrial discovery practices that are primarily designed to intimidate and harass their opponent. They should also refrain from making frivolous objections to pretrial discovery that are designed to hide the truth. In many cases, lawyers can serve a client's best interests by encouraging the client to engage in settlement negotiations, or participate in a mediation process, early in a case or perhaps even before a lawsuit is filed. Early settlements of disputes save the parties considerable money in legal fees and other litigation expenses, reduce the disruption to their personal life and their business, and lighten the burden on our overworked judicial system.

Our experience over the past several years suggests that we cannot simply rely on lawyers to restrain themselves from filing marginal cases and from engaging in abusive pretrial discovery practices. State and federal courts have an important role in curtailing the litigation industry. Judges preside over the cases that are filed. They can manage their dockets and dispose of marginal lawsuits. They can also sanction lawyers for frivolous behavior. Two changes to the court rules governing civil lawsuits would give judges additional tools to help curtail the litigation industry in the United States.

The first change would be to adopt a new court rule requiring an in-person status conference with the court in every civil lawsuit soon after the case is filed. The status conference would give the court an opportunity to manage the case proactively. Issues to be addressed in the status conference would include the allowable scope and timing of pretrial discovery, the timing of settlement negotiations either with or without a mediator, the timing of any pretrial motions that might dispose of the case before trial, and the anticipated length of the trial. The court could play an active role in managing the case on each of those issues, steering the case towards an efficient resolution.

The second change would be to modify the summary judgment standard so it would be easier for the court to dispose of a marginal lawsuit before trial, and perhaps even before substantial resources are devoted to extensive pretrial discovery. Under the current court rules a judge can dismiss a lawsuit fairly early in the process if the allegations in the plaintiff's complaint fail to state a legally viable claim.[513] A judge can dismiss a case later by granting a motion for summary judgment before trial, but only if there is "no genuine dispute as to any material fact" and one of the parties "is entitled to judgment as a matter of law."[514] Summary judgments are difficult to obtain because the parties are usually able to present the court with some disputed factual issues and because a trial court's decision to deny a motion for summary judgment generally cannot be appealed. Many marginal cases survive a motion for summary judgment. The parties continue to devote time and money to additional pretrial discovery. After a while, a nuisance settlement is reached. The lawyers for both sides are happy because they each earned a fee. Yet as taxpayers, consumers of goods and services, and people who pay premiums to insurance companies, we have all subsidized this process. Marginal lawsuits could be resolved more efficiently by raising the standard for allowing a case to survive a summary judgment motion. The summary judgment rule should be changed to allow judges to grant a motion for summary judgment if the plaintiff is highly unlikely to prevail at trial based on the facts of the case and on existing law or a non-frivolous argument for extending, modifying or changing existing law.

In addition to those two changes to the court rules, judges should be encouraged to use their authority under the existing court rules to impose sanctions for certain types of improper behavior by lawyers. In federal courts, Rule 11 allows a court to impose monetary and other sanctions on a lawyer who files a complaint, an answer to a complaint, a written motion or a legal brief that lacks evidentiary support or that is based on a frivolous legal argument.[515] Rule 37 allows a court to impose sanctions on a party that fails to comply with its pretrial discovery obligations. If the party's failure to comply was based on a lawyer's advice, the lawyer can also be sanctioned.[516] State courts have similar rules. Yet the existing court rules authorizing the imposition of sanctions are not used very often. Imposing sanctions on a lawyer puts a blemish on the lawyer's reputation. Lawyers are generally reluctant to seek sanctions against other lawyers unless the misconduct is egregious. They do not want to create enemies within the profession. Most judges are reluctant to impose sanctions on lawyers, particularly in state courts where a judge's tenure may depend on his or her ability to be reelected. As a result, existing tools that could help curtail at least some aspects of the litigation industry are not being fully used. Courts ought to adopt a zero tolerance policy towards frivolous claims, frivolous boilerplate defenses to claims, frivolous discovery requests that are designed to harass, and frivolous objections to pretrial discovery. That policy should be routinely enforced by imposing sanctions for noncompliance.

Lawyers: Choosing Where to Practice

It is important for law school graduates who want to practice law to make a careful and thoughtful choice about where to practice. In making that choice a good starting point for a graduate is to remember why he or she decided to go to law school. What was the motivation, and the inspiration, that led to the decision to embark on a very intense and fairly expensive three or four year course of study? How can the graduate's inspiration be expressed most effectively in the practice of law?

For some, the answer can be found in a career as a prosecutor or as a public defender. Others may want to join the legal staff of a non-profit group that is dedicated to advancing a particular social policy, such as equal rights or environmental protection. Some may want to join the in-house legal team of a corporation and help the company achieve its business goals. Others may want to work as a lawyer in a government agency and help the agency serve the public interest. Most graduates will choose private practice, either by joining a law firm or by starting a law practice as a solo practitioner.

Graduates who decide to practice law as part of an organization ought to be sure that the culture and values of the organization are compatible with their own values. This will be important regardless of whether the organization is a business corporation, a non-profit group, a government agency or a law firm. A lawyer practicing in an organization with a culture that is out of step with the lawyer's own values will feel under constant, though perhaps subtle, pressure to conform to the culture and values of the organization. The tension between the lawyer's values and the culture of the organization will be an ongoing source of stress. If a lawyer compromises his or her integrity in order to conform, the lawyer's conformity will become the ongoing source of stress.

A fair amount of research can be done to learn about the culture and values of an organization. It is worth taking the time to talk with other people such as friends, law professors, practicing lawyers and current employees. An on-site visit will provide valuable information about the professionalism of the organization and the attitude of its employees. The annual report for a publicly traded company or a large non-profit group can provide considerable information. An online search can also reveal useful information about the culture, values and reputation of a corporation, a non-profit group, a government agency or a law firm. The reputation of an organization is important because its employees will be assumed by most people to share that reputation. We really are known by the company we keep.

Graduates choosing the private practice of law have many options. Setting up a law practice as a solo practitioner may be attractive for lawyers who value their independence and want to have a flexible work schedule. Many state and local bar associations offer resources and networking opportunities to help new lawyers establish a solo law practice. Joining a small or mid-sized firm can give new lawyers the opportunity to work with more experienced lawyers and to find a mentor within the firm to guide their development as a lawyer. Newer lawyers in small and mid-sized firms are also likely to have more direct contact with clients than they would have in a large law firm. Large firms, particularly Big Law firms, offer new lawyers more money. The trade-off is that lawyers in large firms are expected to work very long hours in a competitive environment and will be highly unlikely to have any meaningful degree of life balance. In most large law firms, the constant pressure to produce large numbers of billable hours can also restrict the time devoted to mentoring newer lawyers and the time available for *pro bono* activities.

Clients: Being a Smart Consumer of Legal Services

Clients who are thinking about hiring a lawyer can learn a great deal of information before choosing the lawyer they want to hire. They can talk to friends, business associates and other lawyers. They can perform research about lawyers online. They can interview lawyers. By doing this work, clients can learn about a lawyer's skill, experience, personal qualities and reputation before deciding to hire that lawyer. When choosing a lawyer, clients can put themselves in a position to be able to make a well-informed choice.

There are some personal qualities in a lawyer that are essential to an effective attorney-client relationship. Honesty, integrity and loyalty are at the top of the list. Those qualities provide the foundation for a professional relationship based on trust. When clients do not trust their lawyer, the attorney-client relationship cannot work well. Clients should be uncompromising in insisting that their lawyer has these personal qualities. Unless a lawyer has a reputation for honesty and integrity, a client should hire a different lawyer. If a lawyer's loyalty to clients is conditional, as is the case when a lawyer's firm insists on an advance prospective waiver of conflicts of interest, a client should hire a different lawyer.

A lawyer's reputation is also important. A lawyer with a reputation for maintaining high ethical standards will be trusted by other lawyers and will have credibility with judges and with regulatory officials. He or she will be more effective representing clients than a lawyer with a poor reputation. If a lawyer has a reputation for marginal ethical behavior, that reputation will rub off on the lawyer's clients. The lawyer, and the lawyer's clients, will not be fully trusted by judges, regulatory officials or other lawyers.

Lawyers who have certain qualities will tend to be more effective in representing clients than other lawyers. A lawyer who is a good listener will be able to understand a client's broader interests and objectives and provide independent professional advice about the best course of action for the client to take. A good listener will also inspire trust and confidence by demonstrating that he or she really understands and cares about the client's situation. A lawyer who is a good communicator will be able to explain a client's options and give professional advice in terms the client can understand, and will also be an effective advocate on the client's behalf. A lawyer who is a creative problem-solver will be open to exploring different options and finding the one most likely to serve a client's best interests. Clients can develop a sense of whether a lawyer has these qualities by interviewing the lawyer before making a hiring decision.

Whenever clients are seeking legal representation in a civil or a criminal court case they should hire a lawyer who has experience taking cases to trial. A lawyer with a reputation as a skilled trial lawyer will know how to handle the case if it goes to trial and will also help the client achieve a more favorable settlement before trial. To be an effective advocate in a court case, a lawyer needs to believe in the client and in the case that will be presented on the client's behalf. The lawyer needs to have credibility with the court where the case will be heard. For jury trials, the lawyer also needs to have good storytelling skills so the case can be presented in a way that has emotional appeal. It is not necessary for a lawyer to be belligerent and contentious in order to be an effective advocate. To the contrary, a belligerent and contentious lawyer is likely to make it more difficult to resolve the case on favorable terms before trial and is also likely to cost the client considerably more money in legal fees.

Before hiring a lawyer, a client should have a frank conversation with the lawyer about legal fees and expenses. The lawyer should clearly explain how the legal fees will be computed and what expenses the client will be asked to pay. Expenses that will be charged to the client should not include items that one would expect to be part of the lawyer's overhead. The client should be satisfied that the legal fees and expenses will be reasonable. The lawyer should also explain how the client's legal matter will be staffed and obtain the client's agreement to the staffing plan. The client should insist on obtaining at least a rough estimate of how much the legal matter is likely to cost. Hardly anyone would hire a building contractor by saying, "I want you to build a house for our family, or a new corporate headquarters for our company; tell me when you are finished and how much I owe you." Yet clients hire lawyers on that basis far too often.

Very few legal matters are so complex or unique that they need the services of a highly skilled specialist who charges a very high hourly rate. For most legal matters, excellent lawyers can be found who will be far less expensive. They might be solo practitioners or lawyers practicing in small or mid-sized firms, charging significantly lower hourly rates than lawyers in large firms. Small and mid-sized firms are also less likely than large firms to overstaff cases, principally because they do not have the legal staff to do so.

The attorney-client relationship works best for clients who hire individual lawyers with the skills and personal qualities that will serve them well. When a major project or complex litigation requires the services of a number of lawyers, it is not necessary to find all those lawyers in one law firm. From my personal experience, it can actually be more effective to create a legal team consisting of lawyers from different firms who have complementary skills.

After lawyers are hired, clients need to remain actively involved in their representation. Turning a legal matter over to a lawyer and simply hoping for the best is a recipe for an expensive disappointment. Clients ought to insist that they be kept informed about how their legal matter is proceeding and what they should expect. They should understand their lawyer's approach to handling the legal matter and speak up if they disagree with the approach or think a different approach might better serve their overall best interests. They should also speak up if any aspect of the attorney-client relationship is not working well for them.

The legal profession responds to the demands of clients. If clients insist that their lawyers have high ethical standards, and refuse to hire lawyers with reputations for marginal ethical behavior, the profession will become more ethical. If clients insist that the lawyers they hire are honest men and women of integrity who will be loyal to them, lawyers without those qualities will eventually leave the profession and find different lines of work. If clients refuse to hire lawyers who are nasty, belligerent, needlessly contentious and disrespectful of other people, those behaviors will gradually disappear from the profession and civility will return. If clients insist on transparency about the legal fees they are being charged and refuse to pay unreasonable fees, the cost of legal services will decrease. If clients refuse to hire lawyers who do not take the time to listen and learn about their situation and how a legal matter is affecting them or their business, lawyers who take a "cookie cutter" approach to representing clients will either change their approach or leave the profession. These are some of the ways clients can influence the behavior of lawyers and transform the practice of law. In the process, they may help the legal profession reclaim its soul.

About the Author

John Allison has practiced law for 43 years. He built a successful private law practice as a trial lawyer and litigation attorney representing individuals, small businesses, non-profits and large companies. His law practice grew based on repeat business and referrals from satisfied clients. He chaired a committee of the American Bar Association and was a Judge *Pro Tem* in Seattle. He also served in management roles at two different law firms.

After being in private practice for 24 years, John was hired by a Fortune 100 Company as its senior in-house litigation manager. He wrote the guidelines and criteria the company used to hire and evaluate lawyers in private practice. He personally hired and led teams of lawyers representing the company in mass tort, class action and other complex litigation. As Assistant General Counsel, John served on the Office of General Counsel Management Committee and had overall responsibility for the litigation managed by the Office of General Counsel worldwide. He also was legal counsel for the company's Medical Department and Environmental Remediation Program, and advised senior executive management on effective strategies for handling a number of challenging issues.

More recently, John founded The Coach for Lawyers, LLC which is committed to helping lawyers experience the rewards and satisfaction the practice of law can offer and find meaning and fulfillment in their professional lives.

The firm offers business coaching, law practice consulting, professional training and life coaching for lawyers.

John and his wife, Rebecca Picard, live in northern California. He can be contacted by sending an email to john@coachlawyers.com.

Selected Bibliography

Allan, Rick. "Alcoholism, Drug Abuse and Lawyers: Are We Ready to Address the Denial?." *Creighton Law Review* 31 (1997): 265-277.

Altman, James. "Considering the ABA's 1908 Canons of Ethics." *Fordham Law Review* 71 (2003): 2395-2508.

American Bar Association. *ABA Canons of Professional Ethics*. Chicago: American Bar Association, 1908. http://www.americanbar.org/content/dam/aba/migrated/cpr/mrpc/Canons_Ethics.authcheckdam.pdf.

American Bar Association. *ABA Model Code of Professional Responsibility*. Chicago: American Bar Association, 1969. http://www.americanbar.org/content/dam/aba/migrated/cpr/mrpc/mcpr.authcheckdam.pdf.

American Bar Association. "Lawyer Demographics." *ABA Online Summary* (2013). http://www.americanbar.org/content/dam/aba/migrated/marketresearch/PublicDocuments/lawyer_demographics_2013.authcheckdam.pdf.

American Bar Association. *Model Rules of Professional Conduct*. Chicago: American Bar Association, 1983. Accessed May 14, 2015. http://www.americanbar.org/groups/professional_responsibility/publications/model_rules_of_professional_conduct.html.

American Psychiatric Association. *Diagnostic and Statistical Manual of Mental Disorders, Fifth Edition*. Arlington: American Psychiatric Association, 2013.

Aspen, Marvin. "The Search for Renewed Civility in Litigation." *Valparaiso University Law Review* 28, no. 2 (1994): 513-530.

Banning, Lance. *The Sacred Fire of Liberty: James Madison and the Founding of the Federal Republic*. Ithaca: Cornell University Press, 1995.

Bates, John. "Annual Report of the Director 2013." *Judicial Business of the United States Courts.* Washington: Administrative Office of the United States Courts, 2013. http://www.uscourts.gov/Statistics/JudicialBusiness/2013.aspx.

Bennett, Walter. *The Lawyer's Myth: Reviving Ideals in the Legal Profession.* Chicago: The University of Chicago Press, 2001.

Bernstein, Carl and Bob Woodward. *All the President's Men.* New York: Simon and Schuster, 1974.

Bradfield, Bill, ed. *The Book of Ancient Wisdom: Over 500 Inspiring Quotations from the Greeks.* Mineola, New York: Dover Publications, 2005.

Brickman, Lester. "The Use of Litigation Screenings in Mass Torts: A Formula for Fraud?." *SMU Law Review* 61 (2008): 1221-1353.

Burger, Warren. "The Decline of Professionalism." *Fordham Law Review* 63, no. 4 (1995): 949-958.

Carroll, Stephen, Lloyd Dixon, James Anderson, Thor Hogan and Elizabeth Sloss. *The Abuse of Medical Diagnostic Practices in Mass Litigation: The Case of Silica.* Santa Monica, California: The RAND Corporation, 2009.

Chernow, Ron. *Alexander Hamilton.* New York: The Penguin Press, 2004.

Davis, Michael and Hunter Clark. *Thurgood Marshall: Warrior at the Bar, Rebel on the Bench.* New York: Carol Publishing Group, 1992.

Dean, John III. *Blind Ambition: The White House Years.* New York: Simon and Schuster, 1976.

Dinovitzer, Ronit, Robert Nelson, Gabriele Plickert, Rebecca Sandefur and Joyce Sterling. *After the JD: Second Results from a National Study of Legal Careers.* Chicago and Dallas: American Bar Foundation and The NALP Foundation, 2009.

Donald, David Herbert. *Lincoln*. New York: Simon & Schuster, 1995.

Eaton, William, James Anthony, Wallace Mandel and Roberta Garrison. "Occupations and the Prevalence of Major Depressive Disorder." *Journal of Occupational Medicine* 32, no. 11 (1990): 1079-1087.

Edwards, Harry. "The Growing Disjunction Between Legal Education and the Legal Profession." *Michigan Law Review* 91 (1992): 34-70.

Ehrlichman, John. *Witness to Power: The Nixon Years*. New York: Simon and Schuster, 1982.

Emery, Fred. *Watergate: The Corruption of American Politics and the Fall of Richard Nixon*. New York: Touchstone Books, 1994.

Ervin, Sam Jr. *The Whole Truth: The Watergate Conspiracy*. New York: Random House, 1980.

Fehrenbacher, Don, ed. *Abraham Lincoln: Speeches and Writings 1859-1865*. New York: Literary Classics of the United States, 1989.

Fox, Lawrence. "The Gang of Thirty-Three: Taking the Wrecking Ball to Client Loyalty." *Yale Law Journal Online* 121 (2012): 567-588. http://www.yalelaw-journal.org/pdf/1063_eo8auk2m.pdf.

Galanter, Marc. "The Faces of Mistrust: The Image of Lawyers in Public Opinion, Jokes, and Political Discourse." *University of Cincinnati Law Review* 66 (1998): 805-845.

Goldstone, Lawrence. *The Activist: John Marshall, Marbury v. Madison, and the Myth of Judicial Review*. New York: Walker & Company, 2008.

Goodrich, Chris. *Anarchy and Elegance: Confessions of a Journalist at Yale Law School*. Boston: Little, Brown and Company, 1991.

Goodwin, Doris Kearns. *Team of Rivals: The Political Genius of Abraham Lincoln.* New York: Simon & Schuster, 2005.

Gordon, Robert. "The Citizen Lawyer – A Brief Informal History of a Myth With Some Basis in Reality." *William and Mary Law Review* 50 (2009): 1169-1206.

Gordon, Robert. "The Ethical Worlds of Large-Firm Litigators: Preliminary Observations." *Fordham Law Review* 67, no. 2 (1998): 709-738.

Hellerstein, Alvin, James Henderson Jr. and Aaron Twerski. "Managerial Judging: The 9/11 Responders' Tort Litigation." *Cornell Law Review* 98 (2012): 127-179.

Hensler, Deborah and Marisa Reddy. *California Lawyers View the Future: A Report to the Commission on the Future of the Legal Profession and the State Bar.* Santa Monica, California: RAND, 2004.

Holmes, Oliver Wendell Jr. *The Path of the Law.* American Classics Library, 2012. (Reprint of January 8, 1897 speech originally published in *Harvard Law Review* 10 (1897): 457 *et seq.*).

Hopkins, Kevin. "Law Firms, Technology, and the Double-Billing Dilemma." *Georgetown Journal of Legal Ethics* 12 (1998): 95-106.

Hunt, John Gabriel, ed. *The Inaugural Addresses of the Presidents.* New York: Gramercy Books, 1997.

Hyde, Alexander. *Living With Schizophrenia.* Chicago: Contemporary Books, 1985.

Jones, James, Milton Regan Jr., Mark Medice and Jennifer Roberts. "2014 Report on the State of the Legal Market." *Georgetown Center for the Study of the Legal Profession* (2014).

Kronman, Anthony. *The Lost Lawyer: Failing Ideals of the Legal Profession.* Cambridge: Harvard University Press, 1993.

Labunski, Richard. *James Madison and the Struggle for the Bill of Rights.* New York: Oxford University Press, 2006.

LaFountain, Robert, Richard Schauffler, Shauna Strickland, Sarah Gibson and Ashley Mason. "Examining the Work of State Courts: An Analysis of 2009 State Court Caseloads." *Court Statistics Project.* Williamsburg, Virginia: National Center for State Courts, 2011.

Lerman, Lisa. "Gross Profits? Questions About Lawyer Billing Practices." *Hofstra Law Review* 22 (1994): 645-653.

Lincoln, Abraham. "Notes on the Practice of Law." In *Abraham Lincoln: Speeches and Writings 1832-1858*, edited by Don E. Fehrenbacher, 245-246. New York: Literary Classics of the United States, 1989.

Llewellyn, Karl. *The Bramble Bush.* Dobbs Ferry, New York: Oceana Publications, 1960.

Magruder, Jeb Stuart. *An American Life: One Man's Road to Watergate.* New York: Atheneum, 1974.

Maté, Gabor. *When the Body Says No: Exploring the Stress-Disease Connection.* Hoboken, New Jersey: John Wiley & Sons, 2003.

McQuillan, Lawrence, Hovannes Abramyan and Anthony Archie. *Jackpot Justice: The True Cost of America's Tort System.* San Francisco: Pacific Research Institute, 2007.

Meacham, Jon. *Thomas Jefferson: The Art of Power.* New York: Random House, 2012.

Merriam-Webster. *Collegiate Dictionary, Eleventh Edition.* Springfield: Merriam-Webster, 2004.

Mounteer, Joan. "Depression Among Lawyers." *The Colorado Lawyer* 33, no. 1 (2004): 35-37.

Nixon, Richard. *In the Arena: A Memoir of Victory, Defeat and Renewal.* New York: Simon and Schuster, 1990.

O'Connor, Sandra Day. "Professionalism." *Oregon Law Review* 78 (1999): 385-391.

Olson, Keith. *Watergate: The Presidential Scandal that Shook America.* Lawrence, Kansas: The University of Kansas Press, 2003.

Osborn, John Jay Jr. *The Paper Chase.* Boston: Houghton Mifflin, 1971.

Pardau, Stuart. "Bill, Baby, Bill: How the Billable Hour Emerged as the Primary Method of Attorney Fee Generation and Why Early Reports of its Demise May be Greatly Exaggerated." *Idaho Law Review* 50 (2013): 1-21.

"Proposals of Law Firm General Counsel for Future Regulation of Relationships Between Law Firms and Sophisticated Clients." *ABA Commission on Ethics 20/20* (March 2011). Accessed August 21, 2015. http://www.abajournal.com/files/ABA_Ethics_Commission_Proposals_--_3-8-11.pdf.

"Public Esteem for Military Still High." *Pew Research Religion and Public Life Project* (July 11, 2013). http://www.pewforum.org/2013/07/11/public-esteem-for-military-still-high/.

Rakkove, Jack, ed. *The Annotated U.S. Constitution and Declaration of Independence.* Cambridge: Harvard University Press, 2009.

Rhode, Deborah. "Equal Justice Under Law." *Markkula Center for Applied Ethics* (2014). http://www.scu.edu/ethics/publications/submitted/rhode/equal-justice.html.

Rigertas, Laurel. "Post-Watergate: The Legal Profession and Respect for the Interests of Third Parties." *Chapman Law Review* 16 (2012): 98-132.

Riskin, Leonard. "The Contemplative Lawyer: On the Potential Contributions of Mindfulness Meditation to Law Students, Lawyers, and Their Clients." *Harvard Negotiation Law Review* 7 (2002): 1-66.

Rochvarg, Arnold. "Enron, Watergate and the Regulation of the Legal Profession." *Washburn Law Journal* 43 (2003): 61-90.

Sargent, Mark. "Lawyers in the Moral Maze." *Villanova Law Review* 49, no. 4 (2004): 867-885.

Sargent, Mark. "Lawyers in the Perfect Storm." *Washburn Law Journal* 43 (2003): 1-43.

Schaefer, Paula. "Harming Business Clients With Zealous Advocacy: Rethinking the Attorney Advisor's Touchstone." *Florida State University Law Review* 38, no. 2 (2011): 251-302.

Schauer, Frederick. *Thinking Like a Lawyer.* Cambridge: Harvard University Press, 2012.

Scheiber, Noam. "The Last Days of Big Law." *New Republic*, July 21, 2013. http://www.newrepublic.com/article/113941/big-law-firms-trouble-when-money-dries.

Schiltz, Patrick. "Legal Ethics in Decline: The Elite Law Firm, the Elite Law School, and the Moral Formation of the Novice Attorney." *Minnesota Law Review* 82 (1998): 705-792.

Schiltz, Patrick. "On Being a Happy, Healthy and Ethical Member of an Unhappy, Unhealthy and Unethical Profession." *Vanderbilt Law Review* 52 (1999): 871-951.

Sells, Benjamin. *Order in the Court: Crafting a More Just World in Lawless Times.* Boston: Element Books, 1999.

Sells, Benjamin. *The Soul of the Law: Understanding Lawyers and the Law.* Boston: Element Books, 1994.

Senate Report 109-54. *The Role of Professional Firms in the U. S. Tax Shelter Industry.* Washington: U. S. Government Printing Office, April 13, 2005.

Shaffer, Thomas. "Unique, Novel and Unsound Adversary Ethic." *Vanderbilt Law Review* 41 (1988): 697-715.

Simon, James. *What Kind of Nation: Thomas Jefferson, John Marshall, and the Epic Struggle to Create a United States.* New York: Simon & Schuster, 2002.

Sitton, Larry, ed. *Report and Recommendations of the Quality of Life Task Force.* Raleigh, North Carolina: North Carolina Bar Association, 1991.

Summers, Anthony. *The Arrogance of Power: The Secret World of Richard Nixon.* New York: Penguin Putnam, 2000.

Turow, Scott. *One L: The Turbulent True Story of a First Year at Harvard Law School.* New York: Penguin Books, 2010.

Warren, Earl. "Address at the Jewish Theological Seminary of America Annual Awards Dinner (November 11, 1962)." Quoted in Anita Allen, "Moralizing in Public." *Hofstra Law Review* 34 (2006): 1325-1330.

Yarrow, George and Christopher Decker. *Assessing the Economic Significance of the Professional Legal Services Sector in the European Union.* Regulatory Policy Institute, August 2012.

Notes

1. John F. Kennedy, "Remarks at the Convocation of the United Negro College Fund," *John F. Kennedy Speeches – John F. Kennedy Presidential Library and Museum* (Indianapolis, Indiana: April 12, 1959), http://www.jfklibrary.org/Research/Research-Aids/JFK-Speeches.aspx?f=1959.

2. George Yarrow and Christopher Decker, "Assessing the economic significance of the professional legal services sector in the European Union," Regulatory Policy Institute (August 2012).

3. American Bar Association, "Lawyer Demographics," *ABA Online Summary* (2013), http://www.americanbar.org/content/dam/aba/migrated/marketresearch/PublicDocuments/lawyer_demographics_2013.authcheckdam.pdf.

4. U. S. Department of Commerce, "Census Bureau Projects U.S. Population of 315.1 Million on New Year's Day 2013" (December 28, 2012), http://www.commerce.gov/blog/2012/12/28/census-bureau-projects-us-population-3151-million-new-years-day-2013.

5. The Henry J. Kaiser Family Foundation reported that in November 2012 there were 834,769 professionally active physicians in the United States. *See* http://kff.org/other/state-indicator/total-active-physicians/.

6. The number of lawyers in each category is a rough estimate based on the percentages contained in the American Bar Association's data summary. *See* American Bar Association, "Lawyer Demographics" (2013).

7. Ibid.

8. William Shakespeare, *Henry the Sixth, Part 2, Act 4, Scene 2, line 73*.

9. Jon Meacham, *Thomas Jefferson: The Art of Power* (New York: Random House, 2012), 17, 21-22, 39, 100-105; Jack Rakkove (ed.), *The Annotated U. S. Constitution*

and Declaration of Independence (Cambridge: Harvard University Press, 2009), 14-16.

10. Ron Chernow, *Alexander Hamilton* (New York: The Penguin Press, 2004), 138-139.

11. Chernow, *Alexander Hamilton.*

12. Ibid., 167, 229-230.

13. Ibid., 241.

14. Ibid., 243-269.

15. Richard Labunski, *James Madison and the Struggle for the Bill of Rights* (New York: Oxford University Press, 2006), 60-62, 98-99, 103-105.

16. Lance Banning, *The Sacred Fire of Liberty: James Madison and the Founding of the Federal Republic* (Ithaca: Cornell University Press, 1995), 77.

17. Labunski, *James Madison*, 62-63, 158-164, 192-194, 202-203.

18. Jack Rakkove (ed.), *The Annotated U. S. Constitution and Declaration of Independence* (Cambridge: Harvard University Press, 2009), 220-244, 319-320; Labunski, *James Madison*, 254, 259, 265-268, 278-280, 317 n. 21.

19. Labunski, *James Madison*, 259-260, 317 n. 21.

20. 5 U.S. 137, 2 L. Ed. 60 (1803).

21. Lawrence Goldstone, *The Activist: John Marshall, Marbury v. Madison, and the Myth of Judicial Review* (New York: Walker & Company, 2008), 39-41, 100, 151-154.

22. Ibid., 160-173.

23. Marbury v. Madison, 5 U.S. 137, 173 (1803).

24. Ibid., 5 U.S. 177.

25. Ibid., 5 U.S. 180.

26. Ibid., 5 U.S. 174.

27. James Simon, *What Kind of Nation: Thomas Jefferson, John Marshall, and the Epic Struggle to Create a United States* (New York: Simon & Shuster, 2002), 188-189.

28. David Herbert Donald, *Lincoln* (New York: Simon & Schuster, 1995), 149, 154-157, 196-199.

29. Scott v. Sandford, 60 U.S. 393, 15 Law. Ed. 691 (1857).

30. Ibid., 15 Law. Ed. 693-695.

31. U. S. Constitution, Article III, Section 2.

32. Scott v. Sandford, 15 Law. Ed. 698-699 (1857), 698-701, 721.

33. Donald, *Lincoln*, 199-202; Doris Kearns Goodwin, *Team of Rivals: The Political Genius of Abraham Lincoln* (New York: Simon & Schuster, 2005), 190.

34. Donald, *Lincoln*, 202-229.

35. Ibid., 255-257, 301-303, 368-369; Goodwin, *Team of Rivals*, 91, 460; Abraham Lincoln, *Letter to Horace Greeley* (August 22, 1862), in *Abraham Lincoln: Speeches and Writings 1859 – 1865*, ed. Don Fehrenbacher (New York: Literary Classics of the United States, 1989), 357-358.

36. Donald, *Lincoln*, 352-376; Goodwin, *Team of Rivals*, 463, 471.

37. Donald, *Lincoln*, 365, 373-376; Abraham Lincoln, *Final Emancipation Proclamation* (January 1, 1863), in Fehrenbacher ed., *Abraham Lincoln: Speeches and Writings 1859 – 1865*, 424-425.

38. Goodwin, *Team of Rivals*, 499; Donald, *Lincoln*, 377.

39. Michael Davis and Hunter Clark, *Thurgood Marshall: Warrior at the Bar, Rebel on the Bench* (New York: Carol Publishing Group, 1992), 30-31.

40. Plessy v. Ferguson, 163 U. S. 537 (1896).

41. Davis and Clark, *Thurgood Marshall*, 38.

42. Ibid., 47.

43. Ibid., 48-58, 61-62.

44. Ibid., 61, 69-77.

45. Ibid., 78-89.

46. Missouri ex rel. Gaines v. Canada, 305 U. S. 337 (1938).

47. Davis and Clark, *Thurgood Marshall*, 92-95.

48. Missouri ex rel. Gaines v. Canada, 305 U. S. 337.

49. Davis and Clark, *Thurgood Marshall*, 97-98, 105-109, 118-119, 138-147.

50. Brown v. Board of Education, 347 U.S. 483 (1954).

51. Davis and Clark, *Thurgood Marshall*, 155-166, 171-172.

52.   Ibid., 176.

53.   Brown v. Board of Education, 347 U.S. 483, 495 (1954).

54.   Davis and Clark, *Thurgood Marshall*, 234-235, 240, 244-248, 264-265, 277-279, 368.

55.   Ibid., 13; Scott v. Sandford, 60 U. S. 393, 15 Law. Ed. 691, 700 (1857).

56.   *See* Walter Bennett, *The Lawyer's Myth: Reviving Ideals in the Legal Profession* (Chicago: The University of Chicago Press, 2001), 29-35; for a discussion of the related lawyer-statesman ideal *see* Anthony Kronman, *The Lost Lawyer: Failing Ideals of the Legal Profession* (Cambridge: Harvard University Press, 1993).

57.   Bates v. State Bar of Arizona, 433 U. S. 350, 401 n. 11 (1977).

58.   Patrick Schiltz, "On Being a Happy, Healthy and Ethical Member of an Unhappy, Unhealthy and Unethical Profession," *Vanderbilt Law Review* 52 (1999): 871, 907.

59.   "Public Esteem for Military Still High," *Pew Research Religion and Public Life Project* (July 11, 2013), http://www.pewforum.org/2013/07/11/public-esteem-for-military-still-high/.

60.   Arnold Rochvarg, "Enron, Watergate and the Regulation of the Legal Profession," *Washburn Law Journal* 43 (2003): 61-62, 74-84, 87-88.

61.   Merriam-Webster's Collegiate Dictionary, Eleventh Edition (Springfield: Merriam-Webster, 2004).

62.   William Eaton, James Anthony, Wallace Mandel and Roberta Garrison, "Occupations and the Prevalence of Major Depressive Disorder," *Journal of Occupational Medicine* 32, no. 11 (1990): 1079-1087.

63.   Ibid., 1081, 1083.

64. Ibid., 1083, 1085.

65. Ibid., 1086.

66. Rick Allan, "Alcoholism, Drug Abuse and Lawyers: Are We Ready to Address the Denial?," *Creighton Law Review* 31 (1997): 265-266; Schiltz, "On Being a Happy, Healthy and Ethical Member," 871, 876-877.

67. Schiltz, "On Being a Happy, Healthy and Ethical Member," 871, 879-880; *see* Joan Mounteer, "Depression Among Lawyers," *The Colorado Lawyer* 33, no. 1 (2004): 35-36.

68. Larry Sitton, ed., *Report and Recommendations of the Quality of Life Task Force* (Raleigh, North Carolina: North Carolina Bar Association, 1991); Bennett, *The Lawyer's Myth*, 4.

69. Schiltz, "On Being a Happy, Healthy and Ethical Member," 871, 874-875.

70. Ibid., 875.

71. Benjamin Sells, *The Soul of the Law: Understanding Lawyers and the Law* (Boston: Element Books, 1994), 17, 100; Benjamin Sells, *Order in the Court: Crafting a More Just World in Lawless Times* (Boston: Element Books, 1999), 50.

72. *E.g.*, Schiltz, "On Being a Happy, Healthy and Ethical Member," 871, 881-888; Leonard Riskin, "The Contemplative Lawyer: On the Potential Contributions of Mindfulness Meditation to Law Students, Lawyers, and Their Clients," *Harvard Negotiation Law Review* 7 (2002): 1, 10-13.

73. Sandra Day O'Connor, "Professionalism," *Oregon Law Review* 78 (1999): 385-386.

74. Deborah Hensler and Marisa Reddy, *California Lawyers View the Future: A Report to the Commission on the Future of the Legal Profession and the State Bar* (Santa Monica, California: RAND, 2004), 9-13.

75.   Sitton, *Report and Recommendations of the Quality of Life Task Force*; Bennett, *The Lawyer's Myth*, 4.

76.   Schiltz, "On Being a Happy, Healthy and Ethical Member," 871, 939-940.

77.   Debra Cassens Weiss, "After the JD Shows Many Leave Law Practice," *ABA Journal* (April 2014), http://www.abajournal.com/magazine/article/after_the_jd_study_shows_many_leave_law_practice.

78.   Eaton, et al., "Occupations and the Prevalence of Major Depressive Disorder," 1082, 1084; *see* U. S. Department of Commerce, Bureau of the Census, *Alphabetical Index of Industries and Occupations* (Washington: U.S. Government Printing Office, 1980).

79.   Eaton, et al., "Occupations and the Prevalence of Major Depressive Disorder," 1083-1085; *see* U. S. Department of Commerce, Bureau of the Census, *Alphabetical Index of Industries and Occupations* (Washington: U.S. Government Printing Office, 1980).

80.   John Gabriel Hunt, ed., *The Inaugural Addresses of the Presidents* (New York: Gramercy Books, 1997), 417.

81.   Frederick Schauer, *Thinking Like a Lawyer* (Cambridge: Harvard University Press, 2012), 1-2; Karl Llewellyn, *The Bramble Bush* (Dobbs Ferry, New York: Oceana Publications, 1960), 101.

82.   Bill Bradfield, ed., *The Book of Ancient Wisdom: Over 500 Inspiring Quotations from the Greeks* (Mineola, New York: Dover Publications, 2005), 61.

83.   Oliver Wendell Holmes Jr., *The Path of the Law* (American Classics Library, 2012), 13 (reprint of a speech given at Boston University Law School on January 8, 1897 and originally published in *Harvard Law Review* 10 (1897): 457 *et seq.*).

84.   Schauer, *Thinking Like a Lawyer*, 1-2; Sells, *The Soul of the Law*, 35-36.

85.   Kronman, *The Lost Lawyer*, 169.

86.   Ibid., 170-174, 182, 184, 188.

87.   Ibid., 50, 195-199, 201-209, 225-226, 230-232, 240, 245-246, 259-261, 265-270.

88.   *See* ibid., 110.

89.   Based on the novel by John Jay Osborn Jr., *The Paper Chase* (Boston: Houghton Mifflin, 1971).

90.   Kronman, *The Lost Lawyer*, 50, 156, 158-160.

91.   Ibid., 156.

92.   Pleasant Grove City v. Summum, 555 U. S. 460 (2009).

93.   Ibid., 465.

94.   Ibid., 466.

95.   Ibid.

96.   Sells, *The Soul of the Law*, 17.

97.   *See, e.g.,* Sells, *The Soul of the Law*, 13-15; Scott Turow, *One L: The Turbulent True Story of a First Year at Harvard Law School* (New York: Penguin Books, 2010), 75.

98.   *See, e.g.,* Rules 401 and 402, *Federal Rules of Evidence* (2011).

99.   Indiana v. Edwards, 554 U. S. 164 (2008).

100.   Ibid., 170 (emphasis in original).

101.   Ibid., 168.

102.   Ibid., 169.

103.   Ibid., 170-172.

104.   Ibid., 178.

105.   Ibid., 176.

106.   Ibid., 179.

107.   Ibid., 179-180.

108.   Ibid., 180.

109.   Ibid., 181.

110.   Ibid., 181-182.

111.   Ibid., 189.

112.   American Psychiatric Association, *Diagnostic and Statistical Manual of Mental Disorders, Fifth Edition* (Arlington: American Psychiatric Association, 2013), 99.

113.   Alexander Hyde, M.D., *Living With Schizophrenia* (Chicago: Contemporary Books, 1985), 1-2, 11-12, 16-17.

114.   Chris Goodrich, *Anarchy and Elegance: Confessions of a Journalist at Yale Law School* (Boston: Little, Brown and Company, 1991).

115. Turow, *One L.*

116. Goodrich, *Anarchy and Elegance*, 111, 225-227; Turow, *One L*, 74-75, 265.

117. *See* Gabor Maté, M.D., *When the Body Says No: Exploring the Stress-Disease Connection* (Hoboken, New Jersey: John Wiley & Sons, 2003).

118. *See* Sells, *The Soul of the Law*, 102, 176, 181; Bennett, *The Lawyer's Myth*, 99.

119. Kronman, *The Lost Lawyer*, 113-115, 158-159; *see also* Bennett, *The Lawyer's Myth*, 15; Goodrich, *Anarchy and Elegance*, 105, 116.

120. *See* Schiltz, "On Being a Happy, Healthy and Ethical Member," 906-910.

121. Patrick Schiltz, "Legal Ethics in Decline: The Elite Law Firm, the Elite Law School, and the Moral Formation of the Novice Attorney," *Minnesota Law Review* 82 (1998): 705, 721-724.

122. Laurel Rigertas, "Post-Watergate: The Legal Profession and Respect for the Interests of Third Parties," *Chapman Law Review* 16 (2012): 98, 101, 104, 123-124; Rochvarg, "Enron, Watergate and the Regulation of the Legal Profession," 61; Marc Galanter, "The Faces of Mistrust: The Image of Lawyers in Public Opinion, Jokes, and Political Discourse," *University of Cincinnati Law Review* 66 (1998): 805, 812 and n. 40.

123. Fred Emery, *Watergate: The Corruption of American Politics and the Fall of Richard Nixon,* (New York: Touchstone Books, 1994), 132-136, 150-151; John Ehrlichman, *Witness to Power: The Nixon Years* (New York: Simon and Schuster, 1982), 347; Sam Ervin, Jr., *The Whole Truth: The Watergate Conspiracy* (New York: Random House, 1980), 7-8, 153.

124. Carl Bernstein and Bob Woodward, *All the President's Men* (New York: Simon and Schuster, 1974).

125. Ervin, *The Whole Truth*, 154.

126. Keith Olson, *Watergate: The Presidential Scandal that Shook America* (Lawrence, Kansas: The University of Kansas Press, 2003), 70-72; Ervin, *The Whole Truth*, 20-22, 35.

127. Olson, *Watergate: The Presidential Scandal*, 90-91; Ervin, *The Whole Truth*, 30-31, 124-125, 128-129.

128. Olson, *Watergate: The Presidential Scandal*, 92; Emery, *Watergate*, 355-356; Ervin, *The Whole Truth*, 116.

129. Olson, *Watergate: The Presidential Scandal*, 117-118, 121, 156, 187; Ervin, *The Whole Truth*, 239, 244; John Dean III, *Blind Ambition: The White House* Years (New York: Simon and Schuster, 1976), 340.

130. Erhlichman, *Witness to Power*, 411.

131. Olson, *Watergate: The Presidential Scandal*, 149, 154, 157, 187; Emery, *Watergate*, 435, 446-449; Ervin, *The Whole Truth*, 282.

132. Olson, *Watergate: The Presidential Scandal*, 148, 186; Anthony Summers, *The Arrogance of Power: The Secret World of Richard Nixon* (New York: Penguin Putnam, 2000), 482-483; Ervin, *The Whole Truth*, 293.

133. Richard Nixon, *In the Arena: A Memoir of Victory, Defeat and Renewal* (New York: Simon and Schuster, 1990), 96-97, 109, 230.

134. Summers, *The Arrogance of Power*, 217.

135. Ibid., 221-222.

136. Ibid., 231, 260-261, 273-274; Emery, *Watergate*, 10, 37; Nixon, *In the Arena*, 28; Dean, *Blind Ambition,* 21; Bernstein and Woodward, *All the President's Men*, 92-93.

137. Summers, *The Arrogance of Power*, 309, 310.

138. Olson, *Watergate: The Presidential Scandal*, 35-36; Emery, *Watergate*, 110; Summers, *The Arrogance of Power*, 311; Erhlichman, *Witness to Power*, 17-18, 28, 35, 75, 76, 397; Ervin, *The Whole Truth*, 6-7; Bernstein and Woodward, *All the President's Men*, 171.

139. Olson, *Watergate: The Presidential Scandal*, 33-34; Summers, *The Arrogance of Power*, 312; Emery, *Watergate*, 31, 226; Erhlichman, *Witness to Power*, 79, 81, 82, 84; Ervin, *The Whole Truth*, 6, 39, 63; Dean, *Blind Ambition*, 26; Bernstein and Woodward, *All the President's Men*, 9, 24, 171, 215, 257-258, 327.

140. Olson, *Watergate: The Presidential Scandal*, 48; Emery, *Watergate*, 28, 171, 256; Erhlichman, *Witness to Power*, 84; Dean, *Blind Ambition*, 20, 25, 49-50, 104, 291, 352, 385-386; Bernstein and Woodward, *All the President's Men*, 9.

141. Emery, *Watergate*, 73-74; Dean, *Blind Ambition*, 121-122, 125.

142. Summers, *The Arrogance of Power*, 312; Emery, *Watergate*, 55-56; Erhlichman, *Witness to Power*, 81, 84; Bernstein and Woodward, *All the President's Men*, 35.

143. Emery, *Watergate*, 48-51; Erhlichman, *Witness to Power*, 347-348; Ervin, *The Whole Truth*, 9, 15, 187; Bernstein and Woodward, *All the President's Men*, 24-25.

144. Olson, *Watergate: The Presidential Scandal*, 26; Summers, *The Arrogance of Power*, 402; Emery, *Watergate*, 7-8, 31; Ervin, *The Whole Truth*, 3; Jeb Stuart Magruder, *An American Life: One Man's Road to Watergate* (New York: Atheneum, 1974), 144, 158, 215.

145. Olson, *Watergate: The Presidential Scandal*, 26; Emery, *Watergate*, 36; Ervin, *The Whole Truth*, 4; Magruder, *An American Life*, 159-160.

146. Emery, *Watergate*, 76, 286, 296; Ervin, *The Whole Truth*, 32.

147. Emery, *Watergate*, 88; Erhlichman, *Witness to Power*, 317; Maguder, *An American Life*, 220.

148. Olson, *Watergate: The Presidential Scandal*, 30-33, 35-36, 72, 99; Emery, *Watergate*, 95-96, 222, 257; Ervin, *The Whole Truth*, 6-7, 12, 62-63; Dean, *Blind Ambition*, 139-140; Bernstein and Woodward, *All the President's Men*, 273.

149. Emery, *Watergate*, 38, 42-45, 48-49, 58-59, 62, 73; Ehrlichman, *Witness to Power*, 300-302; Ervin, *The Whole Truth*, 105.

150. Olson, *Watergate: The Presidential Scandal*, 18-19, 74; Emery, *Watergate*, 53-58, 201; Erhlichman, *Witness to Power*, 303; Ervin, *The Whole Truth*, 87, 105, 193-194; Dean, *Blind Ambition*, 49; Bernstein and Woodward, *All the President's Men*, 215; Magruder, *An American Life*, 186-187.

151. Emery, *Watergate*, 54-55, 60-61, 374, 440-441; Erhlichman, *Witness to Power*, 400, 404; Ervin, *The Whole Truth*, 105-106, 194.

152. Olson, *Watergate: The Presidential Scandal*, 19-20, 79, 185; Summers, *The Arrogance of Power*, 404; Emery, *Watergate*, 62-69; Erhlichman, *Witness to Power*, 403; Ervin, *The Whole Truth*, 41, 105-106; Bernstein and Woodward, *All the President's Men*, 307.

153. Erhlichman, *Witness to Power*, p. 347.

154. Emery, *Watergate*, 70.

155. Olson, *Watergate: The Presidential Scandal*, 82; Emery, *Watergate*, 354; Ervin, *The Whole Truth*, 106-107.

156.   Ervin, *The Whole Truth*, 107.

157.   Olson, *Watergate: The Presidential Scandal*, 37; Emery, *Watergate*, 79, 80-82; Magruder, *An American Life*, 185-187.

158.   Olson, *Watergate: The Presidential Scandal*, 37, 185; Summers, *The Arrogance of Power*, 400-401; Emery, *Watergate*, 89-93; Ervin, *The Whole Truth*, 68-69, 167; Magruder, *An American Life*, 192, 194-196.

159.   Olson, *Watergate: The Presidential Scandal*, 38, 185; Emery, *Watergate*, 101.

160.   Olson, *Watergate: The Presidential Scandal*, 38; Summers, *The Arrogance of Power*, 402; Emery, *Watergate*, 102-104, 283, 323-324, 361; Erhlichman, *Witness to Power*, 380; Ervin, *The Whole Truth*, 40, 72-73, 83-84, 95, 145-146, 151-152, 159; Dean, *Blind Ambition*, 115-116; Magruder, *An American Life*, 197, 211-213, 319.

161.   Olson, *Watergate: The Presidential Scandal*, 41, 113-114; Emery, *Watergate*, 105, 107; Ervin, *The Whole Truth*, 7, 160, 248; Bernstein and Woodward, *All the President's Men*, 127, 147-149, 152; Magruder, *An American Life*, 207.

162.   Olson, *Watergate: The Presidential Scandal*, 91; Emery, *Watergate*, 78, 112-113, 150, 164, 333; Ervin, *The Whole Truth*, 9, 14-15, 64, 140; Dean, *Blind Ambition*, 100; Bernstein and Woodward, *All the President's Men*, 18, 20-21; Magruder, *An American Life*, 208-210.

163.   Ehrlichman, *Witness to Power*, 380; Ervin, *The Whole Truth*, 14, 40, 95, 153; Magruder, *An American Life*, 229-230.

164.   Olson, *Watergate: The Presidential Scandal*, 39-40; Emery, *Watergate*, 125-136, 162, 188; Ervin, *The Whole Truth*, 7-8, 14, 64-65, 153, 156, 163; Magruder, *An American Life*, 243-244.

165.   Olson, *Watergate: The Presidential Scandal*, 44; Emery, *Watergate*, 141, 162-163; Ervin, *The Whole Truth*, 154; Magruder, *An American Life*, 240, 245.

166.   Emery, *Watergate*, 163; Ervin, *The Whole Truth*, 160, 163; Dean, *Blind Ambition*, 99-100; Magruder, *An American Life*, 245.

167.   Olson, *Watergate: The Presidential Scandal*, 43; Emery, *Watergate*, 144, 179, 208, 365; Ervin, *The Whole Truth*, 8, 40-41, 148, 154, 181; Dean, *Blind Ambition*, 105, 118; Bernstein and Woodward, *All the President's Men*, 59, 90, 170-171.

168.   Olson, *Watergate: The Presidential Scandal*, 48-49; Emery, *Watergate*, 102-104, 168-169; Ervin, *The Whole Truth*, 154, 180-181; Magruder, *An American Life*, 246-248, 264.

169.   Emery, *Watergate*, 148, 158, 171-173, 189-193, 200-201; Ervin, *The Whole Truth*, 9, 40-41, 105, 154, 170; Dean, *Blind Ambition*, 113, 121-122; Magruder, *An American Life*, 250-251, 264, 272.

170.   Olson, *Watergate: The Presidential Scandal*, 48-49; Emery, *Watergate*, 167, 173, 201; Ervin, *The Whole Truth*, 163-164; Dean, *Blind Ambition*, 107-108, 114-115, 119.

171.   Ervin, *The Whole Truth*, 6, 87, 130-131, 192-193.

172.   Ibid., 164-165; Dean, *Blind Ambition*, 121-122.

173.   Olson, *Watergate: The Presidential Scandal*, 72; Emery, *Watergate*, 114, 348-349; Patricia Sullivan, "Watergate-Era FBI Chief L. Patrick Gray Dies at 88," *Washington Post*, July 7, 2005, http://www.washingtonpost.com/politics/watergate-era-fbi-chief-l-patrick-gray-iii-dies-at-88/2012/05/31/gJQA9fX2FV_story.html.

174.   Olson, *Watergate: The Presidential Scandal*, 50, 79, 82, 87; Emery, *Watergate*, 197, 232, 245, 330-331, 342; Erhlichman, *Witness to Power*, 352; Ervin, *The Whole*

Truth, 87, 95-96, 165, 192; Dean, *Blind Ambition*, 169-170, 182, 343; Bernstein and Woodward, *All the President's Men*, 305-307.

175. Olson, *Watergate: The Presidential Scandal*, 140; Emery, *Watergate*, 184; Ervin, *The Whole Truth*, 64-65, 106, 130-131, 172; Magruder, *An American Life*, 243-244.

176. Olson, *Watergate: The Presidential Scandal*, 120; Emery, *Watergate*, 431; Erhlichman, *Witness to Power*, 346-347, 350, 356; Ervin, *The Whole Truth*, 63, 130-131, 172-173, 284, 288.

177. Emery, *Watergate*, 111-112, 188; Ervin, *The Whole Truth*, 64, 140; Dean, *Blind Ambition*, 145; Magruder, *An American Life*, 243-244.

178. Olson, *Watergate: The Presidential Scandal*, 57, 72-73, 87; Emery, *Watergate*, 184, 188, 196-197, 201, 247, 257, 348-349; Ervin, *The Whole Truth*, 62-63, 130-131, 165-166; Dean, *Blind Ambition*, 122, 131.

179. Emery, *Watergate*, 171-173; Erhlichman, *Witness to Power*, 357; Ervin, *The Whole Truth*, 99; Dean, *Blind Ambition*, 112.

180. Emery, *Watergate*, 171-173, 213; Erhlichman, *Witness to Power*, 357; Ervin, *The Whole Truth*, 130-131, 167; Dean, *Blind Ambition*, 112, 131.

181. Olson, *Watergate: The Presidential Scandal*, 69, 186; Emery, *Watergate*, 202, 204; Erhlichman, *Witness to Power*, 360; Ervin, *The Whole Truth*, 10, 156; Bernstein and Woodward, *All the President's Men*, 69; Magruder, *An American Life*, 251, 255, 259-260.

182. Emery, *Watergate*, 232, 257; Dean, *Blind Ambition*, 169-170, 182.

183. Emery, *Watergate*, 199-200, 310, 315, 341; Erhlichman, *Witness to Power*, 69, 359, 397-398; Ervin, *The Whole Truth*, 41, 130-131, 166, 178-179, 183; Dean, *Blind Ambition*, 122-124.

184.   Emery, *Watergate*, 199-200, 220-221, 228; Ervin, *The Whole Truth*, 41, 147, 179-180; Dean, *Blind Ambition*, 140.

185.   Ervin, *The Whole Truth*, 10.

186.   Olson, *Watergate: The Presidential Scandal*, 69-70, 73-74, 186; Ervin, *The Whole Truth*, 14, 16, 169.

187.   Ervin, *The Whole Truth*, 39, 181; *see* Olson, *Watergate: The Presidential Scandal*, 73.

188.   Emery, *Watergate*, 267; Ervin, *The Whole Truth*, 40-41, 52, 181.

189.   Emery, *Watergate*, 196; Ervin, *The Whole Truth*, 130-131.

190.   Erhlichman, *Witness to Power*, 405-406; Ervin, *The Whole Truth*, 96, 98-99, 106.

191.   Olson, *Watergate: The Presidential Scandal*, 84, 186.

192.   Ibid., 120; Emery, *Watergate*, xiv, 434.

193.   Olson, *Watergate: The Presidential Scandal*, 84; Emery, *Watergate*, 352; Ervin, *The Whole Truth*, 109; Neil Lewis, "Elliot Richardson Dies at 79," *New York Times*, January 1, 2000, http://www.nytimes.com/learning/general/onthisday/bday/0720.html.

194.   Olson, *Watergate: The Presidential Scandal*, 92, 186; Emery, *Watergate*, 355-356; Ervin, *The Whole Truth*, 112, 116.

195.   Olson, *Watergate: The Presidential Scandal*, 35-36, 98-99; Summers, *The Arrogance of Power*, 396-397; Emery, *Watergate*, 110; Ervin, *The Whole Truth*, 5, 140, 254-255; Bernstein and Woodward, *All the President's Men*, 194.

196.   Olson, *Watergate: The Presidential Scandal*, 137; Ervin, *The Whole Truth*, 256.

197.   Olson, *Watergate: The Presidential Scandal*, 31, 35-36, 72, 99; Emery, *Watergate*, 112-113, 199-200, 220-222, 228, 257; Ervin, *The Whole Truth*, 6-7, 9, 12, 39, 41, 64, 140-141, 147, 179-180; Dean, *Blind Ambition*, 100, 139-140; Bernstein and Woodward, *All the President's Men*, 273.

198.   Olson, *Watergate: The Presidential Scandal*, 186; Emery, *Watergate*, 34-35; Ervin, *The Whole Truth*, 187.

199.   Olson, *Watergate: The Presidential Scandal*, 117-118, 156, 186-187; Emery, *Watergate*, 372-373, 397-399; Ervin, *The Whole Truth*, 112, 116, 239, 244; Dean, *Blind Ambition*, 340.

200.   Olson, *Watergate: The Presidential Scandal*, 121, 187; Ervin, *The Whole Truth*, 244.

201.   United States v. Nixon, 418 U. S. 683 (1974).

202.   Olson, *Watergate: The Presidential Scandal*, 159; Emery, *Watergate*, 431; Erhlichman, *Witness to Power*, 346-347, 350-351, 356.

203.   Olson, *Watergate: The Presidential Scandal*, 179; Emery, *Watergate*, 482; Dean, *Blind Ambition*, 348; *see* United States v. Nixon, 418 U. S. 683, 687 (1974).

204.   Olson, *Watergate: The Presidential Scandal*, 181; Ervin, *The Whole Truth*, 307-308; Dean, *Blind Ambition*, 395.

205.   Olson, *Watergate: The Presidential Scandal*, 140, 188; Emery, *Watergate*, 440-441, 457; Erhlichman, *Witness to Power*, 344, 394-396, 412, 414; Ervin, *The Whole Truth*, 306-308; Dean, *Blind Ambition*, 395.

206.   United States v. Liddy, 542 F. 2d 76 (D. C. Cir. 1976); United States v. Liddy, 509 F. 2d 428 (D. C. Cir. 1974); Emery, *Watergate*, xii-xvi, 270-271; Ervin, *The Whole Truth*, 306-307.

207. Olson, *Watergate: The Presidential Scandal*, 112, 125, 128, 188; Emery, *Watergate*, 70, 393, 421, 433, 463; Erhlichman, *Witness to Power*, 399; Ervin, *The Whole Truth*, 306-308; Dean, *Blind Ambition*, 340; Bernstein and Woodward, *All the President's Men*, 335.

208. Emery, *Watergate*, 427; Ervin, *The Whole Truth*, 307-308; Dean, *Blind Ambition*, 395; Bernstein and Woodward, *All the President's Men*, 335.

209. Ervin, *The Whole Truth*, 307-308; Dean, *Blind Ambition*, 395; Bernstein and Woodward, *All the President's Men*, 261, 283.

210. Emery, *Watergate*, 427; Ervin, *The Whole Truth*, 307-308; Bernstein and Woodward, *All the President's Men*, 335.

211. Emery, *Watergate*, 375, 440-441; Erhlichman, *Witness to Power*, 399; Dean, *Blind Ambition*, 392.

212. *See* Rigertas, "Post-Watergate: The Legal Profession and Respect for the Interests of Third Parties," 98, 101, 123-127; Rochvarg, "Enron, Watergate and the Regulation of the Legal Profession," 61.

213. Bates v. State Bar of Arizona, 433 U. S. 350 (1977).

214. Ibid., 364.

215. Ibid., 368.

216. Ibid., 371-372.

217. Ibid., 389.

218. Lester Brickman, "The Use of Litigation Screenings in Mass Torts: A Formula for Fraud?," *SMU Law Review* 61 (2008): 1221, 1225-1233.

219. James Jones et al., "2014 Report on the State of the Legal Market," *Georgetown Law Center for the Study of the Legal Profession* (Tarzana, CA: Thomson Reuters 2014), 1 n. 2.

220. "Complete Number of Attorneys Rankings," compiled by Introspect, LLC and reported on its lawfirmstats.com website, accessed March 6, 2015, http://www.lawfirmstats.com/rankings/complete/number-of-attorneys-rankings.php.

221. Jones et al., "2014 Report on the State of the Legal Market," 7.

222. Schiltz, "On Being a Happy, Healthy and Ethical Member," 900.

223. "Complete Profits Per Equity Partner Rankings," compiled by Introspect, LLC and reported on its lawfirmstats.com website, accessed March 6, 2015, http://www.lawfirmstats.com/rankings/complete/profits-per-equity-partner-rankings.php.

224. Schiltz, "On Being a Happy, Healthy and Ethical Member," 891-893.

225. Ronit Dinovitzer et al., "After the JD: Second Results from a National Study of Legal Careers," (Chicago and Dallas: American Bar Foundation and NALP Foundation, 2009), 30-32.

226. "Top Salaries for First-Year Associates Remain Flat at $160,000, But Prevalence Shrinks as Large Law Firm Market Becomes Less Homogeneous," *National Association for Law Placement* (October 9, 2014), http://www.nalp.org/associate_salaries_2014.

227. Harry Edwards, "The Growing Disjunction Between Legal Education and the Legal Profession," *Michigan Law Review* 91 (1992): 68.

228. Jones et al., "2014 Report on the State of the Legal Market," 8-9.

229. Cliff Collins, "Salary Wars," *Oregon State Bar Bulletin* (May 2007), https://www.osbar.org/publications/bulletin/07may/salarywars.html.

230. Peter Lattman, "Suit Offers a Peek at the Practice of Inflating a Legal Bill," *New York Times*, March 25, 2013, http://dealbook.nytimes.com/2013/03/25/suit-offers-a-peek-at-the-practice-of-padding-a-legal-bill/?_r=0; Supporting Affidavit of Larry Hutcher and Exhibits 5 and 7 thereto, filed on March 21, 2013 in *DLA Piper LLP (US) v. Adam Victor*, Supreme Court of the State of New York, County of New York (Index No. 650374/2012, NYSCEF Doc. No. 29), http://s3.documentcloud.org/documents/627381/law-firm-sued-for-overbilling.pdf.

231. Deborah Rhode, "Equal Justice Under Law," *Markkula Center for Applied Ethics* (2014), http://www.scu.edu/ethics/publications/submitted/rhode/equal-justice.html; Edwards, "The Growing Disjunction," 68.

232. Jones et al., "2014 Report on the State of the Legal Market," 8-9; Schiltz, "On Being a Happy, Healthy and Ethical Member," 886-895, 899-900, 902-903.

233. Noam Scheiber, "The Last Days of Big Law, *New Republic*, July 21, 2013, http://www.newrepublic.com/article/113941/big-law-firms-trouble-when-money-dries.

234. Jones et al., "2014 Report on the State of the *Legal* Market," 1-2.

235. *See* "The Layoff List," *American Lawyer*, accessed March 12, 2015, http://www.americanlawyer.com/id=1202425647706/THE-LAYOFF-LIST; Jonathan Glater, "Law Firms Feel Strain of Layoffs and Cutbacks," *New York Times*, November 11, 2008, http://www.nytimes.com/2008/11/12/business/12law.html?.

236. Ashby Jones, "Cadwalader's Layoff Strategy," *Wall Street Journal*, August 6, 2008, http://www.wsj.com/articles/SB121798627846815619.

237. V. Dion Haynes, "Latham & Watkins Cuts 190 Lawyers," *Washington Post*, February 28, 2009, http://www.washingtonpost.com/wp-dyn/content/article/2009/02/27/AR2009022702751_pf.html.

238. Peter Lattman, "Mass Layoffs at a Top-Flight Law Firm," *New York Times*, June 24, 2013, http://dealbook.nytimes.com/2013/06/24/big-law-firm-to-cut-lawyers-and-some-partner-pay/?_r=0.

239. Debra Cassens Weiss, "Jenner & Block Asks About 10 Partners to Leave," *ABA Journal* (October 21, 2008), http://www.abajournal.com/news/article/jenner_block_asks_about_10_partners_to_leave/.

240. Jennifer Smith, "Law-Firm Partners Face Layoffs," *Wall Street Journal*, January 6, 2013, http://www.wsj.com/articles/SB10001424127887323689604578221891691032424.

241. Ameet Sachdev, "Altheimer & Gray to Close," *Chicago Tribune*, June 28, 2003, http://articles.chicagotribune.com/2003-06-28/business/0306280112_1_seyfarth-shaw-retired-partners-firm; James Arndorfer, "Altheimer & Gray to Rest its Case," *Chicago Business*, June 27, 2003, http://www.chicagobusiness.com/article/20030627/NEWS/20009310?template=printart.

242. Jeff Blumenthal, "Wolf Block Decides to Dissolve," *Philadelphia Business Journal*, March 23, 2009, http://www.bizjournals.com/philadelphia/stories/2009/03/23/daily1.html?page=all.

243. Jonathan Glater, "Law Firm that Opened Borders is Closing Up Shop," *New York Times*, August 30, 2005, http://www.nytimes.com/2005/08/30/business/30law.html?pagewanted=print.

244. Dick Dahl, "Case Closed," *Boston Magazine*, April 2005, http://www.bostonmagazine.com/2006/05/case-closed/; Sheri Qualters, "Testa, Hurwitz &

Thibeault Votes to Dissolve," *Boston Business Journal*, January 14, 2005, http://www.bizjournals.com/boston/stories/2005/01/10/daily72.html?page=all.

245.　Nate Raymond and David Ingram, "Lawyer-Turned-Witness Ordered to Prison for U. S. Tax Fraud," *Reuters*, July 30, 2014, http://www.reuters.com/article/2014/07/30/tax-fraud-sentencing-idUSL2N0Q30YL20140730; Department of Justice, Office of Public Affairs, "Former Jenkens & Gilchrist Attorney Sentenced to 15 Years in Prison for Orchestrating Multibillion Dollar Criminal Tax Fraud Scheme," *Justice News*, June 25, 2014, http://www.justice.gov/opa/pr/former-jenkens-gilchrist-attorney-sentenced-15-years-prison-orchestrating-multibillion-dollar; Patricia Hurtado, "Ex-Jenkens & Gilchrist Lawyer Gets 8 Years in Tax Case," *Bloomberg Business*, March 1, 2013, http://www.bloomberg.com/news/articles/2013-03-01/ex-lawyer-donna-guerin-gets-8-year-sentence-in-tax-shelter-case; Katie Fairbank and Terry Maxon, "How Jenkens Lost its Way," *Dallas Morning News*, April 1, 2007, http://www.lfdlaw.com/_files/news/009-jenkins-gilchrist.pdf; IR-2005-83, "Jenkens & Gilchrist Admits it is Subject to $76 Million IRS Penalty," *Internal Revenue Release* (Washington: Internal Revenue Service, March 29, 2007), http://www.irs.gov/uac/Jenkens-&-Gilchrist-Admits-It-Is-Subject-to-$76-Million-IRS-Penalty.

246.　Eric Young, "Ex-Brobeck Boss: Don't Blame Me for Firm's Demise," *San Francisco Business Times*, May 15, 2005, http://www.bizjournals.com/sanfrancisco/stories/2005/05/16/story2.html?s=print; Jonathan Glater, "A Happy Firm's Ending is Anything But," *New York Times*, June 22, 2003, http://www.nytimes.com/2003/06/22/business/a-happy-firm-s-ending-is-anything-but.html?pagewanted=print.

247.　*E.g.*, Andrew Scurria, "Ex-Thelen Attys Lose Bid to Keep Partner Draws," *Law 360* (November 24, 2014), http://www.law360.com/articles/598896/ex-thelen-attys-lose-bid-to-keep-partner-draws.

248. James Stewart, "The Rise and Fall of a Rainmaker," *New York Times*, December 12, 2014, http://www.nytimes.com/2014/12/13/business/the-rise-and-fall-of-a-dewey-leboeuf-rainmaker.html?_r=0; James Stewart, "The Collapse: How a Top Legal Firm Destroyed Itself," *New Yorker*, October 14, 2013, http://www.newyorker.com/magazine/2013/10/14/the-collapse-2.

249. John Bates, "Annual Report of the Director 2013," *Judicial Business of the United States Courts* (Washington: Administrative Office of the United States Courts, 2013), http://www.uscourts.gov/Statistics/JudicialBusiness/2013.aspx; Robert LaFountain et al., "Examining the Work of State Courts: An Analysis of 2009 State Court Caseloads," *Court Statistics Project* (Williamsburg, Virginia: National Center for State Courts, 2011), 3-4.

250. *See, e.g.,* Lawrence McQuillan, Hovannes Abramyan and Anthony Archie, *Jackpot Justice: The True Cost of America's Tort System* (San Francisco: Pacific Research Institute, 2007), 19-22.

251. Edward Re, "The Causes of Popular Dissatisfaction with the Legal Profession," *St. John's Law Review* 68 (2012): 85, 107-110.

252. Rosenberg v. Harwood, Google, et al., *Third Judicial District Court, Salt Lake County, Utah*, Case No. 100916536, Memorandum Decision (May 27, 2011), https://scholar.google.com/scholar_case?case=41116705649085163828&hl=en& as_sdt=2&as_vis=1&oi=scholarr.

253. Honda of America Mfg., Inc. v. Norman, 104 S.W.3d 600 (Tex. App. 2003).

254. Degerolamo v. Fulton Financial Corporation, *United States District Court for the District of New Jersey* (Case No. 1:14-cv-03774-JHR-JS, 2014), *see* Notice of Removal and Exhibit 1, http://www.plainsite.org/dockets/2amy6oh4u/new-jersey-district-court/degerolamo-v-fulton-financial-corporation/.

255. Barbato v. Mercy Med. Crt., 2005-Ohio-5219 (Ohio Ct. App. 2005), https://cases.justia.com/ohio/fifth-district-court-of-appeals/2005-ohio-5219.pdf.

256. Williamson v. Liptzin, No. COA99-813 (NC Ct. App. Dec. 190, 2000), http://caselaw.findlaw.com/nc-court-of-appeals/1042624.html.

257. Amended Verified Complaint filed in Remis v. Fried, Civil Action Index No. 116050/09 (Supreme Court of the State of New York, County of New York, Dec. 9, 2009), http://amlawdaily.typepad.com/files/remis-lawsuit.pdf; Remis v. Fried, 2011 NY Slip Op 50479(U) (Supreme Court, New York County, Jan. 18, 2011), http://law.justia.com/cases/new-york/other-courts/2011/2011-50479.html; Joseph Berger, "Years Later, Lawsuit Seeks to Recreate a Wedding," *New York Times*, November 2, 2011, http://www.nytimes.com/2011/11/03/nyregion/suit-against-photographer-seeks-re-creation-of-wedding-after-divorce.html?_r=4&hp.

258. Tasini v. AOL, 851 F.Supp.2d 734, 741 (S.D.N.Y. 2012).

259. Class Action Complaint filed in Williams v. Kahala Corp., Case No. 10-L-166 (Circuit Court, Third Judicial Circuit, Madison County, IL Feb. 12, 2010), http://www.bluemaumau.org/sites/default/files/Blimpies%20Double%20Meat%20lawsuit.pdf.

260. *"STATEMENT: The Truth About Our Super Stacked™ Subs"* (Feb. 25, 2010), Kahala Franchising LLC, http://www.blimpie.com/press/press/content/2010/pr_double-meat_022510.pdf.

261. In Re: Subway Footlong Sandwich Marketing and Sales Practices Litigation, MDL No. 2439 (Judicial Panel on Multidistrict Litigation 2013), http://www.jpml.uscourts.gov/sites/jpml/files/MDL-2439-Initial_Transfer-05-13.pdf.

262. Plaintiffs' Consolidated Class Action Complaint, In Re: Subway Footlong Sandwich Marketing and Sales Practices Litigation, Case No. 2:13-md-02439-LA (E. D. Wisc. Dec. 31, 2013), 2, http://pdfserver.amlaw.com/nlj/subway-complaint.pdf.

263. *See, e.g.,* Brickman, "The Use of Litigation Screenings in Mass Torts," 1221, 1225-1226, 1229.

264.   In re: Silica Products Liability Litigation, 280 F. Supp. 2d 1381 (J.P.M.L. 2003).

265.   In re: Silica Products Liability Litigation, 398 F. Supp. 2d 563, 580 (S. D. Tex. 2005).

266.   Stephen Carroll et al., *The Abuse of Medical Diagnostic Practices in Mass Litigation: The Case of Silica* (Santa Monica, California: The RAND Corporation, 2009), 24.

267.   In re: Silica Products Liability Litigation, 398 F. Supp. 2d 633 (references to transcript omitted).

268.   Ibid., 596, 601, 603, 628.

269.   Ibid., 581-582.

270.   Ibid., 611-612.

271.   Ibid., 620.

272.   Ibid., 635.

273.   "The American Bar Association Mission," *ABA Mission and Goals* (Chicago, Illinois: American Bar Association), accessed May 14, 2015, http://www.americanbar.org/about_the_aba/aba-mission-goals.html; *see* "About the ABA," *About the American Bar Association* (Chicago, Illinois: American Bar Association), accessed May 14, 2015, http://www.americanbar.org/about_the_aba.html.

274.   American Bar Association, *ABA Canons of Professional Ethics* (Chicago: American Bar Association, 1908), http://www.americanbar.org/content/dam/aba/migrated/cpr/mrpc/Canons_Ethics.authcheckdam.pdf; *see* James Altman, "Considering the ABA's 1908 Canons of Ethics," *Fordham Law Review* 71 (2003): 2395.

275.	American Bar Association, *ABA Canons of Professional Ethics*, Preamble.

276.	Ibid., Canon 15.

277.	Altman, "Considering the ABA's 1908 Canons of Ethics," 2401, 2441, 2452, 2454, 2464.

278.	American Bar Association, *ABA Canons of Professional Ethics*, Canon 12.

279.	American Bar Association, *ABA Model Code of Professional Responsibility* (Chicago: American Bar Association, 1969), http://www.americanbar. org/content/dam/aba/migrated/cpr/mrpc/mcpr.authcheckdam.pdf, Preliminary Statement.

280.	Ibid.

281.	Ibid.

282.	Ibid., Canon 7 ("A Lawyer Should Represent a Client Zealously Within the Bounds of the Law").

283.	Ibid., EC 7-1, EC 7-19.

284.	Ibid., EC 7-2.

285.	Ibid., EC 7-3.

286.	Ibid., EC 7-6.

287.	Ibid., DR 7-101.

288.	American Bar Association, "Preamble & Scope," *Model Rules of Professional Conduct* (Chicago: American Bar Association, 1983), accessed May 14, 2015, http://www.

americanbar.org/groups/professional_responsibility/publications/model_rules_of_
professional_conduct/model_rules_of_professional_conduct_preamble_scope.
html, paragraph 21.

289.   Ibid., paragraph 9.

290.   Ibid., paragraph 2.

291.   American Bar Association, "Diligence – Comment," *Model Rules of Professional
Conduct*, accessed May 14, 2015, http://www.americanbar.org/groups/professional_
responsibility/publications/model_rules_of_professional_conduct/rule_1_3_dili-
gence/comment_on_rule_1_3.html, paragraph 1.

292.   *See* Paula Schaefer, "Harming Business Clients With Zealous Advocacy:
Rethinking the Attorney Advisor's Touchstone," *Florida State University Law
Review* 38 (2011): 251, 253, 256 n. 30, 257.

293.   *See, e.g.*, Smith v. United States, 508 U. S. 223, 228-229 (1992).

294.   Merriam-Webster's Collegiate Dictionary, Eleventh Edition (Springfield:
Merriam-Webster, 2004).

295.   Robert Gordon, "The Citizen Lawyer – A Brief Informal History of a Myth
With Some Basis in Reality," *William and Mary Law Review* 50 (2009): 1169,
1180-1181.

296.   Schaefer, "Harming Business Clients With Zealous Advocacy," 254.

297.   Ibid., 255, 264-265; *see also* Thomas Shaffer, "Unique, Novel and Unsound
Adversary Ethic," *Vanderbilt Law Review* 41 (1988): 697.

298.   Physicians Insurance Exchange v. Fisons Corporation, 122 Wn. 2d 299 (1993),
348.

299.   Ibid., 348.

300.   Ibid., 308, 337-338.

301.   Ibid., 309, 338.

302.   Ibid., 347, 353.

303.   Ibid., 347.

304.   Ibid., 354.

305.   *See* Schaefer, "Harming Business Clients With Zealous Advocacy," 264-265; Mark Sargent, "Lawyers in the Moral Maze," *Villanova Law Review* 49 (2004): 867, 871-872; Mark Sargent, "Lawyers in the Perfect Storm," *Washburn Law Journal* 43 (2003): 1, 31-32; Robert Gordon, "The Ethical Worlds of Large-Firm Litigators: Preliminary Observations," *Fordham Law Review* 67 (1998): 709, 733.

306.   Physicians Insurance Exchange v. Fisons Corporation, 122 Wn. 2d 353.

307.   Malautea v. Suzuki Motor Company, Ltd., 987 F.2d 1536, 1546 (11th Cir. 1993).

308.   Ibid., 1544.

309.   Ibid., 1539.

310.   Ibid., 1540.

311.   Ibid.

312.   Ibid.

313.   Ibid., 1540-1541.

314.   Ibid.

315.   Ibid., 1541.

316.   Ibid., 1546.

317.   Ibid., 1546-1547.

318.   Precision Specialty Metals, Inc. v. United States, 315 F.3d 1346 (Fed Cir. 2003).

319.   Ibid., 1348-1350, 1355-1356.

320.   Ibid., 1355-1356.

321.   Fharmacy Records v. Nassar, 248 F.R.D. 507 (E. D. Mich. 2008).

322.   Ibid.

323.   Ibid.

324.   Ibid.

325.   Fharmacy Records v. Nassar, 572 F. Supp.2d 869, 874-875.

326.   Ibid., 875.

327.   Ibid., 872-873.

328.   Fharmacy Records v. Nassar, Nos. 08-1607, 08-2201 (6th Cir. June 7, 2010), https://casetext.com/case/fharmacy-records-v-nassar.

329.   Fharmacy Records v. Nassar, 729 F. Supp. 2d 865 (E. D. Mich 2010).

330. Fharmacy Records v. Nassar, Nos. 10-1354, 10-2073 (6th Cir. Feb. 23, 2012), https://scholar.google.com/scholar_case?case=6682227887907618104&q=fhar macy+records+v.+nassar+sixth+circuit+2012&hl=en&as_sdt=2006.

331. Matsuura v. Alston & Bird and E. I. duPont de Nemours & Company, 166 F.3d 1006 (9th Cir. 1999); In Re: E. I. duPont de Nemours & Company-Benlate Litigation, 99 F.3d 363 (11th Cir. 1996).

332. In Re: E. I. duPont de Nemours & Company – Benlate Litigation, 918 F. Supp. 1524, 1530 (M. D. Ga. 1995).

333. Ibid., 1531.

334. Ibid., 1535.

335. Ibid., 1534-1535.

336. Ibid., 1545.

337. Ibid., 1534-1536.

338. Ibid., 1546.

339. Ibid., 1551.

340. Ibid., 1556-1558.

341. In Re: E. I. duPont de Nemours & Company-Benlate Litigation, 99 F.3d 369 and note 7.

342. See Matsuura v. Alston & Bird and E. I. duPont de Nemours & Company, 166 F.3d 1006 (9th Cir. 1999); Milo Geyelin, "DuPont, Atlanta Law Firm Agree

to Pay Nearly $11.3 Million in Benlate Matter, *Wall Street Journal*, January 4, 1999, http://www.wsj.com/articles/SB915220245892321000.

343. *See* American Bar Association, "Special Responsibilities of a Prosecutor – Comment," *Model Rules of Professional Conduct* (Chicago: American Bar Association, 1983), accessed May 24, 2015, http://www.americanbar.org/groups/professional_responsibility/publications/model_rules_of_professional_conduct/rule_3_8_special_responsibilities_of_a_prosecutor/comment_on_rule_3_8.html, paragraph 1.

344. Berger v. United States, 295 U. S. 78 (1935).

345. Ibid., 84.

346. Ibid., 88.

347. Coppedge v. United States, 369 U. S. 438, 449 (1962).

348. Brady v. Maryland, 373 U. S. 83, 87 (1963).

349. White v. Helling, 194 F.3d 937, 946 (8th Cir. 1999).

350. Ibid., 945.

351. Wolfe v. Clarke, 819 F.Supp.2d 538 (E. D. Va. 2011).

352. Ibid., 550-551 and note 11, 564-565.

353. Wolfe v. Clarke, 819 F.Supp.2d 538 (E. D. Va. 2011), *affirmed*, 691 F.3d 410 (4th Cir. 2012).

354. Wolfe v. Clarke, 819 F.Supp.2d 538, 555 (E. D. Va. 2011).

355. Ibid., 548 and notes 8, 9, 554.

356.   Ibid., 547, 550, 557 and note 17.

357.   Ibid., 548-549, 551-553.

358.   Ibid., 548 and note 10, 549, 555-563.

359.   Ibid., 571-572.

360.   Ibid.

361.   Ibid., 566-567 and note 24.

362.   Ibid., note 24.

363.   Ibid., quoting from Kyles v. Whitley, 514 U. S. 419, 439-440 (1995).

364.   Ibid., 570 at note 26.

365.   Wolfe v. Clarke, 691 F.3d 410 (4th Cir. 2012).

366.   Ibid., 424.

367.   Ibid., 422.

368.   Ibid.

369.   United States v. Stein, 435 F.Supp.2d 330, 336, 340, 355-356 (S.D.N.Y. 2006).

370.   Ibid., 336-338.

371.   Ibid., 343-349, 352-353.

372.   Ibid., 346-347; United States v. Stein, 541 F.3d 130. 138-139 (2nd Cir. 2008).

373. IR-2005-83, "KPMG to Pay $456 Million for Criminal Violations," *Internal Revenue Release* (Washington: Internal Revenue Service, August 29, 2005).

374. United States v. Stein, 435 F.Supp.2d 349-350; United States v. Stein, 541 F.3d 139-140.

375. United States v. Stein, 435 F.Supp.2d 336.

376. Ibid., 333, 356-357, 359-362, 364-367.

377. United States v. Stein, 495 F.Supp.2d 390, 416-418, 424 (S.D.N.Y. 2007).

378. United States v. Stein, 435 F.Supp.2d 381-382.

379. Ibid., 381.

380. Ibid.

381. Ibid., 393-394, 412-414.

382. United States v. Stein, 541 F.3d 130.

383. Brian Thevenot, "Murder Charges Against Seven NOPD Officers Tossed Out by Judge," *Times-Picayune*, Aug. 13, 2008, http://blog.nola.com/news_impact/print.html?entry=/2008/08/murder_charges_against_seven_n.html.

384. United States v. Bowen, Criminal Action No. 10-204, Order and Reasons (E. D. La. Sept 17, 2013), http://media.nola.com/crime_impact/other/judge%20filing%20re%20bowen%20et%20al.pdf, *appeal pending*, United States v. Bowen, Docket No. 13-31078 (5th Cir., argued Apr. 29, 2015).

385. Ibid.

386.   Brady v. Maryland, 373 U. S. 83; Berger v. United States, 295 U. S. 78.

387.   United States v. Bowen, Criminal Action No. 10-204, Order and Reasons (E. D. La. Sept 17, 2013), 41-42.

388.   Ibid., 37-39.

389.   Ibid., 39.

390.   Ibid., 34-35.

391.   Ibid., 40-41.

392.   Ibid., 49, 99, 113.

393.   Ibid., 8-10.

394.   Ibid., 50.

395.   Ibid., 52.

396.   Ibid, 51, 53.

397.   Ibid., 53.

398.   Ibid., 68.

399.   Ibid., 54.

400.   Ibid., 69.

401.   Ibid., 71, 74.

402.   Ibid., 83.

403.   Ibid., 10-11, 15 and notes 9, 10, 87-89.

404.   Ibid., 10, 15, 24 n. 28; Brendan McCarthy, "Judge Imposes Stiff Sentences on 5 NOPD Officers Convicted in Danziger Shootings," *Times-Picayune*, Apr. 4, 2012, http://blog.nola.com/crime_impact/print.html?entry=/2012/04/judge_imposes_sentences_on_5_n.html.

405.   United States v. Bowen, Criminal Action No. 10-204, Order and Reasons (E. D. La. Sept 17, 2013), 56-62.

406.   Ibid., 16, 20, 56, 63-64.

407.   Ibid., 64, 75-76, 78-79.

408.   Ibid., 65.

409.   Ibid., 6-7.

410.   Ibid., 33.

411.   Ibid.

412.   Edward Robinson, "Refco's Collapse Reveals Decades of Quarrels with Regulators," *Bloomberg Business*, Jan. 5, 2006, http://www.bloomberg.com/apps/news?pid=21070001&sid=a50aqPG7x7qo.

413.   *See* In Re: Refco, Inc. Securities Litigation, 609 F.Supp.2d 304 (S. D. N. Y. 2009).

414.   Ibid.; *see* Robinson, "Refco's Collapse Reveals Decades of Quarrels with Regulators."

415.   In Re: Refco, Inc. Securities Litigation, 609 F.Supp.2d 304 (S. D. N. Y. 2009); Robinson, "Refco's Collapse Reveals Decades of Quarrels with Regulators."

416.   Robinson, "Refco's Collapse Reveals Decades of Quarrels with Regulators."

417.   In Re: Refco, Inc. Securities Litigation, 609 F.Supp.2d 304 (S. D. N. Y. 2009).

418.   Litigation Release No. 21555, "Former Mayer Brown Partner Joseph P. Collins Settles SEC Fraud Action," *Accounting and Auditing Enforcement Release No. 3145* (Washington: Securities and Exchange Commission, June 14, 2010), https://www.sec.gov/litigation/litreleases/2010/lr21555.htm.

419.   United States v. Collins, Case No. 13-2902 (2nd Cir. Oct. 22, 2014), https://casetext.com/case/united-states-v-collins-74.

420.   Press Release, "Joseph Collins, Principal Attorney for Former Commodities Firm Refco, Sentenced in Manhattan Federal Court to One Year and One Day in Prison for Securities Fraud," *United States Attorney's Office, Southern District of New York* (New York: Department of Justice, July 15, 2013), http://www.justice.gov/usao-sdny/pr/joseph-collins-principal-attorney-former-commodities-firm-refco-sentenced-manhattan.

421.   Schaefer, "Harming Business Clients With Zealous Advocacy," 252, 270-271.

422.   David Cay Johnston, "Costly Questions Arise on Legal Opinions for Tax Shelters," *New York Times*, February 9, 2003, http://www.nytimes.com/2003/02/09/business/costly-questions-arise-on-legal-opinions-for-tax-shelters.html.

423.   Paul Braverman, "Helter Shelter," *The American Lawyer*, December 5, 2003, http://www.americanlawyer.com/id=900005537288/Helter-Shelter.

424.   Mike France, "The Rise of the Wall Street Tax Machine," *Business Week*, Mar. 30, 2003, http://www.bloomberg.com/bw/stories/2003-03-30/the-rise-of-the-wall-street-tax-machine.

425. Senate Report 109-54, *The Role of Professional Firms in the U. S. Tax Shelter Industry* (Washington: U. S. Government Printing Office, April 13, 2005).

426. Ibid., 11.

427. Ibid., 12.

428. Ibid., 96-99.

429. Ibid., 45-47.

430. Ibid., 50-55, 96-99.

431. Ibid., 98-99.

432. Press Release, "Three Defendants in Tax Shelter Fraud Trial Convicted of Multiple Counts of Tax Evasion," *United States Attorney's Office, Southern District of New York* (New York: Department of Justice, December 17, 2008), http://www.justice.gov/archive/usao/nys/pressreleases/December08/larsonetalverdictpr.pdf.

433. Press Release, "Three Defendants in Tax Shelter Fraud Trial Sentenced to Prison," *United States Attorney's Office, Southern District of New York* (New York: Department of Justice, April 2, 2009), http://www.justice.gov/archive/usao/nys/pressreleases/April09/larsonetalsentencingpr.pdf.

434. Complaint, Securities and Exchange Commission v. Heinen, Case No. C 07 2214 (N. D. Cal. Apr. 24, 2007), https://www.sec.gov/litigation/complaints/2007/comp20086.pdf.

435. Ibid., 5-6, 8-11.

436. Ibid., 7, 11.

437. Ibid., 12.

438. Ibid., 3.

439. Litigation Release No. 20683, "SEC Settles Options Backdating Charges with Former Apple General Counsel for $2.2 Million," *Securities and Exchange Commission Release* (Washington: Securities and Exchange Commission, August 14, 2008), https://www.sec.gov/litigation/litreleases/2008/lr20683.htm; *see also* Litigation Release No. 20086, "SEC Charges Former Apple General Counsel for Illegal Stock Option Backdating," *Securities and Exchange Commission Release* (Washington: Securities and Exchange Commission, April 24, 2007), https://www.sec.gov/litigation/litreleases/2007/lr20086.htm.

440. Schaefer, "Harming Business Clients With Zealous Advocacy," 254.

441. *E.g.*, Marvin Aspen, "The Search for Renewed Civility in Litigation," *Valparaiso University Law Review* 28 (1994): 513.

442. William Grady, Bill Crawford and John O'Brien, "And Your Clients Wear Combat Boots," *Chicago Tribune*, October 12, 1993, http://articles.chicagotribune.com/1993-10-12/business/9310120275_1_taco-bell-deposition-t-shirt.

443. Schaefer, "Harming Business Clients With Zealous Advocacy," 260-263.

444. Schiltz, "On Being a Happy, Healthy and Ethical Member," 908-910; Patrick Schiltz, "Legal Ethics in Decline," 713-720.

445. Warren Burger, "The Decline of Professionalism," *Fordham Law Review* 63 (1995): 949, 950.

446. Gordon, "The Ethical Worlds of Large-Firm Litigators," 727-729.

447. *E.g.*, Schaefer, "Harming Business Clients With Zealous Advocacy," 279-281.

448. Edwards, "The Growing Disjunction," 68.

449. American Bar Association, "Rule 3.4: Fairness to Opposing Party and Counsel," *Model Rules of Professional Conduct* (Chicago: American Bar Association, 1983), accessed July 2, 2015, http://www.americanbar.org/groups/professional_responsibility/publications/model_rules_of_professional_conduct/rule_3_4_fairness_to_opposing_party_counsel.html.

450. American Bar Association, "Rule 3.3: "Candor Toward the Tribunal," *Model Rules of Professional Conduct* (Chicago: American Bar Association, 1983), accessed July 2, 2015, http://www.americanbar.org/groups/professional_responsibility/publications/model_rules_of_professional_conduct/rule_3_3_candor_toward_the_tribunal.html.

451. American Bar Association, "Rule 3.1: "Meritorious Claims & Contentions," *Model Rules of Professional Conduct* (Chicago: American Bar Association, 1983), accessed July 2, 2015, http://www.americanbar.org/groups/professional_responsibility/publications/model_rules_of_professional_conduct/rule_3_1_meritorious_claims_contentions.html.

452. American Bar Association, "Rule 3.8: "Special Responsibilities of a Prosecutor," *Model Rules of Professional Conduct* (Chicago: American Bar Association, 1983), accessed July 2, 2015, http://www.americanbar.org/groups/professional_responsibility/publications/model_rules_of_professional_conduct/rule_3_8_special_responsibilities_of_a_prosecutor.html.

453. Ibid.

454. American Bar Association, "Rule 3.6: "Trial Publicity," *Model Rules of Professional Conduct* (Chicago: American Bar Association, 1983), accessed July 2, 2015, http://www.americanbar.org/groups/professional_responsibility/publications/model_rules_of_professional_conduct/rule_3_6_trial_publicity.html.

455. American Bar Association, "Rule 4.8: "Misconduct," *Model Rules of Professional Conduct* (Chicago: American Bar Association, 1983), accessed July 2, 2015, http://

www.americanbar.org/groups/professional_responsibility/publications/model_
rules_of_professional_conduct/rule_8_4_misconduct.html.

456.   American Bar Association, "Rule 1.5: "Fees," *Model Rules of Professional Conduct*
(Chicago: American Bar Association, 1983), accessed July 16, 2015, http://
www.americanbar.org/groups/professional_responsibility/publications/model_
rules_of_professional_conduct/rule_1_5_fees.html; American Bar Association,
"Fees – Comment," *Model Rules of Professional Conduct* (Chicago: American Bar
Association, 1983), accessed July 16, 2015, http://www.americanbar.org/groups/
professional_responsibility/publications/model_rules_of_professional_con-
duct/rule_1_5_fees/comment_on_rule_1_5.html.

457.   Stuart Pardau, "Bill, Baby, Bill: How the Billable Hour Emerged as the Primary
Method of Attorney Fee Generation and Why Early Reports of its Demise May be
Greatly Exaggerated," *Idaho Law Review* 50 (2013): 1, 5-6.

458.   Stephen Carroll et al., *The Abuse of Medical Diagnostic Practices in Mass Litigation:
The Case of Silica* (Santa Monica, California: RAND Corporation, 2009), 22.

459.   "Summary," *In Re: Michael A. Murphy, S.J.C. Order of Term of Suspension
Entered by Justice Duffly on September 17, 2012, with an Effective Date of October
17, 2012* (Boston: Board of Bar Overseers, 2012), accessed July 19, 2015, http://
www.mass.gov/obcbbo/bd12-065.pdf.

460.   Pardau, "Bill, Baby, Bill," 9-10; Kevin Hopkins, "Law Firms, Technology, and
the Double-Billing Dilemma," *Georgetown Journal of Legal Ethics* 12 (1998): 95,
99-101.

461.   William Rehnquist, "The Legal Profession Today," *Indiana Law Journal* 62
(1987): 151, 155; *see* Pardau, "Bill, Baby, Bill," 7-8.

462.   Lisa Lerman, "Gross Profits? Questions About Lawyer Billing Practices," *Hofstra
Law Review* 22 (1994): 645, 650.

463. Ibid., 651-652.

464. In Re: World Trade Center Disaster Site Litigation: Cirino, et al., v. City of New York, et al., 754 F.3d 114 (2ⁿᵈ Cir. 2014); Alvin Hellerstein, James Henderson Jr. and Aaron Twerski, "Managerial Judging: The 9/11 Responders' Tort Litigation," *Cornell Law Review* 98 (2012): 127.

465. Hellerstein, Henderson and Twerski, "Managerial Judging," 157-158.

466. Ibid., 158.

467. Ibid., 171, 176.

468. American Bar Association, "Rule 1.7: "Conflict of Interest: Current Clients," *Model Rules of Professional Conduct* (Chicago: American Bar Association, 1983), accessed July 30, 2015, http://www.americanbar.org/groups/professional_responsibility/ publications/model_rules_of_professional_conduct/rule_1_7_conflict_of_inter- est_current_clients.html; *see* American Bar Association, "Rule 1.10: "Imputation of Conflicts of Interest: General Rule," *Model Rules of Professional Conduct* (Chicago: American Bar Association, 1983), accessed July 30, 2015, http://www.americanbar. org/groups/professional_responsibility/publications/model_rules_of_professional_ conduct/rule_1_10_imputation_of_conflicts_of_interest_general_rule.html.

469. American Bar Association, "Conflict of Interest: Current Clients – Comment" *Model Rules of Professional Conduct* (Chicago: American Bar Association, 1983), accessed July 30, 2015, http://www.americanbar.org/groups/professional_re- sponsibility/publications/model_rules_of_professional_conduct/rule_1_7_con- flict_of_interest_current_clients/comment_on_rule_1_7.html.

470. American Bar Association, "Rule 1.9: "Duties to Former Clients," *Model Rules of Professional Conduct* (Chicago: American Bar Association, 1983), accessed July 30, 2015, http://www.americanbar.org/groups/professional_responsibility/

publications/model_rules_of_professional_conduct/rule_1_9_duties_of_former_clients.html; *see* American Bar Association, "Rule 1.10: "Imputation of Conflicts of Interest: General Rule".

471.   Residential Funding Company, LLC v. Decision One Mortgage Company, LLC, and HSBC Finance Corporation, Civil No. 14-1737 (D. Minn. Jan. 23, 2015), accessed August 3, 2015, https://lawyerdisqualification.files. wordpress.com/2015/01/dqed_mayer-brown-dq.pdf.

472.   Ibid., 11.

473.   Ibid., 14, 26.

474.   Roosevelt Irrigation District v. Salt River Project Agricultural Improvement and Power District, 810 F.Supp.2d 929 (D. Ariz. 2011).

475.   Ibid., 952.

476.   Ibid., 985.

477.   Lennar Mare Island, LLC v. Steadfast Insurance Co., No. 2:12-cv-02182-KJM-KJN (E. D. Cal. April 7, 2015).

478.   Ibid., 16-17.

479.   Ibid., 4.

480.   Ibid., 4, 15.

481.   Ibid., 18,

482.   Ibid., 5-6.

483. Ibid., 23.

484. Ibid., 24-25.

485. Young v. Achenbauch, No. SC12-988 (Fla. March 27, 2014), http://www.flori-dasupremecourt.org/decisions/2014/sc12-988.pdf.

486. Ibid., 5, 14.

487. Ibid., 13-14.

488. Ibid., 14; *see also* Merck Aprova AG v. Prothera, Inc., 670 F. Supp. 2d 201, 209 (S.D.N.Y. 2009).

489. 179 F. Supp. 2d 1157 (C. D. Cal. 2001).

490. Ibid., 1169-1171.

491. Ibid., 1165-1166.

492. Ibid., 1164.

493. Ibid., 1166.

494. Ibid., 1169, 1174.

495. *See* Flatworld Interactives LLC v. Apple Inc., 2013 U.S. Dist. LEXIS 111496 (N.D. Cal. August 7, 2013).

496. Ibid., 12-13.

497. Ibid., 21-22.

498. Ibid., 19-20.

499. Ibid., 15.

500. Plaintiff Axcess International, Inc.'s Motion for Judgment, Axcess International, Inc. v. Baker Botts L.L.P., Cause No. CC-13-01301E (Dallas County, Texas June 2, 2014), http://www.axcessinc.com/knowledge/2014/Plaintiffs_Motion_for_Judgment.pdf; Natalie Posgate, "Jury Rules Against Baker Botts, Then Says Company Waited too Long to File Suit," *The Dallas Morning News*, May 15, 2014, accessed August 5, 2015, http://www.dallas-news.com/business/headlines/20140515-jury-rules-against-baker-botts-then-says-company-waited-to-long-to-file-the-suit.ece; Chris Neumeyer, "Jury Finds Firm Negligent to Prosecute Patents for Competitors," *International Technology Law Blog* (Taipei, Taiwan: Asia Law, May 16, 2014), accessed August 5, 2015, http://techlaw.biz/jury-finds-firm-negligent-prosecute-patents-competing-clients-40m-damages/; *see* Axcess International, Inc. v. Baker Botts, L.L.P., No. 05-14-01151-CV (Tex. App. Oct. 27, 2014).

501. Strickland v. Washington, 466 U.S. 668, 692 (1984).

502. *See* Lawrence Fox, "The Gang of Thirty-Three: Taking the Wrecking Ball to Client Loyalty," *Yale Law Journal Online* 121 (2012), 567, 570-571, http://www.yalelawjournal.org/pdf/1063_eo8auk2m.pdf.

503. "Proposals of Law Firm General Counsel for Future Regulation of Relationships Between Law Firms and Sophisticated Clients," *ABA Commission on Ethics 20/20* (March 2011), accessed August 5, 2015, http://www.abajournal.com/files/ABA_Ethics_Commission_Proposals_--_3-8-11.pdf; Fox, "The Gang of Thirty-Three," 567, 574-581.

504. Lao Tzu, BrainyQuote.com (Old Lyme, Connecticut: Xplore Inc., 2015), accessed August 21, 2015, http://www.brainyquote.com/quotes/quotes/l/laotzu121075.html.

505. American Bar Association, "Rule 2.1: "Advisor," *Model Rules of Professional Conduct* (Chicago: American Bar Association, 1983), accessed September 1, 2015, http://

www.americanbar.org/groups/professional_responsibility/publications/model_rules_of_professional_conduct/rule_2_1_advisor.html.

506. American Bar Association, "Advisor – Comment" *Model Rules of Professional Conduct* (Chicago: American Bar Association, 1983), accessed September 1, 2015, http://www.americanbar.org/groups/professional_responsibility/publications/model_rules_of_professional_conduct/rule_2_1_advisor/comment_on_rule_2_1_advisor.html.

507. Letter from Felix Frankfurter to Mr. Rosenwald (May 13, 1927), quoted in Edwards, "The Growing Disjunction Between Legal Education and the Legal Profession," 34; *see* ibid., 34 n. 1, for original source.

508. Edwards, "The Growing Disjunction," 63.

509. Earl Warren, Address at the Jewish Theological Seminary of America Annual Awards Dinner (November 11, 1962), quoted in Anita Allen, "Moralizing in Public," *Hofstra Law Review* 34 (2006): 1325.

510. Lincoln Caplan, "The Good Advocate," *Legal Affairs*, May/June 2004, http://www.legalaffairs.org/issues/May-June-2004/editorial_mayjun04.msp.

511. Abraham Lincoln, "Notes on the Practice of Law," in Fehrenbacher ed., *Abraham Lincoln: Speeches and Writings 1832-1858*, 246.

512. Merriam-Webster's Collegiate Dictionary, Eleventh Edition (Springfield: Merriam-Webster, Incorporated, 2004).

513. *See, e.g.,* Rule 12(b)(6), *Federal Rules of Civil Procedure* (December 1, 2014), https://www.federalrulesofcivilprocedure.org.

514. *E.g.,* Rule 56(a), *Federal Rules of Civil Procedure* (December 1, 2014), https://www.federalrulesofcivilprocedure.org.

515.   *See* Rule 11, *Federal Rules of Civil Procedure* (December 1, 2014), https://www. federalrulesofcivilprocedure.org.

516.   *See* Rule 37, *Federal Rules of Civil Procedure* (December 1, 2014), https://www. federalrulesofcivilprocedure.org.

515. See Rule 11, *Federal Rules of Civil Procedure* (December 1, 2014), https://www.federalrulesofcivilprocedure.org

516. See Rule 37, *Federal Rules of Civil Procedure* (December 1, 2014), https://www.federalrulesofcivilprocedure.org

Index

www.ingramcontent.com/pod-product-compliance
Lightning Source LLC
Chambersburg PA
CBHW061156240326
R18026500001B/R180265PG41519CBX00017B/27